# PRAYER
*and the*
# FIVE STAGES
*of*
# HEALING

# BY RON ROTH, Ph.D.

# PRAYER

## *and the*

# FIVE STAGES

## *of*

# HEALING

## RON ROTH, PH.D.

### with Peter Occhiogrosso

Hay House, Inc.
Carlsbad, CA

*Published and distributed in the United States by:*
Hay House, Inc., P.O. Box 5100, Carlsbad, CA 92018-5100 • (800) 654-5126 • (800) 650-5115 (fax)

*Edited by:* Jill Kramer        *Designed by:* Wendy Lutge

The author of this book does not dispense medical advice or prescribe the use of any technique as a form of treatment for physical or medical problems without the advice of a physician, either directly or indirectly. The intent of the author is only to offer information of a general nature to help you in your quest for emotional and spiritual well-being. In the event you use any of the information in this book for yourself, which is your consti-tutional right, the author and the publisher assume no responsibility for your actions.

Hay House and the author express gratitude to the following publishers and individuals for allowing inclusion of their work in this book:

Excerpts from *Meditations from Meister Eckhart*, edited by Matthew Fox; ©1983, Bear & Co., Santa Fe, NM. Used by permission of the publisher.

"Praying with John of the Cross," by Wayne Simsic. Reprinted from *Praying with Hildegard of Bingen*, by Gloria Durka (Winona, MN: Saint Mary's Press, 1991). Used by permission of the publisher. All rights reserved.

"Praying with Hildegard of Bingen." Reprinted from *Praying with Hildegard of Bingen*, by Gloria Durka (Winona, MN: Saint Mary's Press, 1991). Used by permission of the publisher. All rights reserved.

Excerpts from *Meditations with Hildegard of Bingen*, by Gabrielle Uhlein, ©1983, Bear & Co., Santa Fe, NM. Used by permission of the publisher.

Excerpts from *Hell Bent for Heaven*, by Hilda Charlton, ©1990, Golden Quest, Woodstock, NY. Used by permission of the publisher.

Excerpts from "Prayer of Generational Forgiveness," by Howard Wills. Used by permission of the author.

"God! God! God!" by Paramahansa Yogananda. Reprinted from *Man's Eternal Quest* by Paramahansa Yogananda (Los Angeles: Self-Realization Fellowship, 1982). Used by permission of the publisher.

Quotation by Sri Daya Mata. Reprinted from *Enter the Quiet Heart*, by Sri Daya Mata. (Los Angeles: Self-Realization Fellowship, 1998). Used by permission of the publisher.

**Library of Congress Cataloging-in-Publication Data**

Roth, Ron.
    Prayer and the five stages of healing / Ron Roth with Peter
Occhiogrosso.
        Includes index.        p.        cm.
        ISBN 1-56170-551-9
        1. Mysticism.    2. Prayer.    I. Occhiogrosso, Peter.    II. Title.
BL625.R58    1999
291.4'3—dc21                                                            98-43146
                                                                            CIP


ISBN 1-56170-551-9

02  01  00  99      4  3  2  1
First Printing, February 1999

Printed in the United States of America

*This work is lovingly dedicated to all the saints and mystics who have taught us how to live in a spirit of profound joy; and to Joseph Cardinal Bernardin, who taught us to make the transition to the next life with dignity, grace, and peace.*

# Contents

# Acknowledgments

I am eternally grateful to the many people whose love has empowered me over the years and whose support has taken me to new heights of service. It is my prayer that all of them be continually blessed by God in such a way that they truly recognize that life is not only a gift, but a celebration.

First and foremost, I am grateful to my family and friends, who form my core support group. This includes my spiritual family, who are committed to pray daily for me and the work entrusted to me by the Divine Spirit.

I am also grateful to Peter Occhiogrosso, who is more than a co-worker; he is a true friend and confidant.

To my office manager and secretary, Marilyn Carr, for the efficiency and care she expresses in her work, as well as for being a friend for over 40 years.

To my agent, Muriel Nellis; to my editor, Jill Kramer; to Louise Hay, Reid Tracy, Barbara Bouse, and all my family at Hay House, without whose support for my work this book might not have been realized.

To Kathleen Noone, who has graced my life with her continual love, encouragement, and radiance.

To Rani Stoler, a dear friend whose media expertise has helped bring my message of God's healing love to a wider audience.

To my friends, Carole Dean; Carol Joyce; Alan and Robin Neuman; Dolores Myss, my "other mother," who considers me a member of her own family; and to Toni Boehm; Patricia Treece; Ralph Sariego; and the entire staff of The Conference Works.

To all of you go my prayers for continual blessings and God's peace.

# Introduction

*"One seeks God in books; one finds him in prayer."*
— Padre Pio

*T*hese words of Padre Pio, the 20th-century Italian mystic to whom I feel a close attachment, sum up both my dilemma and my only recourse. No book can supply a surefire road map to the Divine; the best one can hope to do is point pilgrims to the path and help them on their way. The journey will be completed only under God's direction. What I can and do hope to accomplish in this book is to establish the link between prayer and healing, and explore the many ramifications of that connection.

When people ask me how to heal themselves, I tell them to pray for others to be healed. They sometimes look at me askance, as if it couldn't possibly be that simple—or that paradoxical. And yet the link between prayer and healing is so direct that if you take the time to learn just a few basic principles about prayer, along with a few uncomplicated techniques for praying, you can change your life completely.

The first principle we need to accept is that we can no longer look at prayer as some kind of adjunct to life, or as a peripheral aspect of the spiritual path—like that yoga workshop you take every summer, or the occasional weekend retreat. Prayer cannot be something you do only once a week, at church on Sunday, at the temple on Saturday, or at the mosque on Friday. It can't even be something you do for an hour every morning or evening. I am convinced that we cannot make much progress at all along the path unless prayer is as intimately integrated into our daily life as breathing. When St. Paul advised his followers to "pray without ceasing," he didn't mean that in some metaphorical or hyperbolic sense—he meant it literally.

That does not mean that your lips should be engaged in rattling off preexisting prayers every minute of the day. More than words or formulas, prayer is awareness. You can pray while driving to work in the morning, while changing the baby, making dinner, swimming in a lake, or watching television (although I don't recommend the latter). Prayer is a way of invoking the sacred in your life, and once you acquire the habit of prayer, you can make all of your actions sacred acts.

Before you can do all that, however, you need to know how prayer works and how it evolves as your individual spiritual path moves through its own stages of development. Above all, you must understand some basic techniques that can assist you as you move through what I call the five stages of healing.

The first part of this book will explore those stages in detail and will seek to show how you can identify them in your own life. Some readers may be surprised to learn that there are stages to healing in the first place. Particularly in the Christian world, we have become accustomed to the idea that salvation is a one-shot deal. In many born-again Christian churches, you get saved, you get baptized, and that's it. In the Catholic church, after infant baptism, you are required to go to confession and communion only once a year. And since Christians generally do not believe in reincarnation, one baptism or conversion experience is theoretically enough to ensure an eternity of bliss. Although Christians are expected to live a virtuous life and follow the commandments, there isn't much incentive for them to do more in the way of spiritual development. This all tends to foster the belief that our spiritual path is a rather simple yes-or-no, heaven-or-hell affair, without any room for nuanced growth.

Such a belief, however, is neither psychologically nor spiritually realistic. Growth, change, and development are constants throughout our lives. As Elisabeth Kübler-Ross has shown us, we grow through stages of awareness even as we are dying. In the minds of many of the world's mystics, spiritual growth continues after death as well. It is only natural, then, that complex spiritual processes such as enlightenment, healing, and the creation of a meaningful prayer life also go through stages of development.

When I discuss healing, I am not talking merely about the healing of physical maladies. That kind of healing is important, of course.

Although I believe very strongly that we are put here to learn, I do not necessarily believe that we are put here to suffer. Suffering can sometimes be a by-product of learning and sometimes a catalyst for it, but is never an end in itself. Since physical illness has no clear correlation to virtuous living—too many extremely holy men and women have suffered terribly painful diseases and deaths—it isn't always easy to discern the role of sickness and suffering in our lives. In fact, I propose that physical healing is secondary to psychological and spiritual healing.

Of far greater importance is the healing into wholeness of our spiritual nature. For that reason, I have adapted the five stages of enlightenment described by scholar of mysticism Evelyn Underhill, who derived them from her extensive readings of the works of mystics from many of the world's spiritual traditions. I have further adapted these stages based on my own personal journey as well as my experience working with hundreds of people over three decades of my healing ministry.

The second half of my book will describe what I consider to be the most effective ways to pray and to integrate prayer into your daily life. You do not need any prior experience with prayer or any detailed knowledge of specific religious traditions to follow my suggestions. You need only be open to the possibility of healing through communicating with the Divine. I will explore the relationship of prayer to the centers of consciousness known as the chakras, which have been charted by Eastern mystics for several millennia. Based on my own experiences of imitating the prayer life of various saints and mystics of East and West, I will demonstrate how to invoke the energy of our greatest models for successful prayer. I will teach you how to make periods of silence and solitude part of your own prayer life, and will show you in detail how to make that prayer life an intimate part of your everyday existence. Finally, we will examine at length the essential role of forgiveness in opening the heart to genuine prayer.

Throughout this book, generally at the end of each chapter, I present specific prayers and exercises to help deepen your experience of the principles I am attempting to explain, and to help you implement them in your life. As Padre Pio implied, there is a limit to how far words alone can take you. You must be willing to act on those words—indeed, to use them as a springboard to developing an interior life of communion with God that transcends words and even logical thought.

Because Jesus is my spiritual master, I tend to invoke his teachings and his presence more often than any other. Having been raised in the Roman Catholic tradition and having spent 25 years as a Catholic priest before leaving both the institutional priesthood and the church, I am most at home with the sacred Scripture known as both the Hebrew Bible and the Old and New Testaments. But I also have a working knowledge of the world's other great traditions, and have sought to elicit parallels between the Jewish-Christian tradition and those of Buddhism, Hinduism, Taoism, and Islam where they are relevant.

Although most of my prayer and meditation exercises invoke the presence and name of Jesus, I want you to feel free to substitute another name if you are more comfortable doing that. It could be the name of the deity, either male or female, in any other tradition, or the name of any holy person to whom you feel a special connection.

I have quoted from Scripture freely in this book, mostly from the Christian Testaments, although my interpretations are often freer than most. One thing that has always bothered me about the institutional forms of Christianity—and I include Christian Fundamentalism in that category—is the way in which they have quoted Scripture selectively and narrowly for their own purposes. As Peter J. Gomes writes in *The Good Book: Reading the Bible with Mind and Heart,* "One must not use the scriptures as the drunk uses the lamppost—for support rather than for illumination; rather, one reads those inspired words with the very fallible apparatus of fallen human beings." Sadly, institutional Christianity has been in the habit of using Scriptures as a battering ram to attack its opponents, often quoting selectively to bolster its case against homosexuality, birth control, women's rights, or other hot-button issues that are more political than spiritual in nature. One of my goals in writing this book and using Scripture freely is to give my readers permission to read and interpret the Scriptures in ways that make them more loving.

## A Few Words about Meditation

If you have already established a daily practice of meditation, you will find it easy to work with many of my exercises during your daily session. If you have not, I strongly suggest that you use my book as a vehicle to begin daily prayer and meditation, even if at first you spend only ten minutes a day at it. The basics of meditation are very simple, and they apply to just about any form of practice, including the guided visualizations and prayer exercises in this book. (If you feel drawn to deepen your practice, you can always read any of the excellent books on meditation that you can find in any good spiritual bookstore. In the chapter of this book called "Invoking the Sacred," I will give you detailed suggestions for creating a place in your home in which to do your daily meditations and prayers.)

To begin meditating, any quiet corner of the house or apartment will do, including wherever you happen to be reading this book. It's best to sit up straight, because lying down can easily induce sleep. You don't need to assume the full-lotus posture of Eastern yoga; sitting on a chair with your feet planted flat on the floor and legs uncrossed is fine. In time you may prefer to sit on cushions on the floor with your legs lightly crossed, but this is not a prerequisite. Most teachers suggest closing your eyes, unless this tends to make you drowsy. Once you have gotten comfortable in your prayer or meditation posture, spend a few minutes placing your attention on your breath. Begin with a few slow, deep breaths, taking air in steadily through the nostrils and all the way down into the belly. You can even place the palm of your hand on your stomach to feel your diaphragm inflating and deflating as you take the air down into the deepest part of your stomach.

As thoughts flit through your mind—and you can be certain they will—don't try to blank them out or make them leave, but don't get caught up in them either. This delicate balancing act is something that monks have spent years perfecting, but at first you need only follow your breath and watch your thoughts pass by, as the Buddhists say, like clouds reflected in a mirror. Once you get the knack of allowing yourself to *be*, rather than trying to *do* anything during your meditation, you can expand your understanding of the process to take in more conventional prayer forms and the improvised prayers and spiritual exercises you will encounter in this book.

I also hope that those of you who are already accustomed to a daily meditation period will be able to expand your concept of prayer in other ways. Taking a brief prayer break of a minute or two, ten or fifteen times during the day, for instance, represents for me more of an ascetical practice than forcing myself to sit still in meditation for an hour. Without a doubt, sitting for an hour or even half an hour can be extremely beneficial; it can do wonders for your equanimity and composure, not to mention your respiration and heart rate. But keeping God constantly in your awareness is more important in the long run. The ascetics had the right idea, however: By continually denying themselves and doing austerities, they kept their awareness focused on the Divine rather than on the material world. The problem with following their example literally is that by emphasizing denial and self-abnegation, you may end up fixated on the very things you are denying, the way people on a diet can't stop thinking about food.

In describing his own approach to spiritual practice, the Buddha referred to it as the Middle Way, choosing to steer a course between the self-indulgence of the ordinary, ego-driven person and the extreme self-denial of many of the monks and ascetics of his day. He felt that neither approach led to liberation. I feel the same way about prayer: Overlooking the possibilities of prayer is as foolish as torturing yourself in the pursuit of unrealistic goals. I will try to help you steer a middle course that you will be able to live with even as you open your heart and deepen your level of communion with the Divine.

I would be remiss if, along the way, I failed to teach you that God is *for* you and not *against* you. The Western image of God as a stern taskmaster waiting for us to slip up so that He can condemn us to a life of misery on Earth followed by eternal hellfire is a holdover from Puritanical conceptions of a punitive God. So perhaps the first thing you need to heal is your understanding of God. I want to show you that you can change that understanding, which you may have inherited almost unconsciously from your parents and your religious training, as

I did. You can instead begin to see God as the spiritual masters do—that is, as the Father-Mother Creator of the Cosmos, whose deepest wish is for us to prosper and learn on the Earth plane and to continue to do so in the planes that follow this one.

Having said that, I would nevertheless like to direct you back to the roots of your own spiritual tradition by suggesting that you take from that tradition the spiritual elements that work for you. The great traditions in and of themselves all offer viable paths to the Divine. Their founders—the ancient rishis of India, Moses and the Hebrew Prophets, the Buddha, Lao-Tzu, Confucius, Jesus, Muhammad—were enlightened beings who were, generally speaking, far ahead of their contemporaries both intellectually and spiritually. They were driven by compassion to help those around them—not only spiritually, but also in material ways. Jesus practiced physical and psychological healing. Muhammad sought to reform many of the oppressive laws and customs of his time and place, including those against women. The great seers of India passed along many insights regarding health and family life. The compassionate wisdom of these men, unfortunately, was not always shared by their less enlightened followers, many of whom fell back upon the prejudicial customs of their day, especially with regard to the treatment of women. Yet the essence of their teachings, and many valuable elaborations of those teachings instituted by enlightened mystics of succeeding generations, are still available to us if we are discerning.

In some cases, discernment may mean combining different paths in a way that suits you. Let's say you were born into a nonobservant Jewish family with a great respect for secular humanism. The humanistic example of your parents may have outweighed the Jewish rituals they no longer followed. Searching for a spiritual practice outside of Judaism, you may have practiced yoga, Zen meditation, or some other techniques derived from Eastern traditions. Guided by your humanistic background, you may then have returned to your Jewish roots through studying the mystical wisdom of the Kabbalah. Now you can put those paths together and draw on all of them. The same is true of someone raised in a strict Catholic or Protestant church, who at an early age may have rejected the repressive dogma and sexual morality of the church and thrown out the baby with the bathwater. After years of adopting an atheistic or agnostic stance, you may feel the desire to reconnect with the positive aspects of Christianity, especially the social teachings of Jesus.

The most important thing is that you feel free to believe whatever empowers you to be more loving. Any time we use a belief system to pound on other people, we are probably trying to convince ourselves that we are right. As *A Course in Miracles* says, we often take the attitude that we would rather be right than happy. I'm here to remind you that you need to be happy and to learn how to celebrate life. If you can do that, then every moment will be a celebration of love and will be right in the end.

I cannot guarantee how anyone will be healed, whether physically, psychologically, or spiritually, because I am not the healer. Even when I have led healing services before large numbers of people, I could never say who would be healed and who would not. Sometimes a person who brought a friend to one of my services for healing would herself be healed while her friend was not. In any event, I am not interested in the healing of the body, the spirit, or the mind. I am concerned only about "healing into wholeness," by which I mean healing our lives so that we can be whole and exemplify our true nature, which is love. What I call "wholistic" spirituality allows the Holy Spirit, the Spirit of wholeness, to be your only therapist. This doesn't mean you can't use psychologists and psychotherapists, but that you come to the point in prayer when you say to God, as Samuel did in the Old Testament, "Here I am, Lord. Your servant is listening." Alphonsus Ligouri, who wrote the original prayers for the Roman Catholic ritual of the Stations of the Cross, put it another way: "Here I am. Do with me what you will."

That is the most healing prayer you can offer. It is also the one that may frighten you most profoundly. If nothing else, I hope this book will enable you to overcome your fear and open your heart to receive wholly the healing of God.

# PART I

# THE FIVE STAGES OF HEALING

# CHAPTER ONE

# The Prodigal Son and the Five Stages of Healing

*T*he great mystical traditions of the world all share the recognition that spiritual healing and enlightenment take place in a series of overlapping stages. Although different mystics have identified different numbers of stages, they tend to agree on the general progression. The movement upward from the material to the spiritual plane, from the human to the Divine, in effect represents the journey of the soul from its incarnation in a physical body to its reunion with God. The first part of this book attempts to map that journey.

Christian mystics such as John of the Cross and Teresa of Ávila make frequent use of the concept of ascent in their writings. In Teresa's works, for instance, the seven mansions of the "interior castle" follow this call to ascend. When more recent mystics such as Padre Pio speak of an "awakening," they are describing a similar process. In her classic book *Mysticism*, Evelyn Underhill distills mystical awakening into five stages, based on the experiences of many mystics from different spiritual traditions. These she labels the awakening stage, the stage of purification, the stage of illumination, the dark night of the soul, and Divine union. I have adapted her classification for my own purposes, expanding on the stages based on my experience, my personal theology, and the writings of other mystics.

The five stages of healing and enlightenment also represent the growth of an energy that will release the Holy Spirit from within your own being. The Christian mystic Meister Eckhart wrote, "To understand one's vocation as an artist, we should interpret the verse 'The Holy Spirit shall come upon you' (Luke 1:35) to mean 'The Holy Spirit shall come *from within you*'" [my italics]. When I read those words one morning at prayer, I felt as if everything I had learned over the years regarding healing and prayer suddenly came together. The Holy Spirit, I realized, isn't "out there" somewhere. Each of us was created with the spark of Divine energy implanted in our very essence so that we can receive guidance directly from God. Unfortunately, by going to school and church and getting "educated," the knowing element of our being, that direct connection with God, has, to some extent, been wiped away. The result is that we often feel broken, alienated, out of joint, or spiritually ill. Our job in life, in one sense, is to heal ourselves by rediscovering that sense of knowing. We tend to think of enlightenment as an exceptional act of illumination that comes from beyond us. But, in effect, it is something that happens when we heal the essential imbalance within us. To do that, to make such a leap of faith, we need some extraordinary motivation. From where will it come?

Peggy Lee had a big hit years ago with a song called "Is That All There Is?" This is a question that each of us has to ask at some point in our lives, in our relationships with other people, with ourselves, or with the personality we call God: Is this all that I can expect? It is one of the most important questions you will ever ask yourself because it leads inevitably to the two questions that begin your spiritual journey in earnest: Who am I? and Where am I going?

Most people don't ask these questions until they are at least 40 years old, because for the 20 years since becoming adults they have been trying to avoid asking them. They may have been looking at their lives, but in no way will they admit to themselves or others that life is not all it has been cracked up to be. They think, instead, that they just haven't gotten it right yet. But if your life isn't working by the time you're 40, you have to ask yourself how likely it is that it's all going to fall miraculously into place in the next few years.

Once we begin to ask these questions and to take them seriously, we begin to pass from the level of believing—that is, taking on faith certain doctrines and dogmas that may have been handed down to us—to the level of knowing. At this level, we learn to accept our intuitive feelings that certain things are true. At the level of knowing, we experience no doubts. That's why a master such as Jesus could say "Whoever . . . does not doubt in his heart, but believes that what he says will come to pass, it will be done for him" (Mark 11:23-24). The potential is there for everything good to happen, but if you are living according to a belief system that says down deep "I hope this will work," then it is someone else's belief, and 99 percent of the time it will not work for you. As a result, most of us lose our self-confidence because we don't recognize this higher essence of our nature, which is God. We begin to blame God and believe that God is against us, and that prayer doesn't work.

Yet I will demonstrate that prayer does work exactly as it is supposed to work. If you follow the simple principles in each of the five stages as I present them, you will begin to discern how your prayer life can change—and how, in turn, it can change your life.

### The True Meaning of the Parable of the Prodigal Son

On a recent trip to Tustin, California, to conduct a four-day healing intensive on the role of prayer in healing, I had a profound experience that at first seemed coincidental but that I know was anything but. I boarded my plane on Saturday with a calm assurance that the Spirit of God was in charge—not only of this journey, but also of leading me into the teachings I was to present the next four days at the Unity Church of Tustin, beginning with a church service Sunday morning.

The trip was peaceful enough until we began our bumpy descent through some turbulent air over Los Angeles. To take my mind off the turbulence, I picked up the magazine in front of me and began browsing idly through it. I happened to come across an advertisement for an artist named Thomas Kincaid, known as "The Painter of Light." I had never seen his work before, but the illustration caught my eye. It showed a small village with snow on the rooftops, fir trees, houses with their lights on inside, wrought-iron lamps with large glass bulbs, and a single car coming down the snowy roadway. The image reminded me of Christmas in the 1940s, when I was a child and it would be snowing as we were getting ready to go to midnight mass. I was so enraptured with the painting that I hoped I would be able to find out more about Kincaid and maybe purchase one of his paintings. I later learned that Kincaid likes to paint things the way they were in "simpler" times, which is an attitude I can easily embrace. Discovering the painting also had the happy effect of relaxing and calming me during our bumpy landing.

As a way to unwind and reward myself after the Sunday morning service, which went very well, I asked the pastor if she would like to go to one of the nearby malls in Costa Mesa. I'm not a great believer in extraordinary asceticism, as you can probably tell, and I actually find shopping in malls relaxing. It was close to Christmas, and the parking lot of the mall I wanted to visit was so clogged with traffic that we went across the street to a less crowded place called Crystal Court. As we arrived, we were greeted by groups of children singing Christmas carols. I was so delighted by their youthful voices that instead of indulging my desire to shop, I stood there listening to Christmas music for an hour and a half.

As I was waiting for the pastor to return from her shopping, I felt guided to look to my left, where I saw in bright lights the words THOMAS KINCAID GALLERIES. Stunned, I walked over and saw in the window the very painting that I had been admiring in the magazine on the plane. I walked in and had only one question of the gallery people: Do you ship? I didn't care what the price was, because I had to have the painting.

My guidance for that Sunday's message had been to teach the parable of The Prodigal Son related by Jesus in the Gospel of Luke (15:11-32), allowing myself to be guided by the Spirit as to what to say about the key words in that passage. As I awoke early Monday morning for my prayer and meditation time, I received guidance to begin the four-day intensive with the same parable, but to couple it with the guidance of the Spirit leading me to the Kincaid painting. I did not know yet—as I don't for most of my messages in retreats—where this was going to go. But at the end of my teaching that morning, I realized that the story of the Prodigal is not the story of two physical beings, the son and his father, but the story of our return to the essence of our true nature, which is Spirit.

That journey takes many forms and is conceptualized in different ways by different cultures and different spiritual traditions. According to the Vedic map of the human energy system developed by the Hindu tradition, our vital energy is contained in seven centers of consciousness called *chakras*. These energy centers are not actually located in the physical body, as some people believe. The physical body is surrounded by several subtle bodies or energetic sheaths, and the chakras are located within those; they do correspond, however, to certain areas of the physical body, beginning at the base of the spine and moving up to the crown of the head. Through various psychophysical practices including yoga, breath control, and meditation, practitioners have traditionally sought to cleanse the chakras in sequence from bottom to top. This purification of the body facilitates the flow of energy—called *prana* in India, *chi* in China, and *grace* in the Western Christian system—as a prelude to Divine union.

The movement of the individual soul through the stages of healing prior to union with God is described by Indian teachings as the upward movement of energy through the chakras. What in the East is called *liberation, enlightenment,* or *awakening* (*Buddha* means literally "one who has awakened"), in the Western mystical tradition is known as the Divine marriage, the return to God. Although this path has usually been relegated to the mystical literature and has not been promulgated among the public by the institutional religions of the West, it does appear in coded form in the parable of the Prodigal Son.

As I realized that morning in Tustin, this story is not about a father and his two sons, but rather about the growth of spiritual consciousness. The path taken by the younger son, who squanders his inheritance in debauchery, represents a journey away from and then a return to the Father's house, a return to God and the essence of his true nature, which is Spirit. In addition, the parable replicates the five stages of healing, as we will see.

The story of the Prodigal goes like this. A man had two sons. The younger son told his father that he wanted his share of his inheritance without waiting for his father to die. His father agreed to divide his wealth between his two sons. A few days later, the younger son anxiously packed up all of his belongings and took a trip to a distant land, where he wasted all of his money on wild living. About the time his money ran out, a great famine swept over the land and he began to starve. Persuading a local farmer to hire him to feed his pigs, the young man became so hungry that even the husks that he was giving to the pigs looked good to him.

Reduced to such humiliating straits, the young man began to think about his situation. When he finally came to his senses, he realized that while he was dying of hunger, back home even his father's hired men had food enough to spare. He resolved to go home and say, "Father, I have sinned against you and against heaven. I am no longer worthy of being called your child. Please take me on as a hired hand."

So he returned home, and while he was still a long way off, his father saw him coming and was filled with loving compassion and ran to him and embraced and kissed him. His son said what he had rehearsed, but his father simply told the servants to bring the finest robe in the house and put it on his son, and a jeweled ring for his finger and sandals for his feet. "Kill the fatted calf," he added. "We must celebrate with a feast, for this son of mine was dead and is now returned to life. He was lost and now is found." And the party began.

The elder son was distraught at this and asked his father why all this fuss was being made over the son who had squandered his inheritance. "I have stayed and faithfully worked for you all my life, and you have never killed the fatted calf for me."

And the father said, "Son, you are always with me, and all that is mine is yours. But it was right to rejoice in the return of your brother, for I thought him dead, and yet he is alive, was lost and now is found."

The Prodigal has always been one of my favorite stories and teaching tools from the Christian Testament. But over time, certain words and phrases have leapt out at me with special significance when I meditated on this parable of Jesus—phrases such as "distant country," "squandered his wealth," "severe famine," "came to his senses," and "his father saw him and filled with compassion went out to embrace him." I was taught by my Scripture professors in graduate school and in seminary that in studying the sacred writings of any religious tradition, we ought to remember that the ancients generally looked beyond the surface or even the metaphorical level to the mystical level to draw out certain words or phrases that have spiritual resonance.

As I continued teaching the parable of the Prodigal at my intensives since that morning, specific words began to jump out at me again. I expounded on them as if I had studied these particular phrases for years. Reading the words *distant country*, for example, I began to see very profoundly in the depths of my being that any time we feel separated and alienated from the presence of God, from that Spirit at the very core of our being, we are living in a distant country. When we begin to focus only on the material world, we lose sight of our true essence of divinity as if it were far off in the distance. We are then squandering the wealth of our spiritual essence in what could be called "wild living"—living that is off course from our true nature, going in a direction other than love, peace, joy, and spiritual power. We have lost our citizenship in the spiritual dimension and have become a citizen of the material world. That experience alone creates a severe famine within our being, a hunger and a thirst that cannot be filled by any food other than God. Like the prodigal, we need to return, to become aware of our true consciousness.

The father sees his son coming from "a long way off," as if he had been scanning the horizon, no matter how long the boy has been gone, waiting for him to return. This is a perfect example of what God is: always there, always conscious of us, never judging, never condemning, but waiting for the return of His children. Before the son is even close by, the father runs out to greet him and embraces and kisses him and makes him feel that he is truly beloved, in spite of all his misdeeds. As the old mystical saying goes, *If you take one step in God's direction, He will take ten steps toward you.*

Even as the boy tries to express his sorrow to his father, his dad just won't hear of it. He says, in effect, "Son, it's okay." Immediately the father tells his servants to bring "the best robe and put it on him." The boy was probably almost naked or in rags, so the father restores him to his former state and even embellishes his appearance by putting a ring on his finger. In mystical terminology, the ring is a symbol of spiritual authority, and putting the ring on the son's finger is a sign that the young man has realized his true essence. He now sees that he can live in the consciousness of his heavenly Parent. In his position, we might say, "I am an emanation of light. If God is Divine light-energy and love, then as a child of God, I am an emanation of energy and love."

I was struck most forcibly by the fact that the Prodigal's awakening occurs when the young man feels the hunger in his stomach and begins to realize that when he was in the father's house, he never longed for anything. Every need was already met before he even thought of asking for it. Recognizing his hunger, his sense of separation and alienation from his father and his father's house, the boy then comes to his senses.

Like the Prodigal, all of us are incarnated into form and matter and lose our way. Then at some point, usually through some form of crisis, we begin to come to our senses, and this marks the initiation of the unfolding of consciousness. Out of love, the Divine Parent allows certain things to occur in our lives that act as wake-up calls to spur us to return to the essence of our true nature. Ultimately, the Prodigal Son returns from the land of matter and form to the land of Divine energy, light, and life. He hears his wake-up call urging him to confront his fears and illusions, which, just as with our own lives, are so often the basis of all suffering, all inner hunger.

By following the path of this story and its many implications throughout this book, I hope to offer you an opportunity to grow spiritually and heal your sense of separation from God. In my first book, *The Healing Path of Prayer*, I presented an overview of the principles of prayer as it applies to the experience of God's Divine energy (the Holy Spirit) in our lives. Now I would like to take you through the journey of healing and its relationship to our life of prayer. The five stages that we will be looking at are the awakening stage, the purification stage, the illuminative stage, the dark night of the soul, and the stage of Divine union. Although the stages may overlap and are not always clearly discernible, you ought to recognize that spiritual growth and healing are taking place on some level of your being at each stage.

## The Five Stages

The first stage, or **awakening**, is the simplest of the five stages of healing, and yet it can take the longest because we don't usually get the message the first time. We may be cruising along in life, thinking that we have it made, when suddenly something happens that snaps us out of our complacency. On the other hand, we may be stumbling and groping our way along, confused and mentally disheveled, when we hit bottom, as they say in the Twelve-Step Programs, and realize that we need to change our life. During the awakening, a crisis may occur: divorce, the death of a loved one, abandonment, losing your job or all your money, or being diagnosed with a serious or terminal illness. What's important is not the crisis itself, but being brought to the point at which you ask, "Is this all there is in life?"

It makes little difference which scenario we are living when the wake-up calls arrive, because if we are ready and willing to listen to them, they will urge us to turn our lives around. Suddenly our accomplishments seem hollow, the reputation we worked so hard to achieve loses its meaning, and the good life isn't so great after all. We may realize that our life is a mess, that we need to change a job that is stifling us, get out of a frustrating or abusive marriage, or change the habits that are taking us away from God. Once again, the immediate circumstances don't matter as much as the fact that they provide the impetus we need to start to reexamine our lives.

After the awakening has finally taken hold and we have made substantial changes in the way we live, we become so consumed with our awareness of God that we begin to remove every obstacle that keeps us from experiencing God. Following the cold shock of the awakening, the **purification** stage can be a gentle and even blissful period, during which we set about lovingly clearing the dross out of our spiritual life. Some people begin a regular prayer and meditation practice or choose to follow a religious tradition, possibly returning to the birth religion they had long since rejected; others change their diets and start a regimen of exercise or yoga; still others may decide they need to change where they live or the kind of work they do to allow their lives to be more in sync with their newfound desire to be closer to God. Although some amount of sacrifice and uprooting of old patterns may be in order, we generally experience these as satisfying and fulfilling, and the psychic and physical energy that is generated by prayer, meditation, yoga, or exercise is usually more than enough to fuel the most challenging life changes.

In the stage of **illumination,** certain spiritual phenomena and graces begin to express themselves. In certain cases, healings occur, prophecy is given, and people sing or pray in languages they have never learned. Those extraordinary experiences can be dangerous in some ways; they can give you a heady feeling, a sense that you have been singled out for special powers. These *are* powerful experiences, but for that very reason, if you are not prepared for them, they can distract you from your real purpose, especially if you talk about your exploits.

"You spoke in tongues?"

"That's right, I spoke in tongues. Do you speak in tongues? No? Too bad."

I have witnessed people getting caught up in these manifestations of spiritual power, especially at conventions of Charismatic Catholics in which I participated in Southern California and Chicago. They would get up to testify about an experience they had—"testifying" in this context meaning confessing or witnessing an experience of receiving God's grace. That's all well and good, but in some of these situations I was observing, the subtext was often "I have had this experience, and so I must *be* somebody."

The truth is that you already *are* somebody—you just don't know it. Experiences of spiritual powers don't give you anything you didn't have before; they are just manifestations of something good occurring within. They do not bestow healthy self-esteem upon you if you don't already have it. But I guarantee that unless you already possess a sturdy sense of self-worth, you will fall prey to your own ego and could end up submarined by delusions of spiritual grandeur.

Every mystic I have ever studied, from Paramahansa Yogananda to John of the Cross, has warned us to be very careful of spiritual or psychic phenomena because they will rebound on you and destroy you. In India, where advanced psychic powers including telepathy and bilocation have long been accepted manifestations of advanced spiritual progress, the masters continue to warn aspirants to ignore these powers, which they call *siddhis*. The reason is not that anything is inherently wrong with such powers, which are very real and are practiced beneficially by the great saints, but that attachment to them can lead to the misperception that they automatically bestow saintliness on the bearer. When we hear about so-called advanced spiritual masters abusing their positions through financial or sexual misconduct, it is often a sign that they have allowed themselves to be deluded by their own attainments.

That's why the Master Jesus said that when you pray, go into your closet where you are alone with God. He meant both to enter a place of inner connection with God, shutting out outside distractions, and to pray in such a way that you do not call attention to yourself. That way, if you do receive heady spiritual phenomena, you can let them be between you and God. Paul was addressing this issue in his First Letter to the Corinthians (13:1-2), when he said, "If I speak in the tongues of men and angels, but have not love, I am a noisy gong or a clanging cymbal. And if I have prophetic powers, and understand all mysteries and all knowledge, and if I have all faith, so as to remove mountains, but have not love, I am nothing." Spiritual phenomena do not make you great in the eyes of God. What makes you great is love for God, yourself, and others.

I want to make clear, though, that spiritual phenomena need not be anything so obvious as jumping up at a prayer meeting and speaking in tongues, or rolling on the floor in ecstasy, spouting prophecies that may or may not be genuine, or levitating during meditative trance. Spiritual phenomena can and often are as subtle as receiving a hunch or intuition that you ought to do something or call someone, or that you ought *not* do something. It is a question of receptivity. You look at a menu in a restaurant, find something you think you will like, and decide to order it. But then somebody else in your party says, "Wow, the fish special looks good! I think I'll have that." You change your order—and when the dish comes, you hate it.

The **dark night of the soul** is one of the most powerful healing stages one can work through, and yet it is also one of the most harrowing. In the two stages that precede it, *you* are directing the action. During the illumination, you learn to follow your hunches, to recognize the workings of Spirit in your subtlest intuitions. In the purification stage, *you* do the purifying, removing obstacles from your life that you feel are keeping you from a more profound experience of God. You take away from your life what you consider to be bad to replace it with good. But during the dark night, God takes charge and begins to pull the rug out from under you, removing the good things to make you receptive to the best. You may feel that your life is going well materially and spiritually, but God knows that you can be more. So He throws you a challenge, but the scary part is that you don't feel that you're in control anymore.

Because teachings about the dark night are often so misguided, many people are afraid to enter this stage, so they set up blocks to healing. Put simply, the dark night is a period—it can and usually does stretch on for years—during which we feel lost. We have begun in earnest to leave behind our old ways, the old comforts and securities that we have clung to for most of our lives, but we haven't yet reached the far shore, as Buddhism refers to enlightenment. Caught somewhere between our old self, which now seems dry and desiccated, and a new self that hasn't fully formed, we may even feel that God has abandoned us, and we may regret ever having started out on this path. "The mystical path is best not taken," writes Swami Muktananda. "But once begun, there is no turning back."

Once we learn to accept the feeling of wandering in the dark and begin to have faith that God will see us through, we are then ready to enter the fifth and final stage, which is called by various religious traditions *mystical marriage*, the *Divine romance*, or **Divine union**. The Eastern Orthodox Churches may have the best term to define the fifth stage: *deification*. During this stage, you become aware that you are of

God, and once you *know* that, you no longer merely believe it. All beliefs are undercut with doubts. Until you ponder a particular belief and come to know it to be true, it is still only a belief, and it will fill your life with confusion. When you shift during the stage of deification to knowing that God is *for* you, then your life changes profoundly. Your overwhelming assurance of the love of God manifests itself in a strong desire to be of service to others. There ceases to be any significant difference between God's will and your will, because you have become a vessel of his peace, to borrow a phrase from the prayer of St. Francis.

As we discuss these stages, you ought not feel guilty or inadequate, saying, for instance, "I'm only in purification." You must take each level for what it is, be aware of where you are, be grateful for it, and allow yourself to grow into the next level at your own rate of development. Do not think because you have a physical malady that has not healed that you have somehow failed; as I have said, profound healing also takes place on the psychological, emotional, and spiritual levels.

Just as enlightenment and healing usually come in stages, so our receptivity to God's will evolves over time. We make a mistake to try to rush the process or to expect it to happen too quickly. We also learn to pray in a series of stages that, as they unfold, often parallel the five stages of healing and enlightenment, as we will see in part 2 of this book. By coming to recognize and know each stage, learning how prayer affects and is affected by each stage, and becoming acquainted with the potential pitfalls and negative reflections that can crop up in certain stages—what I call the shadow side of the healing process—you will be able to move more mindfully through each stage in turn.

# CHAPTER TWO

# The Awakening Stage

A number of years ago I was stationed in a large parish along with two other priests in order to attend to 3,000 people. Our church was large enough for about a thousand people, and rather than celebrate six masses every Sunday with a half-empty church, we decided to divide up the parish among the three of us and each say one mass on Sunday that would be distinctive. That way the congregation would get to know our personal styles of saying mass and could come back to the priest who most appealed to them. The pastor was an older, traditional man who took the 10:30 mass and kept it traditional. The choir sang the old hymns, and the congregation just listened; they didn't even sing along. This priest even kept a little of the old Church Latin, and the people who came to his mass loved that.

The second priest was from Spain, and he agreed to take the eight o'clock mass and do it in Spanish. We had a fairly large Hispanic population in the parish, including a number of Mariachi musicians who agreed to play and sing the hymns in Spanish. This was a great success, and the mass was frequently full.

I said that I would take the 9:15 mass, although my first thought when I volunteered was, *Why did I say that?* The 9:15 was the worst mass because for some reason, only about 200 people usually came at that hour, and they all sat in the back. Then I heard myself say, "Let's make this kind of a rock mass."

The pastor said, "Wha-what do you mean, a *rock* mass?"

I told him that I would go to the parish school and see how many children, young people, even high school students wanted to be a part of the choir. I ended up with 55 young and enthusiastic volunteers, mostly from high school, who played the drums, the organ, the piano, maracas, tambourines, everything. Within three months, this mass was standing room only. The good news was that there were often capacity crowds at the other masses, too, because the word had gotten out that the priests in this parish were a little more open and spontaneous than most, and we were starting to draw some people from neighboring parishes.

One morning, after about three months of capacity attendance at my masses, as the announcements were made and the lector asked the congregation to rise and sing the opening hymn, I started to walk down the aisle as usual. We always vested in the back of the church and came down the long aisle that led to the altar. It was Laetare Sunday—in the Catholic Church that's the third Sunday in Advent, a celebratory mass when the priest wears pink vestments. Coming down the aisle, I thought, *Listen to those people clapping and singing—over a thousand of them!*

It was hard to remain humble because I kind of felt like Nero walking down that aisle. I held a hymnal, but there was a part of me that wanted to wave like one of those Roman emperors in a Hollywood movie—played by Peter Ustinov, who was about the same body type as I was then. In those days we had luxurious vestments, including a long, white alb that was made of linen, based on a sacred garment worn by high priests in the Old Testament. The linen was as much as a foot longer than the one wearing it, so you had to tuck it up and tie it with a cord called a cincture. These garments were all symbolic; the cincture, for example, was a symbol of the statement that Jesus made to Peter: "There will come a time in which a cord will be wrapped around you, and you will be led where you don't want to go." This means that the Holy Spirit will do the leading; as a priest, you will give up your ego and go where the Spirit leads you.

In the seminary, where you study all manner of odd things, we actually took lessons on how to tie the cincture so it wouldn't come loose. I thought I had tied it properly, but as I was coming down the aisle, unknown to me the knot began to unravel. The altar has six marble steps, with three big marble thrones on top, and the biggest of the three was mine. As I said, it isn't easy to be humble in a situation like that. When I got to the foot of the altar, I looked up at the splendor in front of me and I bowed. And when I bowed, so did the cord; it loosened completely and fell to the floor. As I went to take my first step up the altar, that extra foot of the alb draped itself over my shoe, and in two seconds I was kissing the altar step.

The most humbling thing at that moment was to realize that not everybody in that audience loved me. I had been under the impression that they did, yet when I hit the marble and heard some of the people let out an "Ohhhhhh," I just as clearly heard some of them laughing. At the time I weighed 240 pounds, and I was lying on the floor thinking, *My God, how am I going to get up?* Neither of my altar boys weighed more than 80 pounds. I looked up at the closest one, whose eyes were like silver dollars as he stared at me, and I said, "Pick me up!"

"What?" he said.

"I *said*, pick me up!"

The kid threw up both hands and practically yelled out, "With what?"

He probably meant that he would have to call for a derrick and windlass to hoist my carcass from where it lay. Under the circumstances, I did the only thing possible. I gave myself a quick push up with both arms, picked up the cord and the extra length of alb, and continued walking up those steps. Suddenly I saw the whole scene as if from an overhead camera, and I started to laugh, realizing how funny I must have looked to everyone else. You could say that I expanded my consciousness to include the consciousness of the people watching me, and shared in their laughter. It occurred to me later that God had literally brought me to my knees. At that moment, however, the thought came into my consciousness: *Ronald, you have only two choices in this matter, as you do with all of life. You can become bitter or you can become better; it's up to you.*

That's when the awakening stage began for me. I became a repentant prodigal in my own right and decided that I didn't have to live in depression or despair. I didn't have to continue to live wearing masks filled with fear, which is what the story of the Prodigal Son is all about. I've since had other wake-up calls, because one usually isn't enough, but this was the one that got me started. Like the Prodigal, I had become separated from God, from loved ones, and from all creation. I had entered the priesthood with every intention of serving humanity and growing closer to God, but along the way I had become lost in what the mystical poet Dante famously referred to as the "dark wood of error." I had grown complacent and bloated, both figuratively and literally, and had delusions of my own grandeur. There's nothing like falling flat on your face in front of a thousand people to deflate that particular bubble.

In the awakening stage, whatever happens to us makes us confront our fears, and until we confront our fears, we can never effectively be healed. I don't mean simply a healing of the body, a healing of the spirit, or a healing of the soul, as profound as those are. I mean nothing less than the healing of our whole life so that our life can be a celebration and experience of joy.

The metaphorical story of the Prodigal as the journey of consciousness goes something like this: We have all come from the realm called the heavenly. We are emanations of God's light, but at some point we decide to go it alone. This can be a necessary step in life, of course. The Russian mystic Gurdjieff used to say that before you can lose your ego, you first have to have a fully developed one. At a certain point, we may decide to take control of our lives—a good thing—but we do it in a way that takes us away from God and into the land of illusion. There we may sojourn for some time until the awakening starts us on the path back to God. That's when we learn that there is another way to take control of our lives—by surrendering and turning our lives over to the Holy Spirit.

The story of the Prodigal is the story of moving from the land of illusion back to the land of Spirit. The Prodigal's awakening occurred when the young man felt the hunger in his stomach and began to realize that when he had been in a state of conscious connection to the Divine Parent (living in his father's house), he never longed for anything. Every need was already met before he could even think of asking for it. Then the Prodigal did what we all do at some time in our lives: He left the house of the Father, abandoning the essence of God's love, to become a person who not only lives in the world but is *of* the world. When we do that, we lose our direction and our sense of oneness, which is replaced by a sense of separation. We find ourselves starving to death in the famine of the senses; after the awakening, we begin to move back from the land of matter and separateness to the land of Spirit and light and union with the Divine energy of God.

That is the essence of healing, whether we think that what we want to heal is a physical ailment, a disease or disability, a psychological scar, or even a spiritual malady—a feeling of distance from God or of aridity in our soul. The healing I mean is a healing into wholeness in which no aspect of the human agenda is left unhealed. Those who seek to heal their spiritual separation by turning their backs on the rest of humanity, for instance, are not necessarily healing their lives. They may actually be dividing themselves even more than they had been. Many monastics and ascetics do not necessarily become better people, although they may become more pious. In fact, any time you set up a paradigm of "us" *versus* "them," you no longer sense the oneness of God within you. That's what the story of the Prodigal is about, whatever form it takes in your own life.

When the father in the parable gives a share of the estate to his younger son, the word *share* implies that the fullness is gone. When he was living on his father's estate, he enjoyed the fullness of life. Once he has separated from the estate, however, his fortunes begin to decline. Once in the "distant country," the son squanders his wealth of conscious awareness that he is one with God and every need is met. The moment we pull away and begin to believe we can do this on our own, that consciousness falls apart. "Wild living" or "loose living" here is a symbol of being in the world *and* of the world. "And after he had spent everything," the text continues, "a great famine arose in that country and he began to be in want." Spending everything has fairly clear implications of the utter depletion of one's psychic and spiritual ener-gy. The famine represents the lack of spiritual nourishment that results from distancing oneself from the Father.

What Jesus is attempting to tell us is simple: You must make an effort to remain aware of your oneness with God. But how do you do that? For me, the answer is prayer. That's why prayer needs to be the first pri-ority in our life. People often say they don't have time for prayer. When I was growing up, a song was very popular among my Protestant friends called "Sweet Hour of Prayer." In recent years, I always seem to hear a preacher say, "Now let's have a word of prayer." What happened to the Sweet Hour? Without at least an hour in prayer each day, my work would become a futile effort of intellectual gymnastics. Prayer breaks down countless barriers and makes my work go easier and faster; every minute I spend in it seems to be repaid ten times over. *A Course In Miracles* (20.IV.8.4-6) puts it this way:

> Once you accept [God's] plan as the one function that you would
> fulfill, there will be nothing else the Holy Spirit will not arrange for
> you without your effort. He will go before you making straight your
> path, and leaving in your way no stones to trip on, and no obstacles to
> bar your way. Nothing you need will be denied you.

That text actually paraphrases Isaiah 45:2, in which the Lord says to Cyrus, "I will go before you and will humble the great ones of the earth. I will break in pieces the gates of brass and will burst the bars of iron." That's the way the Spirit speaks to me, saying, in effect, "Ronald, I can do this without any help from you, thank you." All we have to do is surrender and follow the hunches, thoughts, and ideas that are given to us, and the Spirit will go before us making straight our path and leav-ing no obstacles. Nothing we need will be denied us, and all seeming difficulties will melt away before we reach them. This is not to be con-fused with Calvinist predestination, or the born-again Christian notion that once you're saved, you don't have to do anything more. As St. Paul tells us, we have to work out our salvation with a sense of awe. In the Gospel of John (21:18), Jesus says to Peter:

*I assure you,*
*when you were young,*
*you put on your own belt*
*and walked wherever you pleased;*
*but when you grow old*
*you will stretch out your hands,*
*and someone else will put a belt around you*
*and take you where you would rather not go.*

Although this verse is sometimes interpreted as Christ's prediction to Peter of the death that he must suffer to glorify God, I believe it refers to the death that all of us must go through to please God, which is the death of ego dominance—not the death of the ego per se but of its dominance in our lives. In this regard, four Scriptural quotations have changed my life:

*I cry to God who fulfills his purpose for me.*
   Psalm 57:2

*God will perform that which He has appointed for me to do.*
   Psalm 138:8

*God perfects that which concerns me, for the Lord performs that which he has planned for me.*
   Job 23:14

*Man charts the course of his life, but God guides the footsteps.*
   Proverbs 16:9

What all these Scriptures are saying about the journey back to God is that without joy, love, peace, or gratitude, there can be no lasting healing. And these virtues emanate from a life yielded to the Spirit in trust and confidence.

That day years ago when I fell on the altar, I didn't learn the lesson I was intended to. It took another ten years or so for me to realize that the only choices we have when responding to anything that seems to go wrong in our lives are, as I said, to become bitter or to become better. Any awakening is about confronting our fears and allowing God's Spirit to alleviate those fears by yielding to the Spirit's direction as we perceive it within us.

I want to remind you, however, of the essential gentleness and compassion of the Father during what can be the profoundly upsetting time of the awakening. He expects us to discipline ourselves to be alert to Spirit's urgings, but not to beat ourselves over the head. In his wonderfully healing book *How Good Do We Have to Be?*, Rabbi Harold Kushner concludes with a statement that sums up the story of the Prodigal and the story of my own life in a way that makes this point very eloquently: "Life is not a trap set for us by God so that He can condemn us for failing." Kushner writes:

> Life is not a spelling bee, where no matter how many words you
> have gotten right, if you make one mistake you are disqualified. Life is
> more like a baseball season, where even the best team loses one-third
> of its games and even the worst team has its days of brilliance. Our
> goal is not to go all year without ever losing a game. Our goal is to
> win more than we lose, and if we can do that consistently enough,
> then when the end comes, we will have won it all.
>
> In the beginning, in the infancy of the human race as in the infancy
> of an individual human being, life was simple. Then we ate of the fruit
> of the tree and we gained the knowledge that some things are good
> and others are bad. We learned how painfully complex life could be.
>
> But at the end, if we are brave enough to love, if we are strong
> enough to forgive, if we are generous enough to rejoice in another's
> happiness, and if we are wise enough to know that there is enough
> love to go around for us all, then we can achieve a fulfillment that no
> other living creature will ever know. We can reenter paradise.

The point of Rabbi Kushner's book is that we misinterpret Genesis by seeing Adam and Eve as being punished for their sin of eating the fruit of the tree forbidden to them. What they did, he says, was to become human, to enter the world of polarities and difficult moral decisions. The Greek scholar of mysticism Kyriacos Markides likens the state of Adam and Eve to "the state of the Soul just prior to its entrance into the worlds of time and space where experience can be acquired." According to the Teachings, the ancient mystical wisdom to which Markides has been made privy, "Adam and Eve are not being expelled from Paradise, but voluntarily leave the paradisiac state with the blessings of God the Father (or Mother) in the same way that the Prodigal Son (or Daughter) leaves the loving parental palace."

Markides sees the Prodigal, as I do, as a prototype of the seeker, the human soul that has begun the arduous process of awakening and has voluntarily left the sham paradise of ignorance to engage the spiritual path. He will encounter suffering and deprivation and will undergo a change of heart, but the journey will one day lead him back to his Father's estate. "When the Prodigal Son leaves the Palace," Markides concludes, "he does so precisely because in reality he wishes to become conscious of the Palace to which eventually he will return."

In the awakening stage, as I have said, something earth-shattering usually happens—often a crisis that gets your attention and makes you realize that you are not in control. It can be a divorce, the onset of a serious illness, an automobile accident, the death of a loved one, or losing your job or all your savings. Most of us think of these events as disasters, although we could just as easily view them as the opening of the journey of healing and enlightenment. In a few cases, the awakening may be initiated by a religious or spiritual experience. To the person on the Hindu path, whether Indian or not, this would be called the Kundalini experience; to the Christian it might be called the born-again experience. Although the term *born again* has become a negative cliché wrongly associated with certain conservative political views, the conversion experience itself—which may more accurately be described as a rebirth of self-worth—is valid and real, and has nothing to do with political viewpoints. (According to several studies conducted by the prestigious Princeton Religious Research Center, two out of three Americans who identify themselves as "born-again" Christians hold liberal social views and disassociate themselves from the so-called

Religious Right.) A conversion experience can be as simple as going to church at Christmas for the first time in many years and waking up to the fact that God *is*. God suddenly moves through your whole being; you begin to cry without knowing why, and you are suffused by a longing for love and peace and joy. You desire to fill a void in the spiritual dimension, or what I call "the God gap"—a sense of emptiness that only the experience of God's presence can fill.

As for the Kundalini experience, you don't have to be a Hindu to have it, because the literature is full of accounts by Westerners with no background in Eastern religion who have had such spontaneous openings. But like true conversion experiences, they are relatively rare, because most of us are too dense. My experience, both of my own life and of many people I have counseled over the years, is that it often takes something closer to a material or physical crisis than what is commonly referred to as a "religious experience" to start the awakening process. We tend to be so firmly connected to the material world, especially in the West, that we need to have some of our familiar supports pulled out from under us before we are willing to let go. A serious illness, for instance, may change our daily consciousness in remarkable ways. Especially after undergoing a long course of medical treatment involving drugs, surgery, or radiation treatments, people have reported actually feeling separated from their physical bodies in ways that have led them to reevaluate their entire lives.

On a basic human level, someone whose child or loved one almost dies will often report that the experience has made them rethink their priorities; the result may not be a religious conversion but can be as simple as deciding to spend more time with their family and less time in the rat race. After such an experience, men and women in high-pressure careers in business, the professions, or professional sports often decide to cut back on their commitment to their work, to "stop and smell the roses." They would hardly describe this as an awakening, yet in some form it is.

One woman who came to my workshop in California was a typical example. She announced that she had joined the Unity Church two and a half years ago when her 30-year marriage ended. "Up until that time

I had been in complete charge of my life," she told the group. "I had planned everything so completely, and then the bottom fell out. Now I'm learning that it was probably the best thing that ever happened. I'm here to heal and to continue on that path."

Whatever the circumstances, someone who has had an awakening has reached the threshold at which they are finally willing to say, "I'm ready to do something different." They haven't recognized yet that their life up to this point has already been a kind of crucifixion, yet the awakening stage is the symbolic resurrection. They begin to see both themselves and God in a different light. Maybe they become aware of some of the beautiful passages of the Jewish tradition in the Hebrew Bible, in which God is saying, "I lay before you life and death, blessings and curses. Choose life, that you may love God" (Deut. 30:19). Or the passage in the Prophet Jeremiah (29:11) in which the Lord says, "The plans I have for you are not plans to destroy you but to give you a future and a hope." Does that sound like the God you were raised with?

One important aspect of the awakening stage is a rising awareness of the power of choice. Whether we make a momentous decision or not, we do tend to become aware of the options facing us, and this may generate an uncomfortable tension. A psychotherapist once described this situation in terms of baseball. Whether you hit a home run or strike out, your course of action is relatively simple; either you circle the bases and get congratulated by your teammates, or you carry your bat back to the dugout. But if you hit a ball in the gap, as you round first base you have a decision to make: play it safe and stay at first, or try to stretch your single into a double. What you decide to do will depend on a whole range of factors, including how far the ball was hit, the strength of the outfielder's arm, your own speed, and maybe how lucky you're feeling at the moment. Likewise, people who have had an awakening experience may feel exhilarated in some ways, but they may also feel the discomfort that opportunity often presents: Play it safe and stay where you are, or try to stretch things to the next level.

Most people in this scenario remain stuck in the awakening stage until they become aware that it will take some specific action on their part to move out of this stage into the next one. They may be subliminally aware that they need to start moving—hence the feelings of discomfort and tension—but they often find ways to quell those suspicions—at least until the next wake-up call arrives and hits them a little harder.

Unlike the way spiritual conversions have been romanticized by certain movies and books, the awakening stage can be experienced as difficult precisely because it urges us to begin to confront certain issues within us that we have previously ignored or suppressed. Life can no longer go on as usual; it has suddenly and irrevocably been infused with a deep sense of longing, separation, alienation, and aloneness. You may experience this as a confrontation between you and God, between you and others in your life, or between two contradictory drives within yourself. If the conflict is within, it may cause you to come to terms with your own fears and anxieties, real or imagined; as well as your feelings of guilt, shame, depression, despair, and whatever is perceived to have caused those feelings.

### The Role of Prayer

During the awakening stage, you will ask yourself the three questions I posed at the beginning of chapter 1. The "Peggy Lee" question—Is this all there is?—can be the most difficult of the three. Wherever you are in your walk, you have come to the awareness that even after achieving whatever it was you thought you wanted, you don't feel full. You may have been looking for success in your work, for artistic achievement, financial security, a relationship with someone you truly love, a stable family, or just a life of pleasure. You may either have achieved those things or been torn apart in failing to, but the net result is the same: You end up suspecting that there must be more to life than the particular set of habits and conveniences and fears and anxieties that have become part of your everyday awareness.

When you come face to face with these questions, you have two paths of response. You can either go back to where you were before the questions arose—your pre-awakening stage—or you can commit yourself to moving on honestly, no matter how difficult the path may appear. But how do you move on? What can help you make the transition from blissfully (or miserably) ignorant to painfully aware?

One important event that often accompanies the excitement and discomfort of the awakening is a rekindling of prayer. Our prayers usually begin at the most self-absorbed level as prayers of petition: "God, I haven't prayed for so long that You probably don't remember who I am. But I need a job, so could you send one?" Or "I need a healing, or my spouse or child or parent needs a healing. How about it?" We expect God to come to us because we're ringing the temple bell, as it were. The problem with those kinds of prayers is that, because they arise out of fear—fear that we will suffer or be overcome by material forces of some kind—they generate negative energy, which in turn short-circuits the connection between the human and Divine levels.

This may at first appear absurd. Why would a loving God hold it against us that we ask for something rather than affirm that we believe that it is His will for us to have that same thing—whether material prosperity, health, companionship, inner strength, or enlightenment. Yet it makes perfect sense on a psychological level that if we are constantly asking for a handout from the Divine, we will feel as if we are on the spiritual dole. If, in contrast, we acknowledge that we are already in possession of what we need and that the Father wants us to have it, we have moved off welfare and onto spiritual workfare.

One way of looking at prayers of petition might be to say that, because of the short-circuiting effect of our fearful energy, they may never reach the Divine. But even that perception presupposes that the Divine is somehow inaccessible unless you say the right magic words. It may be more accurate to acknowledge that these prayers are ineffectual because we have already made up our mind about precisely what form the answer should take. We want that high-paying job, that new house, that attractive mate, that perfect health, that comfortable life. But we are not open to the possibility that God may choose to answer our prayers in another way, and so when the answer takes an unfamiliar, unexpected, or perhaps an unwelcome form, we ignore it, because we literally cannot see it coming. Out of fear, we close our minds; consciously or unconsciously, we fear that God's answer will challenge us or cause us discomfort. We may say that we want to go forward on our spiritual path, and we may ask God to help us advance. But if the answer is that we first have to lose our job, change our partner, or suffer through a serious illness, chances are that we aren't going to be disposed to hear that answer. In fact, we may feel that God has abandoned us, that our prayers have gone unanswered, and we may stop praying altogether.

Maintaining receptivity is vital to all prayer, but especially so to prayers of petition if they are to rise above the status of what I call "gimme" prayers. If you are going to ask for God's help, at least be sure that you stay open to receiving it, and do everything on your end that you can. It doesn't do much good to pray for a job and then sit home and wait for something to happen, or to pray for healing but then give in to feelings of doubt and hopelessness. Healings do not always occur instantaneously but, like enlightenment, take place over long periods of time. A case in point is a woman named Janice, who does secretarial work for me. She accepted the possibility of being healed, but she still had a lot of work to do to remain receptive to God's message. I'll let Janice tell her own story, as she related it to me recently:

*I had been diagnosed with uterine cancer and was scheduled for surgery. On the way home from the doctor's office, I had an impulse to call two women in your ministry. The first one said that she would pray for me; the other said that she and her husband would come to my house to pray with me the Sunday before my surgery. They didn't even know where I lived, which was some distance away, but they agreed to come anyway.*

*The natural human response for someone in my situation might have been to get really shaken up and go to pieces, but something told me to keep my mind on the positive side. I've learned if you let a little bit of negativity slip into your mind, a whole hurricane can then come rushing in after. Each day when I wasn't working, I kept myself occupied by watching your videos just to maintain a positive mind-set, and I kept the word of God on my mind. At night I listened to guided meditations on a tape player by my bed. If I couldn't sleep because of anxious thoughts, I just kept the meditation tapes going. I wouldn't let my mind get away from me.*

*The Sunday afternoon before my surgery was scheduled, the woman I had called came with her husband to pray with me. I sat between them on the couch as her husband read from the Bible and we sang some of the hymns we used to sing in your services. We prayed a little more, and then her husband looked at me and said, "You know you are going to be okay, don't you?"*

*"What did you say?" I asked.*

*"He has already told us that you're going to be okay," he said.*

*I cried tears of gratitude. That was all I needed to hear. I cleaned my house, did my laundry, and ironed all that afternoon. Everything went very smoothly for me after that. Following the surgery on Monday, I was back to work within three weeks. The surgeon was very pleased with the results of my surgery, and prescribed radiation treatments as a preventive measure. I had 28 radiation treatments, all scheduled on my lunch hour. I was the only patient there who ate her lunch in the car on the way to radiation!*

*I'm very grateful that God is working in my life. There is no doubt in my mind that I did so well because I believed in His promise that I was going to be okay. And I've never doubted it since.*

Janice was not miraculously able to banish negative thoughts or anxieties through prayer alone. Whenever she began to feel fearful, however, instead of indulging the feeling, she countered by watching videos and listening to tapes, sometimes five or six hours at a time. She fed her mind with the videos and tapes, and she fed her spirit by seeking out other people for prayer and comfort. And then she helped her soul, as Thomas Moore might put it, by cleaning, washing, and ironing—activities that seem mundane but that can also be very grounding and comforting in times of crisis.

## Medjugorje

We can all remember those mornings from our childhood when our mothers would try to get us up for school and we kept falling back to sleep. Maybe it was a big test that we weren't prepared for, or the bully we didn't want to face, or just a sleepless night that was making it so hard for us to wake up. It's a little like that with the awakening stage of healing, which can cover 20 years or more in some cases as you go through one wake-up call after another before you finally get the message. Each call takes you a little farther along the path until the calls reach a kind of critical mass and you finally realize what is at stake. In my own case, as I've said, it took several wrenching episodes before I truly woke up.

One of my major wake-up calls occurred while I was still a Catholic priest in a small Midwestern parish, but many years after my humbling on the altar steps. My associate, Paul, who was also the lay minister in charge of our parish, told me one morning that the Blessed Mother was appearing to people in a town called Medjugorje in what was then known as Yugoslavia. Although I was a fairly traditional priest, I had been seeing physical healings as a result of some of the healing services I had been doing in my parish. Still, I didn't make the connection that the same power that was behind those healings, the Spirit of God, might also be behind the apparitions. Although I wouldn't admit it at the time, I was afraid to look too closely at such phenomena. When I was a child growing up in a German-Polish household in Illinois, I had occasionally seen relatives of mine walking in the parlor of our house—which would've been fine, except that these relatives had died. When I told my devoutly Catholic mother what I had seen, she said that whatever I did, I was never to mention these apparitions to anyone, especially the priest. Now I was a priest myself, and I still didn't have a very positive feeling about visions and apparitions.

So I told Paul to go to Medjugorje and have a good time. My excuse for not going myself was that I was a pastor, and my parish was just getting ready to celebrate Holy Week. I could hardly leave my parishioners in the church to go off in search of something that you might expect to find on an episode of *Unsolved Mysteries*. With a feeling of profound relief, I saw him off, and buried myself in preparations for Holy Week.

As it happened, I was relaxing in my living room when Paul returned on the evening of Holy Thursday. He entered the house looking somewhat disheveled, and when I asked him about his trip, he began to describe some of the inconveniences—the absence of indoor toilets, the poor food, and things like that. I decided that under no circumstances would I be going to this little town in the hills of Yugoslavia. Even his ensuing accounts of spontaneous healings and the sun appearing to spin in the sky didn't do much to overcome my reluctance, which was nothing but ill-concealed fear.

Over the next few months, however, I had cause to rethink making a pilgrimage to Medjugorje. I was at a point in my life when I felt that I wasn't growing spiritually as a pastor because I was too involved with the day-to-day activities of the parish and the world. Even the healings that had occurred around me had come to seem mechanical, and I realized that joy was missing from my work. So one day I announced to Paul that I would be going to Medjugorje after all. I insisted that I wasn't going to see the external phenomena like the sun dancing in the sky; I wanted only to discover the perfect will of God for myself. I had to know the ultimate purpose of my living on this planet, and I believed that I would find the answer in Medjugorje. What I didn't realize at the time, though, was that it would take four trips for me to discover the answer—not because God wasn't defining the purpose of my life, but because I was still too stubborn to listen and surrender to what He had to tell me.

Since I can never seem to do anything in a small way, I ended up taking Paul and 18 members of my parish who wanted to go along. My journey of personal discovery had turned into a community outing. The apparitions had begun in 1981, and when we arrived in Medjugorje two years later, the town was still largely the way it had been for hundreds of years. There was none of the circus atmosphere that often develops around so-called sacred sites after the word gets out. I could feel a different level of consciousness as soon as the plane landed and I stepped into that ancient world. (By my fourth and final trip there, over a decade ago, they had built some amenities, including indoors bathrooms to accommodate the crowds, and a small religious goods store for pilgrims who needed prayer books and rosaries. From what I hear, however, they have not turned it into another Lourdes.)

At first I tried to absorb the spiritual energy that seemed to permeate the town, especially around the Church of St. James. I kept in contact with God throughout the day, talking consciously to Jesus and Mary and feeling inexplicably elated. I was still in what I would call a state of primitive ecstacy when I was approached on the street by a nun who was serving as spiritual supervisor to the five young people who were having the visions of Mary. Although she did not know me, she looked directly at me and asked if I would like to come to the room where the apparitions were occurring. I followed her to a simple room in the Franciscan monastery, where I found a nice seat in the corner next to a big table and sat down.

Prior to this trip, I had stopped praying the rosary because it no longer made intellectual sense to me. Nonetheless, I did buy a new rosary to take with me just in case I decided to begin praying it again, and, materialist that I am, I made it an expensive coral and crystal one with a sterling silver chain. When the visionaries entered the room, they stood before the crucifix on the wall and began to pray the rosary. In good Catholic priestly fashion, I pulled out my rosary beads and joined in. As I was sitting there fingering the beads, grateful for my foresight, a blinding flash of light appeared and knocked me off of my chair and underneath the table, and I lost consciousness. I don't know how long I was out, but when I opened my eyes, I realized that I was looking up at the bottom of the table that had been next to me. My ruling emotion, however, was not awe but embarrassment, certain that everyone must be staring at me. It hadn't occurred to me that people were so intent on praying the rosary, experiencing God and perhaps a vision of Mary, that they would hardly be concerned about another visiting priest.

As I slowly opened my eyes and scanned the room, I saw that nobody was paying the least bit of attention to me, so I pushed myself to my knees and continued to pray the rosary along with them. Looking down at my rosary as I prayed, I noticed that the silver chain had turned completely to gold. When I realized what had happened, my first thought was that I must be special.

And so began my latest wake-up call. Shortly after my experience in that room, as I was reading the Scriptures, I found a passage explaining that as God's children we are to be refined as pure gold. In that moment I realized that the silver chain turning to gold was simply a call from God. It was telling me that the gold of the spiritual life consists of acquiring the Holy Spirit. I then intuitively knew that prayer, fasting, meditation, and chanting would help to bring the Holy Spirit's presence into my life.

I saw many things that moved me deeply in Medjugorje. Like others there, I saw the sun appear to spin in the sky, although that didn't move me as much as simple gestures such as older Slavic women giving up their pew so young American visitors could sit down. Such expressions convinced me that the prayers of the people were leading them to become more loving, kind, merciful, and forgiving. And I realized that precisely that kind of healing was what I wanted for myself.

Returning to my parish, I told myself that from this point on I was going to do nothing but concentrate on the message of peace, reconciliation, and forgiveness that I had seen practiced in Medjugorje. I told my parishioners that we were going to allow the power of these revelations to transform us. In that little country parish, the last one I served before departing from the institutional priesthood, just about every Monday night for the next eight years I conducted a healing service. Our church held at most 400 people if we set up extra chairs, but soon we had 500 or more showing up on Mondays, with the overflow standing outside the doors.

One day while the musical introduction was being played and I was getting ready to come out for the healing service, I heard a tremendous commotion in front of the church. Paul came running in and said breathlessly, "You have to come outside!" I said that I was getting ready for the healing service and didn't have time to go outside. I don't like to have my energies scattered when I'm preparing for a sacred service, but Paul was insistent. As I kept refusing to go outside, Paul calmly informed me that 75 people were out there crying hysterically. I wanted to know why.

"Because," Paul said, "the sun is spinning over the church." As I stood in the sacristy, I heard a voice say within me, "Get excited about God, not about the phenomena." I knew in my heart that I was not to go out. Especially at a time when people are so hungry for God, it's tempting to put one's whole focus on spiritual phenomena—visions, voices, blissful states. But that makes God into a Disneyland experience, when the spiritual path is actually about everyday effort. Nonetheless, I thanked God for the experience, because it did help some people in the parish get their minds refocused on the presence of God.

The story doesn't end there. The next morning at daily mass, I noticed that some of the women looked shaken. When the Eucharist was finished, these women came to me as a group, and each in turn said that something remarkable had happened to her husband. My congregation was made up mostly of farmers, and although the men came to church on Sunday, I seldom saw them at the Monday night healing services. So while the women were standing in front of the church the previous evening, their husbands had been out in the field plowing. They, too, had witnessed the sun spinning over the parish church, and it had frightened them out of the fields. When their wives returned from the service that night, they had related their own experiences, and the confirmation had strengthened whatever doubts any of them may have had.

This event was beginning to have all of the earmarks of a spiritual awakening—not just for me, but also for members of my parish. We were being called by God in a very gentle way to begin to see ourselves as we really are—beloved children of God filled with the Holy Spirit. It was, you might say, a kind of group awakening.

The awakenings continued for some time, both for me and for my parishioners. During the latter stages of this period, however, I began to realize—or perhaps in retrospect it became clear to me—that I was beginning spontaneously to adopt certain practices that were new to me. These practices, it turned out, were typical of the next stage of healing, known as the purification.

## MEDITATION AND CHANT: THE SACRED SOUND

This meditation will help you become spiritually grounded at the beginning of the day so that you will be open to the guidance of God throughout the rest of the day. That requires getting in touch with what I call Spirit in the form of hunches and instincts. To begin this practice, you only need about ten or fifteen minutes. You do not have to get up at three o'clock in the morning and sit for hours. You may do that later, but if so, it will be because you love the experience of communion with God. God looks at your heart, not the hours you spend. You can use the modest preparations that open this meditation and chant before any of the exercises in this book or not, as you desire. They are suggestions, not requirements.

When I first get up in the morning, after I wash my face to help myself wake up, I usually do the holiest thing I can—I make a cup of coffee. If you prefer tea or a glass of orange juice, please drink those instead. Somehow we have absorbed the notion that you can't snack when you commune with God, but you can. Most teachers feel that meditation on a full stomach is not optimal, and that may be, but trying to sit still with hunger gnawing at your innards will not make you more spiritual either. Some people enjoy the feeling of clarity before they have anything to eat or drink in the morning, but I'm not one of them. So have a piece of toast or something light if you like.

The next thing I do is sit down and focus my awareness on my breath for two or three minutes. I am aware that every breath I take is keeping me alive and energizing me, because it is the breath of God, and that is at the core of my being. You don't have to try to remember all these things and repeat them; just relax and follow your breath, in and out. If you tend to get tense when you meditate or are afraid you're not doing it right, remember that God is *for* you, not *against* you.

After breathing for a few minutes, I might affirm various truths that are significant for me, such as "God is the only power. That power resides at the core of my being. God is the only love. That love resides at the core of my being." Sometimes I use prayer beads to help with my affirmations. Most of the great traditions make use of beads in some fashion for prayer or meditation. Catholics say the Hail Mary, Hindus and Buddhists use a rosary called a *mala* to count repetitions of various mantras, and some Muslims, especially Sufis, use beads as well. You do not have to follow a set way of using your beads; you can be creative with them. Nor does it matter if you use a Catholic rosary divided into five decades of ten beads apiece or a mala of 28 or 108 beads; use what feels best to you.

To pray most effectively, you need body, mind, and spirit working congruently, not getting caught up in mental activities or being distracted by physical sensations. The beads can release your mind from having to keep track of the number of times you've said a certain prayer or affirmation. I usually say mine for 30 to 40 minutes, but that is after years of practice; other people may stay at it for longer or shorter periods of time. You do whatever you feel comfortable with at whatever stage you are in your life.

After saying my affirmations, I usually chant the various names of God, or some brief phrase or sound such as "God Is; I am" or "Om." The Hindu Scriptures teach us that "Om" was the primordial sound of the universe, and that all creation emanated from that sound. To a Westerner, that's the equivalent of saying that Om is a name of God, since in the Jewish-Christian-Muslim concept, creation emanated from God the Father, who is identical with the Jewish Yahweh and the Muslim Allah. The first chapter of Genesis tells us, "And God said, Let there be light: and there was light." In a sense, the Bible is agreeing with the Vedic Scriptures that sound initiated creation. The *Katha Upanishad* says,

> *This syllable OM is indeed Brahman. This syllable is the highest. Whosoever knows this syllable obtains all that he desires. (1:2:15-16)*

*Brahman* is the Hindu name for the Godhead. Many Westerners believe that Hinduism is a polytheistic religion because Indians revere so many different images of gods and goddesses, including Shiva, Vishnu, Kali, and Durga. Yet at its core, Hinduism teaches that there is only one God. The vast impersonal Brahman manifests in many different personal forms, both male and female, so that the people can relate to God in different ways that meet their needs. And the cosmic sound is an integral aspect of their understanding of God. The *Mandukya Upanishad* begins,

*OM! This eternal Word is all: what was, what is, and what shall be, and what beyond is in eternity. All is OM. [Mascaró trans.]*

When we examine the world's religions side by side, we often find that they have more elements in common than in opposition, beginning with moral codes that are virtually identical. For some reason, however, most of us have been taught to emphasize the divisions between religious traditions, despite the fact that they all tell us in some form to love our neighbor and to treat others as we would have them treat us. So in the spirit of loving one another, the following exercise may help you accept other spiritual paths along with whatever path you may be following now.

Begin by relaxing yourself as much as possible. Then take a deep breath and bring into your consciousness the word *omnipotent*, which means "all-powerful"; the word *omniscient*, which means "all-knowing"; and the word *omnipresent*, which means "existing everywhere."

With that awareness, take another deep breath and as you exhale, begin to say softly *Ommmmmm*. Without forcing it, let the sound linger as long as it can on your breath. Then pause long enough to breathe in deeply again, and repeat the sound, *Ommmmmmm-nipotent*. Take another deep breath and exhale, *Ommmmmmm-niscient*. And take another deep breath, and breathing out say, *Ommmmmmm-nipresent*. Continue to breathe normally as you say this prayer:

*O God, absolute pure Being, our heavenly Father-Mother, Creator of the Cosmos, your love, the essence of your being, vibrates throughout the universe. Let my heart and mind be open to catch your thoughts, your ideas, your wisdom, and your knowledge. For you are all-powerful, all-knowing, and everywhere present. As I set my mind to receive your thoughts, my will also aligns with your will; they become one, and your will is done.*

Now take a deep breath and exhale, *Ommmmmmm*. What you have just prayed is the essential meaning of the beginning of the Lord's Prayer: *"Our Father, who art in heaven, hallowed be thy name. Thy kingdom come, thy will be done, on earth as it is in heaven."* Be aware that even as you breathe, you are God-breathed. The Spirit of God is the very breath that moves through you, all-powerful, all-knowing, and everywhere present. God is our life. God is our peace. God is. *Ommmmmmm.*

When you have finished, continue to breathe normally and recognize that whenever you invoke the names of God, you begin to feel a sacred spiritual energy. In another exercise, we will invoke the names of God used by different religions speaking different languages, originating in different historical eras and in various parts of the world. God has given all these traditions to humanity to know Him and love Him according to their own languages, cultures, and specific needs. To despise or ridicule another religion is to shun God.

# CHAPTER THREE

# The Purification Stage

*E*very morning after awakening and getting out of bed, we perform what are sometimes called our morning ablutions. In plain English, most people wash their face, brush their teeth, and, if they're lucky and their bodies are in good working order, they rid themselves of the accumulated waste and impurities from the previous day and night. Mundane as it all may sound, this is not unlike the second stage of healing. After we receive enough wake-up calls to rouse us from our spiritual torpor, the next step is generally to begin house cleaning. We have seen the error of our ways, and now we want to cleanse and purify ourselves in order to create a pure vessel for the workings of the Holy Spirit.

So like a pioneer family getting their new homestead in order, we begin to examine our lives and look for areas that we can clean up and rearrange. Fueled by the energy of our awakening, we begin to work on those things that we feel keep us from God in any number of ways. Usually we begin with the most obvious material impurities and work our way up from there. We may realize, for example, that we are drinking or eating too much; or that we have a problem with drugs, sex, or gambling. Sometimes the answer to these material impurities is relatively simple: a decision to cut down. In more serious cases, we may need to seek professional help or join a Twelve-Step program, or both.

On a somewhat less material level, you may begin to see that you are not able to control your temper, that you explode for no apparent reason, or that you are impatient with everyone around you. If you can see these things without condemning or judging yourself, it can result in a healing moment, because then you can accept your shadow side as part of who you are. That doesn't mean that you don't try to change things; on the contrary, you begin to examine even small behaviors, like hoping the driver who cuts you off in traffic has an accident or gets a ticket. Thoughts like that are perfectly human, but if you want to progress spiritually, you will have to learn to recognize negative thoughts as they arise, and, without judging yourself for having them, release them.

At the same time, we need to distinguish between having impulses and acting on them. When you catch yourself mentally cursing someone for having poor driving habits or just a bad attitude, you have a choice. You can indulge your retributive thought impulses, or you can remind yourself, as author Dan Millman once suggested, that whoever has offended you is just another passenger on spaceship Earth who happens to be having a bad day—or maybe who always has bad days. He isn't your problem, as long as he isn't endangering your life. The problem is allowing yourself to fall into a judgmental mode and letting that person throw you off balance and off center. By forgiving and letting go of your judgment, you can more easily return to center and reclaim your balance.

I have found that if you genuinely desire the spiritual path and you arrive at the purification stage, changes will begin to happen spontaneously. Certain people who may no longer be appropriate for you will leave your life because they cannot grow with you. As the saying has it, you don't *go* to heaven, you *grow* to heaven. And you grow through stages of healing until life itself becomes the state that we call heaven.

You may find yourself drawn to acts of service more than at any previous time in your life. I will have more to say about service in a later chapter on Divine union, but even at this stage, such an impulse may already begin to manifest, and it may have a synergistic effect on your development. Any action of service you undertake may spring from the growth in your own healing process, but it also fuels further spiritual growth. Service to others may help you catch a glimpse of your noble side, and that glimpse will alleviate a great deal of the guilt and shame that have accumulated in your life over the years. Most of our physical illnesses can be traced back to guilt, shame, and fear—especially the latter. If you are jealous, for instance, what is actually driving you is fear of another's success, and your relatively lower level of success. Maybe you are also fearful that you won't know what to do if you do become successful. In a similar fashion, any emotion that is positive can be traced back to love. A large part of progressing through the purification stage consists of recognizing that you have to learn to handle only two emotions: love and fear.

If love is the driving force of the purification stage, then fear is the emotion that dominates what I call the shadow side of purification. This fear often manifests during the cleansing process as a kind of misguided zeal. We begin to think that our goodness is proportional to the number and intensity of the austerities we perform; or the amount of time spent praying, fasting, or attending religious services. Self-cleansing soon devolves into self-righteousness, which represents a fear that we cannot be good enough, that God will not approve of us unless we push ourselves to the max. In a curious way, it may also signal a fear that others will outdo us in a kind of competition for the Lord's affection, as if God were the kind of parent who plays favorites.

When I entered my purification stage, in addition to fasting, I began kneeling in prayer at length every day without benefit of any padding. Then I thought that perhaps I should put glass under my knees because that would add to the level of austerity that I imagined God finds pleasing; I thought better of this, however, since I have a low threshold for pain. When I went home to visit my mother during this phase, I would go to my old bedroom with my Bible and beads so that I could do all the things that would signify that I was now a truly "holy" person. Each morning I would stay in my room reading my Bible and having what I thought were blissful experiences, although in retrospect they were nothing but ego trips. As I was interpreting the Scriptures in such a way that they made me look even holier, my mother would knock on my door with a cup of coffee she had made for me. I would announce piously that I was praying and reading Scripture.

"Yes," she said, "I know. I brought you some coffee."

"Not now, Mother," I said. "I'm praying!"

Of course, the gesture she made was more about expressing love and nurturing than it was about coffee. What I was saying, in effect, was that I didn't need her love. She just went back to the kitchen and nothing further was said. The next time I was home, I did the same thing, and she let it pass again. Finally, around the third or fourth time this happened, when I told her that I was busy praying, she threw open the door and said, "Well, then, go to hell!"

And in my state of purified self-righteousness, my first thought was, *I'll pray for you, Mother.* I would have done better to pray for myself at that point. I had managed to thwart her need to nurture her own child by implying that I didn't need her or her love—a greater "sin" than her disturbing me at prayer.

This stage lasted about five years, during which time I began to notice that my personal relationships were becoming fewer and less intense. When I entered a room, the crowd parted like the Red Sea, but I just thought it was because they were all sinners going to hell. I knew that I was the only righteous one in the whole bunch. If you find yourself with this attitude, my advice to you is to get over it as soon as you can. Don't fall in love with your own sanctity. Develop some humility.

As I progressed through the purification stage, I began to realize that I had been judging my family in other ways as well. To my newly "enlightened" mind, my parents were still worshiping the old-fashioned way, with no understanding of how God loves us all. They were praying to the old judgmental God, the One who is waiting for us to slip up so He can cast us into hell. In my own way, of course, I was being just as judgmental as the image of God I had long since rejected. Even though I still believe that this image of God is detrimental, I should have accepted that my parents weren't about to change at that late stage of their lives, and furthermore, that they were comfortable with their image of God. What I had to learn was to be comfortable with *them.*

Then I came across a Christian mystic who had said everything I wanted to believe. St. Irenaeus, who served as the bishop of Lyons, France, around the end of the second century, is best known today for his treatises against the Gnostic Christians of his day. I don't appreciate his attacks on the Gnostics, but in one of his writings he said, "The glory of God is found in the person who is fully alive." When I see the word *glory*, I think of *Shekhinah*, the actual energy of the Divine presence. What that means in plain terms is that to be enlightened in the true sense—to be filled with God's light—means to live a life of love toward oneself and others.

As you are growing in awareness of the presence, love, and power of God, the temptation is to pull away from people and become, if not a hermit, at least less sociable. You may feel that your friends and associates don't share your exalted view of spirituality or your close connection with the Divine. You will need to make a distinction at this stage between those people who are engaged in activities that can pull you down or reverse your spiritual progress, and those who are moving at different levels of spiritual progress from you. I certainly wouldn't advocate continuing to hang around with your old pals who like to get blitzed on Saturday night and go to  strip clubs; or the business associate who is constantly urging you to join him in cutting corners, misleading clients, or doing shoddy work. Those calls are relatively easy to make once you have enjoined the purification process. But I would advise against pulling away from people who may, in fact, need your help—including family, friends, and business associates. Sometimes that desire to pull away is not a desire of Spirit, but merely the desire not to be bothered by others. I'm not saying that there is no place for those who want to spend their days in a state of solitude, contemplating God; for some that may be the only way to achieve spiritual growth. But as more and more people seek to follow the mystical path, it is increasingly counterproductive for them to believe that they need to leave the workaday world to go on the spiritual journey. It may be advisable to relocate from the city to the country or to change the kind of work you do, but withdrawing from society altogether is rarely the answer.

The early mystics called the purification stage "desert spirituality," yet we can learn to practice this kind of spirituality without going to the desert. All we need is to adjust our attitudes by being simple in our approach to God in our prayer life, practicing silence, and listening for the voice of God to speak from within. Having a quiet room or place to sit in meditation and prayer each day is helpful. At times you may choose to get in the car and drive to the mountains or seashore to be alone with God, or just go for a hike on a country trail. Weekend retreats or workshops where the focus is on meditation or healing prayer may appeal to you, but balance is essential. If your family needs you to stay home with them, you can't keep running off to retreats because you want to be "spiritual." And yet you also need to recharge your batteries on occasion. Like most things in life, balance may require compromise.

Through the practice of simplicity, silence, and solitude, we eventually learn how to surrender. These disciplines of desert spirituality, which I will discuss in another chapter, fuel the furnace of transformation that leads us to perform acts of love for others. The Desert Fathers, early Christian mystics who lived in solitude or small communities in the deserts of Egypt and Syria beginning in the third century, learned that the practice of silence and solitude can generate the spiritual power necessary to overcome the negative undertow of the material world and our own egos. As the fourth-century Desert Father Ammonas said, "I have shown you the power of silence, how thoroughly it heals and how fully pleasing it is to God."

We can now take what these early mystics have discovered over the centuries and apply it to a life lived in close contact with others so that we develop silence and solitude as states of mind rather than physical conditions. The great Indian master Nisargadatta Maharaj was once asked if he lived in the same world of people who think as everyone else, since he had proclaimed that the very act of perceiving shows that you are not what you perceive. "Yes," Nisargadatta replied. "I appear to hear, see, talk, and act, but to me it just happens as to you digestion and perspiration happen. The body-mind machine looks after it but leaves me out of it, for in my world nothing ever goes wrong."

Nothing ever goes wrong once you realize that you are Spirit and that what happens to your body and your mind is not happening to you. The essence of you—the Holy Spirit alive within you—cannot be touched by external disasters. As Lord Krishna tells Arjuna, the prototype of the spiritual seeker, in the *Bhagavad Gita*:

> I say to thee weapons reach not the Life,
> Flame burns it not, waters cannot o'erwhelm,
> Nor dry winds wither it. Impenetrable,
> Unentered, unassailed, unharmed, untouched,
> Immortal, all-arriving, stable, sure,
> Invisible, ineffable, by word
> And thought uncompassed, ever all itself—
> Thus is the Soul declared.
> (II:23-25, Sir Edwin Arnold translation)

The Buddha put it this way:

> Those who are unawakened grasp their thoughts and feelings, their body, their perceptions and consciousness and take them as solid, separate from the rest. Those who are awakened have the same thoughts and feelings, perceptions, body, and consciousness, but they are not grasped, not held, not taken as oneself.

This is what peace is all about, the peace of God that fills our life when we surrender to God and realize that we are not physical beings separate from other people and from God, but spiritual beings intimately connected, through God, with all humanity and with nature itself.

In the purification stage, you will make a sincere attempt to stop condemning and judging yourself and others, and start very slowly but precisely to disconnect from all negative feelings and fears. Your prayer is not words to or at God, but communion, a sense of oneness with the eternal Being, the Source of all life. All that matters now is love and an identification of the heart with all creation.

## EXERCISE: SELF-EXAMINATION AND WITNESS CONSCIOUSNESS

I can think of no better exercise for the purification stage than the ancient mystical practice of daily self-examination, sometimes called the *examen*, from the Latin word for the tongue of a balance used in ancient Rome for weighing gold. In the Roman Catholic tradition, this practice has been reduced to the formulaic "examination of conscience" preceding the sacrament of Penance, during which one is instructed to tot up one's sins as if making out a laundry list. The implication of self-flagellation in this approach is so strong that it probably outweighs any beneficial effect. The process I am talking about is both less judgmental and more demanding than that.

Before going to sleep at night, while you are in a relaxed state but prior to drifting off, review your actions that day. To begin with, I recommend choosing one particular action that stands out either in a positive or negative way: an argument at work or at home, or a satisfying interaction on the job or with a loved one.

Without attempting to judge your actions as good or bad, just try to recall the thoughts and feelings that went through you as the event was happening. Next, sense how much your ego was involved in your thoughts and feelings, and how your survival mechanism colored or directed your actions. If it was an argument, for example, ask yourself how much your hurt feelings at something your boss, a co-worker, parent, child, or spouse said to you triggered a protective response on your part. Did you go into what some therapists call a "consolation" mode, reverting to feelings or attitudes that you used as a child to console yourself at being attacked? The extent to which your ego became involved will probably determine in large measure the level of objectivity you were able to bring to the encounter.

The same goes for positive appeals to your ego, through flattery, blandishments, or seductive behavior. The key here is not to praise or blame yourself, but merely to view the interchange as objectively as possible. Then, to the extent that you were able to transcend either positive or negative ego reactions, reinforce your behavior by asking the Holy Spirit to help you repeat those constructive behaviors that minimized ego involvement, and to help you reduce those destructive behaviors that fed the fires of anger, aggression, or self-loathing.

The idea is to achieve a balanced evaluation of your actions, as implied by the root meaning of the word *examen*. You need to become a neutral observer, a role that is not as easy as it sounds. In Vedanta, a system of thought and practice developed over thousands of years in India, this role is known as the Witness. In explaining the Witness, the great ninth-century Indian sage named Shankara distinguished between the Self, or the presence of God within each of us, and the body-mind complex commonly known as the ego (or lower-case "self").

One must understand the Self, he writes, "to be distinct from the body, sense-organs, mind, intellect and its tendencies, and always a witness of their functions, as a king." Shankara is saying that just as a king is aware of everything that goes on in his domain yet remains above it, one can learn by meditation to focus on the pure Awareness that "witnesses" all phenomena. "The Self is the Witness, beyond all attributes, beyond action," Shankara writes. This concept of the Witness became the keystone of his version of Vedanta: "You are pure Consciousness, the Witness of all experiences. Your real nature is joy. Cease this very moment to identify yourself with the ego."

Cease this very moment to identify yourself with the ego! We could hardly ask for a more precise and profound delineation of the heart of the spiritual path. Seen through that lens, learning to view one's life with detachment becomes perhaps the most potent spiritual activity imaginable. Ah, but if it were that simple, we wouldn't need sages like Shankara and Jesus to show us the way.

You may also wish to practice Witness consciousness at other times during the day, rising above whatever situation you are in to observe yourself and your actions as objectively as possible. Especially when someone pushes your buttons and you feel an emotional reaction coming on, try getting outside yourself and watching both you and the other person. This may feel awkward or "unreal" at first, but it may also give you some perspective on the situation. You may see that your confrontation is not the axis of the world, and that maybe you can afford to be a little more flexible, or to take things a little less personally. Part of the purpose of going into Witness consciousness is precisely to loosen the grip that ego continually exerts on us, if only for a time. The more we practice getting outside of ourselves both during and after our actions, the less we will be attached to following the dictates of the ego.

If we can't cease identifying with the ego by a sudden act of will, perhaps we can gradually metamorphose, like the caterpillar in the cocoon. In that fashion, the cathedral of self-observation can be constructed of small bricks over a period of time, just as the great cathedrals of Europe were built over centuries. Practicing self-examination and Witness consciousness on a regular basis will bear results in less time than you imagine. Just remember to retain your objectivity so that your self-examination doesn't become a nightly exercise in self-criticism. Purification can be as refreshing as a cleansing shower, as long as the water isn't either too hot or too cold.

# CHAPTER FOUR

# *The Illumination Stage*

*I*n most people's minds, illumination is associated with the extraordinary events described in the mystical literature or idealized by certain schools of modern Christianity: elaborate visions, speaking in tongues, deep trance states, levitation, and out-of-body experiences. I find it increasingly challenging to compete with those descriptions and write about illumination in a way that will relate to the ordinary person, one who is not the recipient of so-called powers. And yet when I talk about illumination, I also mean "inspiration," the breathing into ourselves of Divine Spirit in a way that all of us can receive. Webster's New World Dictionary defines *illumination* this way: "To give light to, to make clear; explain; inform." To experience illumination in the spiritual sense means not only to receive extraordinary phenomena, but also to be alert to the simple grace of insight, hunches, dreams, and intuitive guidance of all sorts.

To my mind, illumination includes works of creativity, art, music, teaching, and philosophy. When Paul speaks of the gifts of the Spirit in the passage from First Corinthians that we examined earlier, he says plainly that the gift of "prophecy" should be regarded above all others. "Those who speak in tongues speak to God, but not to other people, because nobody understands them," Paul writes. "They are speaking in the Spirit and the meaning is hidden. On the other hand, someone who prophesies speaks to other people, building them up and giving them encouragement and reassurance" (14:2-3).

But what exactly does Paul mean by prophecy? We might think that he is talking about the ability to predict the future, since that is the dominant modern usage of this term. But the Greek word for prophet, *pro-fetes*, can mean one who proclaims a revelation or interprets an oracle, since it comes from roots meaning literally "to speak forth." A beloved Scripture teacher I had in the seminary used to say that rather than thinking of prophecy as "foretelling" the future, we should think of it as "forth-telling." In this sense, one who speaks her heart before a group of people is as much a prophet as one who utters predictions about the future. If we examine the works of the Hebrew prophets, we find that they were more concerned with rectifying the present and calling their own leaders to account for their actions than in merely predicting the fate of Israel.

It is true that during the third stage of healing, some of the world's saints, seers, and healers had profound experiences of God that manifested as spiritual phenomena including visions, levitation, and the stigmata. Yet my experiences have by and large been rather ordinary, consisting mainly of intuition, guidance, and hunches. In certain situations, especially with people who come to me for spiritual guidance, healing, or a blessing, I have an inner knowing of what to do and say that comes to me as clearly as if someone were speaking in my ear.

Padre Pio (1887–1968) was one of the most renowned Western mystics of the 20th century. Born of humble parentage in southern Italy, he joined the Capuchin Friars at the age of 15 and was ordained a priest at 23. At the age of 31, he received the stigmata, the wounds of the crucified Christ in his hands, feet, and side, becoming the first stigmatized priest in the history of the Catholic church. Pio's stigmata, which bled constantly, made him a figure of some repute, and yet he considered his ability to read the hearts of other people in confession and in spiritual counseling far more significant than his wounds.

Likewise, there is nothing profound in the life of Thérèse of Lisieux apart from the spiritual path she discovered based on a childlike confidence in God. She is not noted for founding or reforming a religious order like some other saints. She died at the age of 24 with no tangible achievements to her credit apart from her trust that nothing can separate us from God, yet she is revered today as one of the greatest saints of the 19th century. Thérèse was deeply influenced by passages from Scripture that talked about what she called the "little way" of childhood. In Isaiah 66:13, for instance, the Lord says, "As one whom his mother comforts, so I will comfort you. . . ." In the Book of Proverbs, God creates Wisdom, a feminine personality that seems to exist on a different plane from the rest of creation. In Proverbs 9:4, Wisdom says, "Whoever is simple, let him turn in here." Moved by such passages, Thérèse became the saint of the Little Way, the Path of Spiritual Childhood, characterized by a simple trust in God.

As a young man in the early 16th century, Ignatius of Loyola was much more interested in courtly life, romance, and military exploits than the life of a cleric that his father hoped he would follow. Recuperating from a leg wound received in battle, Ignatius asked for adventure and romance novels to read, but the library in the castle where he was healing had only the *Imitation of Christ* by Thomas à Kempis and some books on the lives of the saints. Ignatius found that when he read the stories of St. Francis and St. Dominic, he experienced an exhilaration and energy that eventually urged him to pursue the spiritual life. And so this fortuitous incident in his life started Ignatius on a path that ultimately led him to write one of the outstanding works of Christian contemplative literature, the *Spiritual Exercises*.

Talking about great saints and mystics may create a misleading impression that only people of great fortitude and courage are capable of turning their lives around or reaching out to others to help change *their* lives. But this happens all the time to perfectly ordinary people like you and me. One night many years ago as I was experiencing my own stage of illumination, I had grown weary of the dry periods of conventional prayer in which I usually did all the talking. *There has to be a better way,* I thought, and with that I just let go and sat still. I felt a stirring within me, as if someone or something were trying to get my attention. Although I did not recognize it then, I now realize that it was the voice of God who dwells within us all. I did not "hear" a voice somewhere actually speaking, but I distinctly sensed a directive to take up paper and pen and be prepared to write down whatever came to me. As I did, I was filled with peace and serenity, at times so profound that I broke down and sobbed. I began to see visions of Jesus performing various acts in the course of his ministry, and I imagined the responses of those around him at the time.

These visions turned into written meditations on Jesus of Nazareth as seen through the eyes of his contemporaries, such as the Canaanite woman, the man healed at the pool of Bethesda, Thomas the disciple, and several others. I often wrote from nine at night until three in the morning, imagining how people I had never met would talk about Jesus. While performing these meditations, I became aware of my need for inner healing into wholeness, along with a need to change my belief system from negative to positive, to be free and to celebrate life, and, above all, to heal the doubt, fear, and anxiety that were plaguing me.

I did nothing with these writings for 15 years, but in 1986 I decided to compile the meditations into a slim, self-published volume called *I Want to See Jesus*. Those acts of illumination started me on my way to believing that I could influence others through my writing. I didn't levitate or bilocate or literally see visions and hear voices, but I did open myself up to the possibility of letting God's healing love flow within me. In the foreword to that volume, I wrote:

> This book can be therapeutic as you immerse yourself in the different personalities presented to me by the Holy Spirit. Immerse yourself in the "personality" of the Scriptural character and let the therapy of the Holy Spirit work upon your life. Remember, "therapy" comes from the Greek *therapeia* and *therapeuein*, which mean "to cure"; in essence, then, the Holy Spirit is the only therapist.
>
> As you reflect on these messages, you will be aware of peace and love and the presence of God's Holy Spirit.
>
> Don't struggle, just rest in His presence and allow Jesus to bring you healing.

When I am asked to define healing, I describe it as experiencing the peace and love of God in all areas of our lives. These meditations have brought healing to various areas of my life. I'm not whole yet, but I am closer to wholeness and holiness as I submit more and more to the Voice of God within me (the Holy Spirit) who loves, guides, leads, and protects me.

It sounds simple, but submitting to that voice of God within us can take years of practice, of learning to remain open and listen for His guidance in even the darkest, most confusing times. I can't emphasize enough that illumination does not require elaborate spiritual powers or psychic abilities. The Tibetan Buddhist lama Chögyam Trungpa Rinpoche, who founded the Naropa Institute in Boulder, Colorado, coined the term *spiritual materialism* to describe the pursuit of spiritual practices and powers as if they were exotic collectibles. He warned that they can clutter our spirit the way too many antiques can clutter a room that was originally clean and simple. We can do much the same thing by letting ourselves get caught up with the spiritual "gifts" that may arise during this stage. I prefer the term *grace* to *gifts,* because we are all graced to benefit ourselves and others in some way. The voice of spiritual materialism says instead, "I received this spiritual gift, and now I want more."

The shadow side of this stage is a kind of self-importance or spiritual hubris; if you are not careful, you can become possessed by your own pursuit of spirituality and begin to be choked by it. When I went to Los Angeles and Chicago as a priest some years ago to speak, I discovered that some of the churches there had what they called the Gifts Ministry. Members of the congregation who had had revelations or had received certain powers would sit on stage, and the rest of the people would look up and get their prophecy from the chosen few. I immediately sensed that something was wrong with that arrangement, because it implied that those people on stage must be special. What the church was saying, by extension, was that a few special individuals could provide prophecy and anything else the rest of the people needed.

That was as dangerous for the "special" people as it was for the others, who were in effect giving up their spiritual self-reliance and depending on somebody else to be their conduit to the Divine. In a sense, it can be just as dangerous to think of ourselves as "special," possessed of highfalutin' powers, instead of ordinary people blessed by God.

Rather than focus on spiritual powers that may or may not accrue to you, you can concentrate on becoming aware of the power of love. You may not practice this awareness all the time, but you may begin to practice it in at least a minimal way. Begin to take seriously what mystics of all religious traditions teach: We are to love God, and we are to love ourselves. In my previous book, I expanded on an idea originated by Dr. Herbert Benson that we are all "wired for God." This means that our inner circuitry, or, if you prefer, our DNA coding, predisposes us to have a spiritual life and to make God an active part of that life. Denying our wiring or coding—as many people tend to do during those wild middle years between childhood and maturity—only causes us continued suffering.

One of the ways we are wired for God is that we are one. Ask yourself if you have ever been taught by your religious tradition that you are one with all creation or one with God. Probably you have. Now ask yourself if you were also taught to compete against others. Were you taught that your religion was the only true way, or at least superior to other religions? And were you also taught that to excel in life you had to compete with others, to do a better job at all costs? The problem is that you are not wired to compete. If you buy into the belief that to be happy you have to be better than your sister or brother or anyone else, you are probably going to get sick.

Nor are we wired for victimhood. Watch any talk show today, and you are likely to see a fascinating array of people who identify themselves as victims. I'm not saying that if you were abused in some way as a child or even as an adult, you should not talk about that. But if you are over 18, *do* something about it. Change your thinking and get on with life. You're not wired to hold on to what my good friend, medical intuitive Caroline Myss, calls "woundology," by which she means defining yourself by old wounds. If you continue to cling to those wounds, you are going to destroy yourself. We are wired to release negativity.

We are wired in these spiritual ways, and yet when we look at our lives, we see that we are competing, we are unforgiving, and we are victims. Still, we can't understand why life is so miserable! We can't understand why, with all of that stress and anxiety, we are sick. I'm here to tell you that you don't have to live that way anymore. When you enter the stage of illumination, you have the opportunity to say, "That's enough." Once you forgive yourself and release yourself from this terrible negativity, you will be able to release others, and you can get on with your life. You can begin to experience a joy you have never known before.

Let me relate a brief story that may help to illustrate the power of forgiveness. Jeff is a professional writer who was working on a book that would be significant for his career, yet he found himself unaccountably "stuck." He wasn't sure what the problem was, but when his brother suggested he come to one of my workshops on prayer and healing, he felt reluctant. He did come, however, and later described his experience there and afterwards:

> Some years ago, I became aware that my spiritual pipes were clogged with anger, and my heart was closed. When my brother invited me to attend an all-day seminar on prayer and healing, I agreed, with some hesitation. I was writing a book on deadline and wasn't sure that I could take time away from the project. And yet I had encountered a serious writer's block, and I realized that my reluctance to go had very little to do with time, since I had written virtually nothing for months. This was more than mildly embarrassing, since my book was supposed to be about how to end stress. I had sold my proposal to a major publisher, only to find that I was having great difficulty completing a first draft. I knew I had a book in me, one that had the potential to help thousands of people conquer their stress. Yet the ironic result of my inability to get it down on paper was that I had succeeded in creating just what my book was supposed to help alleviate: stress and more stress.
>
> I had tried everything I could think of to get my creative juices flowing, including a writer's workshop and visits to psychics, with no tangible results. And so I went with my brother to the healing workshop, ostensibly skeptical while embracing a secret hope that something might move in me so that I could

*at last express all that I knew I had to say. Within the first hour or two of being at the workshop, I was able to allow myself to quiet the nagging voices in my head. I became aware of how much psychic energy these voices—which original- ly had belonged to my parents and teachers but which I had long since internal- ized—were draining from my system. They were making so much noise that, as my mother used to say, I couldn't hear myself think.*

*As the voices gradually subsided, I began listening more closely to how the Holy Spirit was speaking to me, calming and reassuring me that what I had to say in my book was both original and valuable. By the time the heal- ing prayer portion of the workshop arrived that afternoon, I was open enough to accept at least the possibility of healing my writer's block. As Ron started praying, he asked us to forgive. I tried, although at first I wasn't sure exactly who or what I was supposed to forgive. Then, as the prayer continued, it suddenly occurred to me to ask God to help me forgive. When I asked Him what He wanted me to forgive, I felt a strong intuition that I should begin by forgiving myself.*

*I was astonished, because such a simple idea had never occurred to me, and yet it felt so appropriate that I knew this intuition could only be the voice of the Holy Spirit working within me. More than anything, though, I was astonished that I had spoken to God, and He had answered through His Spirit. I couldn't remember the last time that had happened to me, because as I had struggled with my book, I had begun to feel increasingly alienated from the Divine.*

*As we chanted different Holy names of God, Ron's assistants walked through the crowd, placing their hands on certain individuals and praying for them. Ron told us that it wasn't necessary that his assistants actually touch us to be healed. I accepted this, since on an intellectual level I told myself that we are all one, yet still I asked God for someone to come directly to me. As soon as I let that thought escape, I began to judge myself for being so pre- sumptuous. Even as I was struggling with this self-criticism, however, I felt someone place his hands simultaneously on my heart and head. Unaccountably, I felt a burning sensation in my chest and realized that my heart was opening. I can't tell you exactly how that happened—a pretty strong admission for a writer—but all I can say is that I felt alive for the first time in years. Once again, I was astounded that God had answered me.*

*In the days that followed the seminar, I couldn't stop writing. I still can't. My book is pouring out of me like a fountain that has been turned on after it had seemed to be dried up and barren. Writing is what I've always wanted to do, what I knew even as a child I would someday do, and so the deep satisfaction I feel now is almost ineffable.*

*I am grateful that God is finally talking to me again—maybe because we are talking to each other. Life is also talking to me, and I am certain that is because I am listening. With those nagging voices in my head reduced to a murmur, I can hear more clearly what life wants to tell me. Awe and a sense of wonder have returned, and it feels like spring after a long, bitter winter. I have finally found my writing voice, the particular tone of expression that is the most crucial aspect of any writer's work. And this can only be because I have learned to accept God's voice in me.*

## Exercise: Chanting the Names of God

When we pray or chant using the name of God, as we did at the workshop Jeff attended, we receive access to the storehouse of Divine energy inherent in that name. The Hebrew Testament book entitled *Song of Songs*, attributed to Solomon, says of God (1:3), "Your name is like perfumed oil poured out." And the living Indian saint Sai Baba says this of the prayer of the name, which he calls *namasmarana*:

To start with, the name and the form go together in *namasmarana*. They are the reverse and obverse of the same coin. Recite the name and the named will be before you. Picture the named and the name will leap to your lips. The name should dwell on the sweetness that it connotes. It should ruminate on the beauty of the form that it remembers, the perfume that it spreads. *Nama*, the name of God, and *Nami*, the form, should have constant and continuous contact with the devotee's mind. Then just as two branches of a tree, by continuous contact and friction, are able to produce fire, the continuous contact of the name and the named produces the fire of *jnana*.

In Sanskrit, *jnana* (pronounced *GYAH*-nuh) means "knowledge" or "spiritual wisdom," but as used by Indian masters, it means specifically knowledge of Ultimate Reality, the transcendent realization that Atman (the God-spirit within each of us) is Brahman (the Godhead). This is the highest realization to which Indian spirituality aspires, and so for a sage of Sai Baba's stature to say that *jnana* can be attained by reciting the name of God is extraordinary tribute to that form of prayer.

Moreover, in a book entitled *Harmony*, Sai Baba speaks of *namasmarana* as a way to cleanse the elements of Nature herself. "Today the air, water, soil, sound, and light are all polluted by human activity," Sai Baba says. "Man has today created negative vibrations in the atmosphere. This is pollution. We can purify these sound waves and other negative vibrations by singing *bhajans* [devotional songs] aloud in groups."

When we set out to say, chant, or sing the names of God, we can draw from quite a few different religious traditions. I suggest beginning with the name that is most meaningful for you, whether it's God, Yahweh, Allah, Rama, Jehovah, Shiva, Ra, or some form of the Goddess. You can also use the form of a human being who you feel carries most perfectly the essence of Divine humanity, be it Buddha, Krishna, Ishua (the Aramaic name of Jesus), or Mary. While chanting or pronouncing whichever name you choose, listen to the sound of "ah" that all these names of God have in common. That is the sound of creation, the sound of the Spirit, the breath of God creating only good in our body, soul, and mind. In all the ancient spiritual languages, the sound of "ah" was common to the names of God, either at the beginning of the name, as the name itself, or at the end. And so now take a deep breath and on let the sound "aaaah" come out of your mouth as you exhale. Take a deep breath and stretch it out this time: *aaaaaaah*.

Now let's raise it a level. Take a deep breath and exhale at a slightly higher pitch: *aaaaaaah*. Take a deep breath and let it out again: *aaaaaaah*. Breathe normally, take your little finger and ring finger, press them against your thumb, and place your hand on your heart. Take a deep breath and exhale.

Now take a deep breath, and this time exhale the name of God in Aramaic, *ALAHA*, stretching it out to sound like *aaah-laaah-haaa*. Repeat the name two more times. Then take a deep breath, and this time say the name in Arabic, *ALLAH*. *Aaah-laaah*. Again and with each new name, repeat it twice more. Then take a deep breath, and this time say the name in Hebrew, YAHWEH. *Yaaah-wehhhh.*

The ancient religions of the Middle East used many names for the Goddess, the Source of all life, including Astarte, Ishtar, and Inanna. Choosing one, take a deep breath and exhale: *In-aaah-naaah.* Or chant: *Aaah-staaahr-te.*

Now take a deep breath and say the name of Jesus in Aramaic, ISHUA. *Ihhh-shuuu-waaah.* Take another deep breath, and say one of the many names of God in Sanskrit, KRISHNA. *Kriiish-naaah.* Be aware of the vibrations going on in your body, especially in the area where your fingers and thumb are over your heart.

Technically, Buddha ("Awakened One") is not a name of God, yet the Buddha in several different manifestations is revered by Buddhists the world over with much the same reverence others show to God, along with other figures from Buddhist theology, such as Tara and Padmasambhava. In Sanskrit, the first syllable of the Buddha's name rhymes with "good," and the second syllable begins with "h": *Buuud-haaaa.*

Another way to pray the names of God is to use names that are actually attributes of God. To begin, let's take the name *Rapha*, which in Hebrew means "God is my health." Take a deep breath, and exhale *Raaah-phaaah.* As you do so, feel the energy of health vibrating through your body. This is the presence of God being released from within. You are not calling upon it from the outside but are calling forth that presence from within to move out into your world, creating only that which is good— in this case, good health. *Raaah-phaaah.*

Remain silent for a few moments and express your gratitude to God for that loving presence of His-Her energy vibrating in you, through you, around you. Sometimes a simple "thank you" from the heart will suffice. Thank you, our Father-Mother, Divine Parent. You may also say the following prayer:

*Lord God, Adonai, our Father-Mother who loves us unconditionally, I release that presence now from within my heart to move outward and consume me with your love. At the same time, I ask you to consume my loved ones with your love, and even those I perceive to be my enemies. Let this love rise up as a cloud of glory to the ceiling until it not only interpenetrates the walls but moves through the walls down the streets outside.*

Rest with that for 30 seconds or so, then say the Prayer of St. Francis:

*Lord, make me a channel of your peace.*
*Where there is hatred, let me sow love.*
*Where there is injury, pardon.*
*Where there is doubt, faith.*
*Where there is despair, hope.*
*Where there is darkness, light.*
*And where there is sadness, joy.*
*O Lord, grant that I may not so much seek to be consoled as to console,*
*To be understood as to understand,*
*To be loved as to love.*
*For it is in giving that we receive,*
*It is in pardoning and we are pardoned,*
*And it is in dying that we are born to eternal life.*

At this point, I generally pick up the Bible and read wherever I am drawn. If your tradition is Islamic, you may pick up the Quran; if it is Jewish, the Talmud or Torah, and so on. Bring to your consciousness a sacred phrase or verse and rest in that. For me it is usually something like this passage from Paul's Letter to the Corinthians, chapter 13, part of which we have already discussed:

If I speak in the language of men and angels but have not love, I am only a resounding gong or a clanging cymbal. If I have the gift of prophecy and can fathom all mysteries and all knowledge, and if I have a faith that can move mountains, but have not love, I am nothing. If I give all I possess to the poor and surrender my body to the flames, but have not love, I gain nothing. Love is patient, love is kind. It does not envy; it does not doubt or boast. It is not proud or rude, it is not self-seeking. It is not easily angered, and it keeps no records of wrongs. Love does not delight in error but rejoices with the truth. It always protects, always trusts, always hopes, always perseveres, and love never fails.

This ode to love is also a description of the attributes of God, and because I am made in the image of God, I follow this reading by putting my name in every phrase or sentence that starts with love. Whether it's true or not at this moment doesn't matter. It becomes true as it becomes a part of our consciousness. For instance, I say, "Ron is patient. Ron is kind. Ron does not envy," and so forth.

Close this exercise with a prayer of gratitude:

*Thank you, God. Thank you, Adonai, Jehovah, Yahweh. Thank you for this wonderful sense of love and peace and joy that is present in my life now.*

# CHAPTER FIVE

# The Dark Night of the Soul

*F*ollowing the eye-opening exhilaration of the awakening stage, the springlike ardor of purification, and the unexpected graces of the illumination, the dark night feels like a slap in the face from God. So much has been written about the *dark night of the soul*, a term that gets tossed around rather freely these days, that we may be in danger of losing its meaning. The expression was invented by John of the Cross, the 16th-century Spanish mystic who was a contemporary of Teresa of Ávila. As John described it in his poem of the same name, the dark night is a period of spiritual wandering and transformation, a bridge between the illumined state that follows awakening and the final, unitive state of identification with the Divine. John writes in *The Dark Night of the Soul*:

> That which this anguished soul feels most deeply is the conviction that God has abandoned it, *of which it has no doubt*; that He has cast it away into darkness as an abominable thing. . . . The shadow of death and the pains and torments of hell are most acutely felt, and this comes from the sense of being abandoned by God, being chastised and cast out by His wrath and heavy displeasure. All this and even more the soul feels now, for a terrible apprehension has come upon it that

thus it will be with it forever. It has also the same sense of abandonment with respect to all creatures, and that it is an object of contempt to all, especially to its friends.

In his book *The Springs of Carmel*, the Carmelite author Peter Slattery describes three signs that John of the Cross gives by which we can know that we are in the dark night. To begin with, although we do not find consolation in prayer and the things of God, neither do we find consolation in other pursuits. If we have been following the spiritual path, we may suddenly find it so arid and unrewarding that we turn to "other enjoyments," only to find these just as arid and unfulfilling. We may actually feel duped or betrayed. After all the time and energy we have expended on the path, to be so badly lost can only seem like a great waste of effort. It does not help that even our closest friends seem oblivious to our dilemma; either their spiritual lives are going fine, or they are relatively uninterested in the level of spiritual commitment we have made. They may be having a grand old time doing the sorts of things that no longer bring us much satisfaction, and you start to feel like the time you stayed in to study for a final exam while all your friends went out to dinner and the movies.

Second, although our minds are focused on God, we feel that we can't find Him and are not serving Him. We become hyper-aware of our repeated failings, our uncontrolled outbursts of anger or cruelty at a time when we thought we had put such imperfections behind us. The third sign is a loss of the ability to, in John's words, "meditate and make use of the imagination as was one's previous custom." This can seem like the greatest betrayal of all. The very medium that had in the past brought you such consolation—that had, in fact, brought you to where you are now—suddenly feels stale, flat, and unprofitable. Given this situation, John of the Cross recommends that one not try to meditate as one used to but simply rest in the presence of God. Of course, resting feels like the last thing you want to do.

As you move through this stage, you may feel like a ship at sea on a moonless, overcast night. You are far from home, yet your destination seems just as far off, and there are no stars or lights to steer by. Such a situation requires faith that God is doing the steering, but even your faith begins to desert you at times.

Reading John of the Cross or Peter Slattery, we may get an image of the dark night being experienced by a monk or nun shut away in a cell, lips parched from long hours of solitary prayer, longing for a word of comfort from a distant God. But in reality, the dark night descends on most of us in everyday situations and mundane settings, and is no less torturous for it. I was ordained a Catholic priest in 1966, yet within two years I had unaccountably begun to feel that I wasn't going to stay in the priesthood for long. Believing from the start that I had made a life-long commitment to spiritual practice, I naturally found these intimations very upsetting. One day I heard the voice of God within my inner being telling me that although I was following the priestly path for now, I would eventually move on to a different path of spiritual fulfillment. When a few more years went by and my path didn't seem to change, I began to ask God what was happening. In another "conversation," I was told that before I could make the transition to my new path, I had to let go of my bitterness and resentment.

I immediately recognized the truth of this intuition, and yet it floored me. Why was I, a priest who had vowed to devote his life to helping others, feeling so much bitterness? The most obvious reason, in retrospect, is that I was still applying such a harshly judgmental standard to my own behavior that there was no way I could be pleased with myself. Among other things, a number of personal relationships had gone awry and I blamed myself for their failure. The most damaging of these was a relationship I had formed while still a parish priest with a woman I will call Rosalie. I had been taught that celibacy meant that, as a priest, you were not to love a woman in any way, and yet my love for Rosalie was such that it made me a better priest. I became more compassionate and more patient with my parishioners than at any time before I was involved with her. Still, for much of the time we were together, I wrestled continually with the question of whether I could love this woman and still serve God. Unfortunately, at that point in my development, I reduced the terms of this question to whether I should marry Rosalie or remain a priest. I began to wonder why God (although by "God" I really meant the Church) would not want this love in my life, given the positive results. At the time, I had no answer to this quandary.

I avoided the inevitable question of marriage because I became convinced that if I continued the relationship, I would have to abandon serving God. I was not prepared to do that, and I could not yet envision serving God outside of the institutional priesthood. The irony, of course, is that I eventually came to precisely that realization, but by the time I did, it was too late. Guilty and conflicted, I ended the relationship after only eight months. Rosalie was confused and hurt by my decision, and I was devastated because I was still deeply in love with her, and remained so for a long time.

Compounding my disgust with myself for making what I couldn't help thinking at the time was a decision based on fear, I was also feeling great jealousy toward certain priests and religious leaders of other denominations who were having more success with their ministries than was I. Each time I became aware of these petty jealousies, I came down on myself even harder. Healings had begun to occur around me, and I had somehow gotten it in my head that for the flow of healing from God to continue, I had to be perfect. Christ's injunction to "be perfect, even as your Father in heaven is perfect" had come to haunt me. Some years later I discovered that a poor translation had obscured the real meaning behind those words of Jesus. The original meaning of the word translated as "perfect" is closer to "complete" or "all-inclusive." In this context, "all-inclusive" means "compassionate," because compassion is the state of including all other beings in our feelings. So Jesus was actually telling us to imitate the compassion of God. At the time, however, I was wracked with guilt. If I was supposed to be perfect, how could I allow myself to feel angry or jealous? And so I suppressed my growing rage, which only caused it to mount under the surface.

In that emotionally charged atmosphere, it was probably to be expected that my resentment would find a target in church politics, given the way in which some of my superiors seemed to be trying to thwart my attempts to expand my healing ministry. Jesus had built his ministry on healing love, but the idea that a follower of Jesus should try to effect healings within his own community somehow threatened the local hierarchy. Their resistance did not help my generally low opinion of authority in general. I might have been right in theory, but my anger was not productive; suppressing it only made matters worse, both physically and spiritually.

My distrust of authority figures had begun years before with my father, who was an alcoholic and from whom I had inherited feelings of inferiority and insufficiency. As a young man, he had assembled clocks for the Westclox company in Peru, Illinois. After he was fired, he taught himself how to operate graders and other heavy road-building equipment, and went on to become a highway construction engineer. That he was essentially self-taught impressed me even as a child growing up, especially when he would drive those huge machines home and take me for a ride on them. Yet my father never had a very high opinion of himself or of his own achievements. He would come home in the afternoon and sit outside with his friends from the neighborhood and drink beer. With a brewery located right in town, the beer was always fresh, potent, and plentiful, and those guys would polish off a quart or two each at a sitting. My father was German-American, and his father had been the brewmaster at the brewery for many years. Beer being part of the German tradition, nobody thought that there was anything amiss with his drinking. But my father simply drank too much, and when he drank, he often flew into a rage.

Often the smallest thing would set him off. When my mother announced one evening at dinner that she was going to get a job, Dad exploded in a fit of anger that left food and dishes on the kitchen floor. His manhood had been threatened, and he responded in the only way he knew how. Although I didn't drink myself, I tended to respond to any situation in which I felt my masculinity was threatened in much the same fashion. As a priest, if I had a conflict with my colleagues, I would fly into a rage like his, figuring I could just shout down the opposition. I have since realized that during those early years of my priesthood, I was being propelled more by fear than by love. But since I was repressing any conscious awareness of my bitterness and resentment, I had little chance of coming to terms with my inherited behavior, as I desperately needed to do.

Without being aware of it, I was moving into a state of clinical depression. My mother's death, followed by the deaths of four close friends within as many months, had drained me of my energy to such an extent that I could barely get out of bed in the morning. Part of my depression no doubt stemmed from having to come to terms with mortality as I got older, but I don't believe I feared physical death as much as the death of the ego. For the first time in my life, I contemplated suicide. At the urging of a friend who was a nurse, I went to see a psychiatrist to discuss my problems and possibly get medication.

The psychiatrist was extremely helpful, and although he prescribed a popular antidepressant drug, I took it for only a few days before I realized that I didn't need the drug at all. What I really needed was to have someone be present for me as I talked out my feelings of resentment toward my father, and some of the other disturbing events of my early life. I was gradually able to acknowledge that I also had good feelings and memories about him, like those times when he took me out for rides on the grader. Before my father died, I was able to resolve most of my anger toward him, although this occurred slowly over many years, and did not culminate until he was on his deathbed.

From the time I heard that inner voice telling me to get over my negative emotions, nine years went by before I could largely resolve my problems and heed the call to be more loving and less judgmental. Those nine years constituted my dark night of the soul, even though I was not fully aware of it at the time. I remained a priest for 25 years in all, but those 9 years were such a struggle that I often didn't feel very spiritual at all. I had given in to the forces of negativity that constituted my own personal demons, and it took me that long to extract myself from their pull. I will discuss in detail the lure of negative energies in the chapter that follows, but first we need to examine an important principle that I feel is key to prevailing in the dark night.

### The Be-Do-Have Principle of Life

Both our secular and religious educations were based on a principle that is absolutely incongruent with the way our internal circuits are wired. We were all raised with this tenet, which I call the Have-Do-Be Principle. From the time we were small children, we were taught to ask the so-called important questions—not "Do I have enough to eat?" but "Do I have new toys, and are they the same new toys that the other kids have?" Later the question becomes "Do I have nice clothes, an attractive partner, a high-paying job, a new car, a big house?"

As soon as we start asking those questions, of course, we then have to ask what kind of career will pay enough money for us to have what we want. That usually includes a job we hate, or one that forces us to compromise our ethical beliefs just to succeed. "But by God, it will pay what it takes for me to have all those things, so I'm taking it! Because if I *do* what it takes to *have* what I want, then I'll finally *be* somebody."

We have known for some time that more people have heart attacks on Monday morning than at any other time of the week, presumably because they just can't face another week at the same dispiriting job. Setting their sights on having certain things, they have gone on to do what society requires of them, and they pay the price. They are following the paradigm of Have-Do-Be.

Countless millions of people pursuing that game plan remain unhappy and unfulfilled in the midst of prosperity. Andrew Delbanco, a professor at Columbia University, has put forward a fascinating thesis based on the observations of the 19th-century French philosopher Alexis de Tocqueville about democratic nations in general and the United States in particular. Tocqueville noticed that in the American democracy, as opposed to the monarchies and oligarchies of Europe, people could easily attain a certain equality of living standards without ever actually obtaining as much as they desired. Delbanco writes of their vision of the good life:

> It perpetually retires from before them, yet without hiding itself from their sight, and in retiring draws them on. At every moment they think they are about to grasp it; it escapes at every moment from their hold. They are near enough to see its charms, but too far off to enjoy them; and before they have fully tasted its delights, they die.

Prof. Delbanco attributes the "strange melancholy that haunts democratic countries in the midst of abundance" to the "illusion that equality could eradicate" the envy that the average person felt for the fortunate few in the Old World system of privilege. Perhaps, ironically, people were better off under the old system, where they knew their place in society; the poor and working classes could envy the rich without being tormented by fantasies of living that way. Yet in America, as Tocqueville keenly observed, although many of us already live as well as the upper classes of Europe did 200 years ago, we continue to feel melancholy, depressed, unfulfilled, and egged on by the dream of having more than we already have. Such hopes are illusory, Tocqueville realized, because "the incomplete joys of this world will never satisfy [the human] heart."

The problem that Tocqueville so aptly identified springs from the faulty premise that *having* should be our primary goal. We get the progression exactly backwards, because our internal circuitry is set in the opposite direction. We are wired for Be-Do-Have. The Be-Do-Have Principle goes something like this. Because I am made in the image and likeness of God, I already *am* somebody. Once I recognize that I am somebody, whatever I am called to *do* in life will flow out of that "I am." I will be guided primarily by principles of unity rather than of separation, or what the feminist historian Riane Eisler calls the mode of cooperation rather than domination. This is akin to what Buddhism refers to as "right livelihood," doing work that fulfills us, makes a contribution to the evolution of society, and does not harm others.

If we do all that, not only will we feel better about ourselves, but we will also have the things we need to live life abundantly. That is the truth in the often repeated saying of Jesus: "Seek first the kingdom within, and everything else you need will be added to you."

The truth behind the Be-Do-Have Principle is the awareness that from childhood on we are already emanations or localized expressions of God in this particular moment. The Gospel of Matthew begins the public ministry of Jesus with the Sermon on the Mount, in which Jesus says to the people:

> You are the salt of the earth. . . . You are the light of the world.
> A city set on a hill cannot be hid. Nor do men light a lamp and put it
> under a bushel, but on a stand, and it gives light to all in the house
> (5:13-14).

Jesus isn't saying to them, "If you do what I tell you right now, you are going to be somebody one day." He is assuring them that they *are* somebody already.

The Sermon on the Mount begins with the Beatitudes, but it goes on to encapsulate most of the radical teachings of Jesus, his expansion of the Mosaic law, his emphasis on love and compassion, and the Lord's Prayer, among other things. As soon as Jesus finished teaching, he came down the mountain and was greeted by a leper. This is a loaded situation to begin with, because Scripture scholars tell us that, depending on the nature and severity of their affliction, many lepers were forbidden from coming within a certain distance of the general public. It raises the question of why this man was allowed to get so close to the crowd listening to Jesus preach. But if we read Scripture to be transformed, we have to look beneath the literal story to the basic truth it is meant to convey. I believe that whoever wrote this story wanted to get across what the will of God was, and the way he chose was to take one of the most feared diseases of the day, which was leprosy, and present it in the context of the Sermon on the Mount.

The leper was standing close enough to Jesus to hear the words of wisdom being uttered from the mind and heart of this sacred being. Sacred words carry sacred vibrations, especially when they emanate from the heart of love, and those words caused to arise in this poor outcast's heart the belief that all things are possible. So he approached Jesus and said, "Lord, if you want to, you can heal me."

That's the imperfect way most of us pray. We say, "If you want to, Lord," because, like the leper, we are not sure what God wants. We figure that we have been bad and deserve to be punished, so that's probably what God wants. But what does Jesus say? He does not say, "I'm not sure, I'll have to pray about it. I don't know what Dad wants to do. Come back tomorrow." He says, "I want to; be healed."

It is that simple—not because Jesus is God, but because Jesus knows the will of the Divine Father-Mother, which is to demonstrate love in every situation in such a way that it will produce fulfillment in the life of the creature. In some situations, the will of God may not look like love. A child who is fascinated by a gleaming kitchen knife may cry bitterly when her mother pulls the knife away, yet another adult looking on will immediately understand that the mother has acted out of love. If you think that's a silly example, try to recall how you felt the last time a loved one was taken from you, or you lost a job, a lover, or a lot of money. Your first reaction was probably one of anger or disbelief: Why would a loving God let such a thing happen? But then follow the course of your life from that point on and see if you eventually learned from your loss; if, on some level, perhaps years later, your life became better or you developed coping skills you may not have known you possessed.

In the dark night, we are taught by God how to leave the Have-Do-Be Principle behind and enter into the world of Be-Do-Have. That transition is precisely what makes the dark night such a difficult stage through which to move. We are being led to change a whole belief system that is based on the faulty principle that we must do certain things so that we can have certain things, and only then can we be somebody. That is also why this stage requires such supreme confidence, because God is leading us through the dark, from point A (Have-Do-Be), which is receding behind us, to point B (Be-Do-Have), which we can't yet make out in the distance.

The Sanskrit word for prayer, *pal al*, means "to see ourselves as wondrously made." Once you realize that you are wondrously made, you start becoming aware of the cues that are being presented to you. You begin to receive thoughts or hunches—to write a letter, make a phone call, visit someone, or send your résumé somewhere. In plain language, you start to *be*, and then the doing flows out of your being without any struggle. The doors begin to open for you effortlessly.

You then begin to meditate or contemplate, without worrying about exactly what those terms mean. It doesn't matter if you have never meditated before. As an experiment, for the next week or two, I would like you to bring into your consciousness just two words: "God is."

Don't do anything else during the time you set aside to pray or meditate, whether it's ten minutes or ten hours. As you begin to focus on "God is" for five, ten, or fifteen minutes, you begin to remind yourself that God is always present. Whatever you need to have revealed to you about the personality or the being of God will be revealed. If you have gone through a lot of grief or sadness, all of a sudden a sense of peace wells up within you. You take a deep breath and you are so overwhelmed that you think, *My Lord, what happened?* That's the energy of God revealing what you need to experience at that moment.

At another time, you may have gone through a traumatic divorce or lost a loved one. You are feeling lonely, separated from the world, and alienated from God. But you start to meditate on "God is." After several days, you begin to experience a feeling of oneness; all of a sudden you don't feel separated, fragmented, or alienated from God. Why this simple phrase? Any definition of God will begin to limit who God is. As helpful as it is to say "God is light" or "God is love," or to list the attributes of God, they don't fully describe Him. What describes God is your experience with God. Because you cannot understand this notion with your head, you must do the following exercise to get the idea into your heart. Only then will you understand that this process leads directly into the fifth stage of healing.

### Exercise: God Is

Take a deep breath and get as comfortable as possible. If you like, put on some music that relaxes you. When I meditate at home, I often put on background music, and not necessarily chants. (In fact, I may have scandalized readers of my last book when I revealed that I use music by Kenny G in my meditations.) Let the atmosphere around you be filled with the presence of God. Take another deep breath, and on the inhale, think "God." Then on the exhale, think "is." Find the rhythm in what you are bringing into your consciousness and how you're breathing. Breathe in, *God*; breathe out, *is*. In, *God*; out, *is*.

Breathe that way for eight or ten full breaths: God. Is. God. Is.

Then follow it with the phrase "I am." Breathe in, *I*; breathe out, *am*. In, *I*; out, *am*. I. Am. I. Am. Continue for another eight or ten complete breaths, and then combine the two phrases. Breathe in, "God is"; breathe out, "I am." In, *God is*; out, *I am*. God is. I am. God is. I am.

As you continue breathing, allow yourself to drift. Everything we have been taught tends to make us want to do things actively and precisely, to be in control at all times. I suggest that you let go of control for the time being. You may drift into a beautiful cloud or a mist of gold and silver light. Or you may float into the arms of some image of the Divine, either male or female. It may be Jesus, Buddha, or Krishna; or it may be Mary, Tara, Kali, or any of the other feminine aspects of God.

Now, just stay with that presence, that light. Allow yourself to be in that presence. *God is. I am.* The most important thing is to allow your body, spirit, and soul to be one as you read the following prayer-poem by the Indian mystic Paramahansa Yogananda and allow it to vibrate through every part of your being. You may prefer to record the poem beforehand and play it back so you can take it in with your eyes closed, breathing evenly.

*From the depths of slumber*
*As I ascend the spiral stairway of wakefulness,*
*I whisper*
*God! God! God!*

*Thou art the food*
*And when I break my fast of nightly separation from thee,*
*I taste thee and I mentally say*
*God! God! God!*

*No matter where I go, the spotlight of my mind*
*Ever keeps turning on Thee,*
*And in the battle din of activity my silent war-cry is ever:*
*God! God! God!*

*When boisterous storms of trials shriek*
*And worries howl at me,*

*I drown their noises loudly chanting*
*God! God! God!*

*When my mind weaves dreams with threads of memories,*
*On that magic cloth*
*I do emboss.*
*God! God! God!*

*In waking, eating, working, dreaming, sleeping,*
*Serving, meditating, chanting, Divinely loving,*
*My soul constantly hums, unheard by any:*
*God! God! God!*

For a moment, allow that essence of God with which you were just in contact to bring into your consciousness those people who are in need of your prayers today. They may be people you know or don't know, but for whom you feel you ought to pray. As these names or images arise in you, consciously or unconsciously, you may want to pray silently "God! God! God!" As the sacred power that you are invoking comes into consciousness, become receptive to the love of God. The desire is growing stronger. You truly want to be of service to God and to others. Allow these words to move through every aspect of your spiritual wiring.

Understand that invoking God's presence will help you through the dark night. This is the way to come to a realization that there is light in the dark night. Orthodox Christians refer to God as the "bright darkness." In the darkness is the light, and you are just a short way from home. There is a way out. *God is. I am.* Wherever God is, I am. You may want to repeat that in a whisper: Wherever God is, I am.

Then express your gratitude to God. Thank you, God, for revealing to me and to all of us your children that we already are somebody. We are called to a specific purpose in life and if we only enter into and rest in your presence, our purpose is revealed as the doors open, as the mountains are leveled, as the brass gates and the obstacles in our path are removed. O God, how wonderful is your name, Adonai, Jehovah, Yahweh, Rama, Elohim, Allah, Alaha, Abwoon.

# CHAPTER SIX

# The Lure of
# Negative Energies:
# Demons and Elementals

To speak of the dark night as having a shadow side may sound like bringing coals to Newcastle, since this stage could be characterized as primarily shadow. However we think of the energies that are unleashed during this stage, they represent a formidable roadblock to our progress through the dark night, and we need to understand their nature and substance in some detail to be able to neutralize their impact.

The anger and bitterness I felt toward my father and his alcoholism are examples of the powerful negative energies that one begins to experience during the dark night, energies that some might even call demons. The Greek word *daemones*, which has been translated as "demons" or "devils," and which in early Jewish and Christian usage referred to unclean spirits that could inhabit a human soul, was used by the Greek pagan philosophers to refer to deities regarded as supernatural powers. These negative spiritual energies were seen as exerting influence over the lives of men and women, often seemingly against their will. In her perceptive book *The Origin of Satan*, Elaine Pagels points out, "Although many pagans had come to believe that all the powers of the universe are ultimately one, only Jews and Christians worshiped a single god and denounced all others as evil demons. Only

Christians divided the supernatural world into two opposing camps, the one true God against swarms of demons; and none but Christians preached—and practiced—division on earth."

Christians especially believed that "spiritual energies, demonic and Divine, can dwell within human beings, often without their knowledge, and drive them toward destruction—or toward God." This is precisely what Paul is warning his followers about in his Letter to the Ephesians (6:12), when he writes that "our contest is not against flesh and blood, but against powers, against principalities, against the world-rulers of this present darkness, against spiritual forces of evil in heavenly places."

Pagels goes on to explain that this belief that "unseen energies impel human beings to action" was "nothing new; it was universally accepted throughout the pagan world." Over time, the pagan belief in "spiritual energies" became the Christian belief in "Satan." Even today, though, the two beliefs often echo each other, as in an expression popularized by comedian Flip Wilson some years back with his refrain, "The devil made me do it!"

These *daemones*, or spiritual energies, positive and negative, do not inhabit the body so much as the energy fields surrounding the body. They gain access to us through various phobias or confused psychological states. The early Christian mystics referred to our fears and phobias as access points or open doors by which these negative energies can possess us. If we are giving vent to anger, for instance, angry energies will more readily be able to gain access to our energetic fields and ratchet up the levels of anger and bitterness within us. That is precisely what was happening to me during those nine years of my dark night. My father's rage induced so much fear in me that it opened the door for more angry energy to enter my system, which was then manifested through my rages at people who didn't agree with me.

And so we must confront our "demons," which are not to be thought of as devils or personal beings, but as our negative attitudes, phobias, jealousies, and hatreds. In the first three stages of healing, we are confronting external elements—attempting to rid our lives of the people, places, and things that are leading us away from God. But when the dark night occurs, what we are facing is within us. God directs us to look inside and acknowledge our own internal negativity. The early mystics believed that one can be possessed by negative spiritual energies of one's own device, which they called "elementals." In his book *The Magus of Stravolos*, the Christian mystical scholar Kyriacos Markides gives a detailed description of elementals as explained by his teacher, the Greek mystic Spyros Sathi, known as Daskalos.

According to Daskalos, elementals take on a life of their own independent of the person who originally projected them, like those thought-forms that are said to be visible to psychics and clairvoyants. Annie Besant and C. W. Leadbeater, two clairvoyants associated with the Theosophical Society, claimed to have observed differently colored shapes emanating from the auras of individuals they knew, and presented full-color drawings of them in their book *Thought-Forms*, originally published in 1901. Besant and Leadbeater ascribed these thought-forms to the same general cause that Daskalos and Markides do—namely, desires. They wrote:

> Each man travels through space enclosed within a case of his own building, surrounded by a mass of the forms created by his habitual thoughts. Through this medium he looks out upon the world, and naturally he sees everything tinged with its predominant colors, and all rates of vibration which reach him from without are more or less modified by its rate. Thus until the man learns complete control of thought and feeling, he sees nothing as it really is, since all his observations must be made through this medium, which distorts and colors everything like badly made glass.

We can produce these thought-forms or elementals subconsciously or consciously, and though we project them outward, they eventually return to our own subconscious. If we direct negative thoughts of hatred or anger toward someone else who is not receptive to them, those elementals may bounce off them and return to us with increased force. The more we create and project these negative elementals, the more sustenance they take from our unconscious, until they possess us. "The tendency of elementals to return to their source makes the law of

Karma possible," Markides writes. "An individual sooner or later will be confronted with the elementals that he consciously or subconsciously creates."

This idea represents an elaboration of the opening verses of the *Dhammapada*, an ancient collection of the sayings of the Buddha.

> All that we are is the result of what we have thought: it is founded on our thoughts, it is made up of our thoughts. If a man speaks or acts with an evil thought, pain follows him, as the wheel follows the foot of the ox that draws the carriage. . . . If a man speaks or acts with a pure thought, happiness follows him, like a shadow that never leaves him. (Max Müller translation)

As Markides explains in a subsequent book, *Riding with the Lion*, "an evil elemental that we project against an individual or a group will eventually return to us either in this or a future life. Therefore, when we harm someone, in reality we harm ourselves. Similarly, when we do good to someone, in reality we do it to ourselves." This ancient principle explains the continual reappearance of the Golden Rule ("Do unto others as you would have them do unto you") in some form or another throughout the history of religion, beginning with Confucius in the sixth century B.C., through Rabbi Hillel, Jesus of Nazareth, Muhammad, and others.

In addition to the elementals that we ourselves create, some elementals may be induced in us by others who direct negative thoughts against us—what we might call curses or negative prayer. Human beings who have died but who, because of their negative energies, remain stuck on the earth plane can besiege us with those energies. People who have not resolved certain issues with their deceased parents often speak of being "possessed" by their angry or restless spirits, as Hamlet is haunted by the ghost of his father, who demands that his murder be avenged.

Most traditional cultures recognize such spirits in various forms. The Chinese, for instance, call them *kwei*, and pray to their departed ancestors to intercede in their behalf with the *kwei*. Arabic culture has its *jinn*, which originally represented hostile, unsubdued forces of nature close to the Greek *daemones*, but which under Muslim belief later assumed the nature of supernatural, rational, intangible beings. Buddhist tradition includes a category of beings called *pretas* (literally, "departed ones"), also known as "hungry ghosts." According to Buddhist belief, those who die still possessed by greed, envy, and jealousy can be reborn as *pretas*.

Similar concepts appear in Christian belief, although only Catholics acknowledge directly the existence of states of being between Earthly and heavenly life, such as limbo and purgatory. Padre Pio consciously worked with the spirits of deceased humans who had not completed their afterlife journey. He used to say that his masses were attended by more people from the other side than from this side.

Whether negative thoughts, desires, and feelings come from within us or are induced in us by restless departed souls, they can cause our energy field to vibrate at certain frequencies, which in turn determine the type and quality of the elementals we create. We must learn to create elementals of love that will dissolve the negative elementals, no matter where they come from. Just as we are always surrounded by God's grace, which is available to us if we learn to tune into it through prayer, we are also surrounded by environmental thought energies that are less than positive. If we open ourselves to these energies through our own negative thoughts and attitudes, they can assume a life of their own and possess us in somewhat the same way that a bad habit possesses us: The longer we entertain the energy of a bad habit, the harder it is to break.

Since mystics are more experienced in navigating the spiritual byways than most of us, they tend to encounter the negative energies on a more conscious level, leaving us with instructive and often hair-raising accounts. Hilda Charlton, an Anglo-American mystic who lived in the 20th century and about whom I will have more to say in a subsequent chapter, writes in her autobiography about one such memorable encounter. At the time, Hilda was taking instruction on the dreamlike inner plane from a number of what are known as Ascended Masters—realized beings who have left their physical bodies but continue to work with us in various ways. She writes:

One night the Masters took me on the inner plane and had me face evil forces in the form of small people on a lower plane of consciousness. I saw these tiny people, who at first looked innocuous. Standing naively and innocently there, foolishly allowing them to come closer, suddenly I realized they were not what they were pretending to be— they were an evil force. The horror overpowered me, and I came down into my physical body and found it drenched with perspiration. The Master commanded, "Go in again." I found myself in a dilemma meeting evil with force. On the inner plane I desperately picked up objects to fend off the evil. In one case, I saw a bottle. Grabbing it, I held it in my hand and began to chase them to protect myself, but it was to no avail. They just stood there, unmoved by my counteractive force. Their force was ineradicable. I came back into Earth awareness, my whole body trembling with fear, only to hear, "Go back, Daughter." I went back into the fray again and again, until at last I caught on. I merely stood there tall and firm and used the greatest weapon of all: love. I stood and looked at these evil people, breathed into my heart center, and sent, on an outgoing breath, a wave of love. They ran, scrambled and disintegrated. A feeling of triumph ending in peace came over me. Love, I knew, was my shield against the battle of life from then on. Evil cannot stand against love. Gratefulness filled me as I thought how patient my teacher was. What a lesson! It would last a lifetime.

Hilda had learned firsthand what Jesus meant when he said, "Do not resist one who is evil" (Matt. 5:39). The same principle applies to evil or uncharitable thoughts and emotions. We are not to resist them directly or to judge ourselves for having them, but to observe them dispassionately, then dissolve them in light and love. That sounds easier than it is, of course, and requires patience and practice.

Although we may be unaware of negative energies entering our systems, they may be quite apparent to those around us. Once when I was conducting a healing prayer service, a young man in his early 20s made his way to the front, looking for me to touch and bless him. As I did so, he began to scream and jerk violently until he fell down on the floor. I was too stunned to realize that I might be dealing with something out of the ordinary, so as he lay writhing on the floor, I made the sign of the cross over him. His body suddenly became as rigid as if it were laid out on a marble slab and began to levitate two or three inches off the ground. I blessed the young man again, and as his body returned slowly to the floor, he opened his eyes. Although it was the middle of winter, he was sweating profusely. Looking at me with a blank stare, he asked, "What happened?"

When I spoke with this man some weeks later, whatever difficulty had been possessing him seemed to have passed, and he reported that he felt fine, although he had no recollection of what had happened. He did say, however, that prior to the experience, he had felt as if he was wandering through life with no direction.

On another occasion, I was asked by a Roman Catholic priest to pray with a young woman from his parish. I went to his church, where I met the woman and her family along with the priest and two nuns. The woman seemed perfectly normal to me, and I was asking her general questions about her spiritual condition when all of a sudden her pupils rolled up so that I could see only the whites of her eyes, which were becoming bloodshot. At that moment, a voice about an octave lower than hers emanated from her body and said, "I will kill you!"

She flailed her arms at me, aiming for my eyes. Catching me totally off guard, the woman probably would have connected, but there seemed to be a protective wall that kept her from reaching me and scratching my eyes out. I had brought a large crucifix with me, thinking that I might give it to her to hold. But as she continued flailing and abusing me in that guttural voice, I yelled at her to stop, tapping her on the head with the crucifix, whereupon she fell to the floor. I hadn't hit her hard enough to knock her down, so she may have fallen under the power of the Holy Spirit. When the woman came to, she looked quite normal again. "What am I doing here?" she asked as she pulled herself up off the floor.

Finally, I was saying mass at a retreat center not far from where I live, and just as I got to the consecration, elevated the host, and pronounced the ritual words "This is my body," I heard all hell break loose out in front of me. A woman had stood up and had begun to yell obscenities at me. Two men on my staff rushed to her and tried to calm her down, but found that they could not even contain her as she jumped and thrashed about with enormous force for a woman of her size. I recognized her as one of the quietest women on the retreat, someone I had seen walking around with downcast eyes much of the time. Halting the service, I went down, touched her gently, and said, "Stop." She immediately became quiet and returned to her seat, seemingly unaware of what had just transpired. For the remainder of the retreat, this woman was still soft-spoken, but appeared more confident and joyful.

These incidents were sufficient to let me know that I was dealing with a real energy that was, for lack of a better term, evil or dark. After studying exorcism and its authentic place in healing ministry today, I began to have more of these experiences and to realize that they were not uncommon. One reason they may manifest during the dark night is that this is when we are likely to experience strong feelings of separation from the Divine. I believe that a deep sense of alienation or abandonment by God does leave one open to the negative elementals, and that we then act as magnets for fearful energies that are in the atmosphere.

In this context, we would do well to revisit the accounts of the great healer Jesus of Nazareth. The context in which Jesus' miraculous healings took place is as significant as the cures themselves. The Jews of Palestine had been under Roman occupation for a century. The Jewish peasantry was dirt poor, with barely enough to eat; and virtually no health-care facilities, hospitals, asylums, doctors, or medicines. "When a healer appeared—a man who could perform miraculous cures and did so for nothing," writes the venerable Biblical scholar Morton Smith in his book *Jesus the Magician*, "he was sure to be mobbed. In the crowds that swarmed around him desperate for cures, cures were sure to occur."

Other scholars have made the point that the numerous cases of demonic possession in Palestine may have resulted from years of colonial occupation, during which the spiritual and physical possession of their bodies by an all-powerful demon mirrored the possession of their land and lives by a stronger outside force. Jesus offered the possessed and otherwise afflicted a release from their overwhelming sense of colonial oppression by showing them the existence of a "kingdom of God" within themselves, more powerful than any exterior force, and freely accessible to any willing to follow his path.

As Elaine Pagels understands it, moreover, the monastic communities of Jesus' day, most notably the Essenes, "saw the foreign occupation of Palestine—and the accommodation of the majority of Jews to that occupation—as evidence that the forces of evil had taken over the world and—in the form of Satan . . . or the Prince of Darkness—infiltrated and taken over God's own people, turning most of them into allies of the Evil One." And so what has come down to us as the Judeo-Christian personality of Satan, the devil, actually derived from a personification of alien forces at work within the ancient Jewish community, along with a sense of struggle against possession by those forces.

Although many of us have rejected, and rightly so, the notion of the Evil One leading us into "sin," the fact remains that any number of impersonal negative energies—elementals or thought-forms—that in many cases we generate ourselves, can and do militate against our spiritual development. We need to become aware of their presence and how we generate them, and to take steps to inhibit their activity.

Some years ago when I was still a Catholic priest, I was asked by a diocese in Southern California to celebrate a healing mass with a healing service there. When the mass was over, I went down into the audience and began laying on hands and asking God to heal those members of the audience who were ailing in a variety of ways. At one point I suddenly felt a strong intuitive impulse to touch the ears of two women standing next to each other in the crowd. The women then informed me that they both had problems with their ears. One had been deaf in one ear from childhood and the other had been totally deaf for over ten years. So I said very simply and quietly, "This spirit of infirmity, come out!"

Within moments, the women began to jump up and down with joy and declared that they could now hear quite clearly. As this was happening, I happened to catch sight of the church leaders who had invited me to lead the service and saw that they were frowning. Afterwards, I was informed that the bishop of the diocese disapproved of what I had done, which he interpreted as "calling out demonic spirits," an activity that the church restricts to the ritual of exorcism. What I had been doing, however, was not exorcism, but *deliverance*. Exorcism is a ritual that often calls for penance, fasting, and other austerities on the part of the exorcist prior to the ritual itself, and should be performed only by one trained in the ritual—namely, a Catholic priest. Deliverance, by contrast, is a simple act of calling out a negative energy that has been drawn to a person and taken up residence within. That is not the devil, or Satan, or any personal being, but an energetic force of the kind I have been discussing. I believe that what Jesus did in most of his healings was not exorcism, but deliverance. Although there remains a need for exorcism, this is far more rare than the need to call out energetic spirits of infirmity.

Over time these negative energies can accumulate within an individual until they become a major obstacle to experiencing God. We might refer to such an obstacle as a *satan* in the original sense in which that term was used in the Hebrew Bible, as Elaine Pagels describes it, meaning an adversarial force used by God to block or obstruct one's path. In modern terms, think of people who are given to negative thoughts about themselves but who then continue to indulge in these thoughts to the extent that they become habitual, and ultimately lead to a major depression. Such cases may call for medical or psychiatric treatment, or, in extreme situations, for the ritual of exorcism.

The Catholic church has traditionally made a distinction between so-called venial and mortal sins, mortal being the kind of serious sin that could, if unrepented, condemn one to hell. According to this theory, no amount of venial sins added together can equal the destructive power of a single mortal sin or succeed in separating one from God. I disagree with this distinction, because I believe that if you continue to commit small, negative acts over a long period of time, they become so obsessive that they possess you and can in fact become major. I observed this in my father's progressive anger, which eventually turned into drunken rage. He wasn't always a yeller; when I was a small child he would play with me often, and the yelling didn't start until I was around 12 years old. Maybe I had become more of a threat to him as I approached manhood, or maybe his love of drinking beer had gotten out of hand. By the time I was into my teenage years, the yelling escalated into throwing things around, including bowls of food from the dinner table. Yelling had become his way of silencing any opposition, because at first we all trembled silently.

As I got older and began to sass him back, he yelled louder and threw even more things. Had he lived longer, his fits of temper might have led him to physical violence and even to the kind of incident we read about all too frequently today, when a man goes berserk and starts shooting people. We often find out later of such spree shooters, like the man who shot two police officers in the Capitol building in Washington in 1998, that their rage had been simmering for some time before it exploded into bloodshed.

In just this sense, I believe that acts of deliverance can serve to defuse certain infirmities, physical and psychological, before more serious intervention is required. We can do this for ourselves or for others. Very experienced holy people have been known to take on the ailments of their disciples by filtering those ailments through their own energy systems and dissolving them. I was told by a monk who had been with Yogananda that the great Indian holy man occasionally had to use a wheelchair. I expressed surprise, since I was not aware that Yogananda had ever been ill. The monk explained that after healing services, Yogananda often seemed to age to such an extent that he needed to rely on a wheelchair for several days.

Tibetan Buddhism has a practice called *tonglen,* by which one visualizes the sickness and suffering of others as a kind of dark, viscous substance and filters it through one's heart as if through an air conditioner. The Tibetan teacher Sogyal Rinpoche tells the story of a lama who performed this practice for a recently deceased friend of his whose spirit he intuitively knew was caught in a purgatorial state between this life and the next. (Tibetan Buddhists, like Catholics, believe in the ability of those on Earth to help the souls of the departed on their journey after death. Although they believe in reincarnation rather than an eternal afterlife, they also believe in hell-like, purgative states quite similar to those in Catholic theology.) After several days of performing tonglen while focusing on his friend's trapped spirit, this lama's body broke out in boils. The man took this as a sign that he had been successful in taking on his departed friend's suffering and liberating him from his purgatorial condition.

Such events are different only in degree from what happened when Jesus took on the negative energies of the world on the cross. Whether tombs actually opened and the temple veil was rent in two, as described in the Gospels, is not important. The truth underlying those accounts is that when negative energy is transformed by being filtered through the system of a highly realized being, enormous power is released.

## PRAYERS OF PROTECTION FROM NEGATIVE ENERGIES

If you feel that you are being besieged by negative energies of any sort, the following prayer will serve as your shield of protection from them. It may be said by a group for an individual, or, by changing the wording slightly, you may say it for yourself:

Come, Spirit of the living God. Come, Holy Spirit, Spirit of love, Spirit of light. We thank you for surrounding this your child/me with your wall of protective fire so that nothing can harm him/her/me. Holy, Mighty God, Adonai, by your power, by your authority, you have set him free, you have brought back another soul and healed the memories that have haunted this individual for the past few years. I thank you, God, for the release of this dark energy. Let it be sent now back to the light where it can be dealt with by you, O Lord. Peace is your gift to us. Peace is what we receive now. There is nothing around us but tranquility, peace, and harmony, for you, Lord, fill the whole universe with the essence of your light and life, your Holy Spirit.

If you feel that someone may have put a curse on you or a loved one, say the following:

Spirit of the living God, come now and destroy this curse. Dissolve it by the light of your love, by the light of your presence. With the power and the authority given to me as a spiritual being, I break this power. I break this bondage now by the power of the cross, and from this day forward, only the peace of God shall flow through (name). So all negative energies, all *daemones*, depart now and do not return.

Now, O Lord, the heart of this individual is open for your continual presence and light to shine from (name). May the vibrational energy of your Holy Spirit bring harmony now to every aspect of his energy field that has been in disarray.

## PRAYERS OF DELIVERANCE FOR HEALING AND WHOLENESS

Lord in Heaven, for myself, all my living immediate family members, all other relatives, and all our ancestors back through all time, back through all our lives: For all the people we have hurt, I apologize for our wrongs and ask for forgiveness. Lord in Heaven, I ask that you help all the people we have hurt to forgive and release us completely and totally.

Thank you, all you people, for forgiving and releasing us, completely and totally back through all time with God's help. Thank you, Lord in Heaven.

Lord in Heaven, for myself, all my living immediate family members, all other relatives, and all our ancestors back through all time, back through all our lives: I ask that you help us to forgive and release, completely and totally, all the people who have hurt us in any way, at any time back through all time. And we do forgive and release completely and totally all the people who have hurt us, in any way, at any time, back through all time, all with God's help. Thank you, Lord in Heaven.

Lord in Heaven, for myself, all my living immediate family members, all other relatives, and all our ancestors, back through all time, back through all our lives: I ask that you help us to forgive and release ourselves, completely and totally, for all the times that we hurt ourselves or hurt others. And we do forgive and release ourselves, completely and totally, for all the times we hurt ourselves, or hurt others, back through all time, back through all our lives, with God's help. Thank You, Lord in Heaven.

With this release, freedom, peace, power, and new life, Lord in Heaven, we rejoice and give thanks for your Love, Life, Light, and Perfection, which we are now receiving through your grace and blessings. Thank you, Lord in Heaven. Thank you, Lord, thank you. Amen.

# CHAPTER SEVEN

# *Divine Union*

*H*aving weathered the tumultuous dark night, surprisingly little can be said about the final stage of healing. Once you experience the "I AM" of God, you have entered the stage the Eastern Orthodox refer to as *deification*, or what some religious traditions call the state of bliss. The latter word can be terribly misleading, however, since we tend to imagine bliss as a state of passive enjoyment or peace. In the Eastern spiritual traditions, it is variously described as ecstatic communion with the Divine, as in Hindu *samadhi*, or the extinguishing of all separative egoistic desires, as in the Buddhist concept of nirvana.

The stage of Divine union, as I understand it, is something quite different, and we ought not to even use the word *bliss* to describe it. For this is a state that compels one to action. We have been taught that Eastern religions are more about learning to "be" than about doing. And although there is great value to emphasizing "being" over "doing," especially in the West where we often seem to use our constant busyness as an excuse not to stop and look within, too much emphasis on "being" seems to open the door for a certain passivity toward one's less fortunate neighbor. Some even invoke the excuse that it is the karma of those less fortunate to suffer, and that one must not interfere with karma, the cosmic law of cause and effect. That is so much pious nonsense. Although it is true that much of Indian religion has not traditionally emphasized caring for one's neighbor in the direct material way that Western religions preach—even if we don't always practice it—individual mystics from the Indian tradition have always manifested their spiritual development in the form of service to others. Once you begin to commune with God on a profound and continual level, you will overflow with love, and that overflow will take the form of wanting to be of service to others.

The lives of mystics and spiritual teachers from all the world's traditions have shown that one of the corollaries of enlightenment is the desire to serve humanity. In his book *Padre Pio: The True Story*, C. Bernard Ruffin writes:

> Far from distancing the mystic from human affairs, [his] increasing absorption in God is almost always accompanied by increased physical and social activity. While the mystic experiences deep intimacy with God, he is imbued with a greater desire—and ability—to serve humankind. The more intense [one's] spiritual life, the more intense his response to the needs of mankind.

In his Letter to the Philippians, written from prison, Paul makes a telling point while weighing the possibility of his death:

> Life to me of course is Christ, but then death would be a positive gain. On the other hand again, if to be alive in the body gives me an opportunity for fruitful work, I do not know which I should choose. I am caught in this dilemma: I want to be gone and be with Christ, and this is by far the stronger desire—and yet for your sake to stay alive in this body is a more urgent need (1:21-24).

Like the Buddhist tradition of the *bodhisattva*, the realized being who chooses to put off nirvana to return and work for the liberation of all sentient beings, Paul finds it more compelling to stay "in this body" and be of service to others than to move on to what he expects to be certain union with Christ in heaven.

Our image of the mystic as someone isolated in a monastery, ashram, or temple, meditating in silence, studying Scripture, and chanting endless prayers is not necessarily the only image or even the most appropriate one. In the past, monks and mystics have played a crucial role by supplying spiritual oxygen to the rest of the world through their prayers and meditations. Their prayers may well have kept the world from destroying itself or sinking into permanent night. The story of spiritual development in the last century, however, has been the gradual shift of the mystical impulse from the ashram and monastery to the home and workplace of everyday life. It is increasingly up to each of us to assume the roles once played by men and women in solitary or closed communities.

We need to reinterpret the classical description of mysticism for the modern day, which requires a more holistic understanding of what it means to be a mystic. In the past, people worked on either the body, the emotions, or the spirit. They focused all their attention on health or material well-being—for example, accumulating wealth, power, and/or a healthy and beautiful body. Or, they focused on emotional states, attempting to achieve happiness through marriage and family and all the comfort and sense of fulfillment that domestic life can bring. Alternatively, they often chose to "give up" the material and emotional fulfillment of work and family to focus entirely on the spiritual path. This meant perhaps entering an ashram or monastery; becoming a monk, nun, or priest in one of the many religious traditions; and seeking fulfillment through spiritual practice. Some traditions have allowed clergy to follow a spiritual path while having a family and a modicum of material success. But people who chose that path were not generally considered to be mystics; mystics were supposed to renounce the world utterly.

The stage of Divine union makes it possible to have a fully developed spiritual life without ignoring the body and the emotions. Whereas some mystics went on to become hermits or ascetics, most became actively involved in the world. You can go off by yourself and develop a solitary life of prayer and meditation, or you can translate your experience of inner peace into a life of service to others.

The perception that spiritual masters give only spiritual help and comfort, moreover, is misguided. They do that, of course, and they may try to show us the folly of being attached to material things, but that does not mean that they somehow look down their mystical noses at those who are in need or in danger. Padre Pio was a great mystic, but he often made himself available to help others in material ways. The account of how he used his mystical powers to save a village in Italy from being bombed during World War II, after its inhabitants appealed to him for help, has been well documented. The story is also told that the great Indian saint Ramana Maharshi, whose face clearly glows with love and compassion in the few photographs we have of him, once saw a dog about to attack a squirrel. Ramana threw his walking stick at the dog to distract it long enough for the squirrel to escape. But since Ramana needed the staff to walk, he himself fell and injured his hip. Even though it was the dog's nature to kill squirrels, Ramana felt compassion for the endangered animal and acted on that feeling.

St. Martin de Porres, born into poverty in 16th-century Peru, was known as "the Flying Brother" because, like Padre Pio, he had the power to be in two places at one time. The illegitimate son of a Spanish knight and a poor black woman, he became a Dominican monk and spent most of his life healing the poor. Likewise, Catherine of Siena ministered primarily to prisoners sentenced to death and to people suffering from the Black Plague.

In the present day, any number of teachers have made prominent contributions to the idea of expressing spiritual illumination as service to others. That is the message of the American spiritual master Ram Dass outlined in his books *How Can I Help?* and *Compassion in Action*. It is also the message of John Wimber's Vineyard church in Anaheim, which regularly distributes clothing and food to the needy; Bo and Sita Lozoff's Prison Ashram program, which instructs inmates in yoga and meditation; and Joan Halifax's work with the terminally ill. One of the most fascinating examples of compassion in action is Bernie Glassman, the former abbot of the Zen Center of New York and the founder of the Greystone Foundation and more recently the Zen Peacemaker Order. Born into a nonobservant Jewish family in Brooklyn, Glassman went on to become an aerospace engineer with McDonnell Douglas, helping to plan space voyages to Mars. While working there, he became involved with Zen Buddhism, studied with the great Japanese Zen master Maezumi Roshi, was ordained a monk, and now holds the title of Roshi himself.

Not satisfied with the practice of Zen isolated from the rest of society, Glassman Roshi has worked for years to apply the compassionate feelings generated by his own spiritual experiences to serving others. He began by moving the Zen Center of New York from a donated mansion north of Manhattan to one of the poorest areas of Yonkers, New York. He began a bakery to help support the Zen Center, hiring local people to work alongside his own monks. Later he renovated abandoned buildings to create permanent housing for the homeless while devising a program to help those who were motivated to get off welfare and reenter the workplace.

We have been talking about spiritual masters, and once again you may think that what I am saying can't possibly apply to you because you are not "enlightened." But let's be careful how we use that word. As with bliss, the words *enlightened* and *enlightenment* tend to be used inappropriately and to conjure images that do not correspond to reality. In recent years, too many supposedly enlightened masters have been shown to have peculiarly unenlightened attitudes toward money, sex, and power. I suspect that on any given day there are precious few genuinely enlightened beings active on the physical plane. I prefer to think of enlightenment as an ongoing process. If you learn nothing else from this book, I hope you will take from it the realization that we do not go overnight from poor, unenlightened egoists to selfless saints. Even the awakening stage, as we have seen, usually requires many years and many false starts before it takes hold of us.

And so you may feel small urges or twinges of compassion as you progress through the stages leading to Divine union. When you do, pay attention to them and try to act on them as best you can. When this feeling of love and its attendant impulse to help overtakes you at any point, direct that impulse toward some person or place that touches your heart, whether it's a children's hospice, a volunteer food delivery service for homebound people, a family shelter, a neighbor who is sick, or someone who is in prison. Act on the impulse as a way of preparing for the state of Divine union, when most of your energy will go into service.

Divine union will make itself known to you without your doing anything in particular. Once you enter this stage, everything is the way it is supposed to be. You will have understood what real spiritual healing and growth are all about. At last you know what your purpose in life is: to be a success in the true sense of the word, as the great American Transcendentalist philosopher Emerson defined it:

> To laugh often and much, to win the respect of intelligent people
> and the affection of children. To earn the appreciation of honest critics
> and endure the betrayal of false friends. To appreciate beauty, define
> the best in others. To leave the world a bit better, whether by a
> healthy child, a garden patch, or a redeemed social condition. To
> know even one life has breathed easier because you have lived. This
> is to have succeeded.

Attaining Divine union, however, does not mean that all your work is over—in some sense, your real work is just beginning. What it does mean is that you are becoming aware that you can live on a transcendent level while in the body. You have attained the highest level of healing, because physical healing is no longer your primary goal. Your soul and spirit are healed, and in that state, nothing can truly harm you. It is as we have already seen when Krishna says to Arjuna in the *Bhagavad Gita*, "Weapons reach not the Life, Flame burns it not, waters cannot o'erwhelm." Even if your body suffers physically at this stage—as was the case for certain saints and mystics of both East and West—your heart and mind cannot be diminished.

In the first four stages, you may experience some sense of union with God, but it is temporary and intermittent. In the fifth stage, the sense of union is continuous. Likewise, although we strive for forgiveness in all the stages, in the last stage we experience an ease and immediacy with the impulse to forgive. Those elements of yourself that are no longer life-giving, for instance, will present themselves to your awareness during prayer and meditation, and you will be directed to let them go. You will do so because you recognize that if you do not, you will suffer more than anyone you may fail to forgive. In the parable in which Jesus likens the kingdom of heaven to a king who wants to settle accounts with his servants (Matt. 18:21-35), Jesus tells of a kindly king who forgives his servant a huge debt, only to have the servant turn around and persecute a fellow servant who owes him a vastly smaller sum. When the king learns of the servant's lack of forgiveness, he turns him over to the tormentors to be tortured until he should pay back all he owes.

I think of the tormentors in that parable not as human torturers, but as our own inner awareness that we have knowingly caused suffering to another. In the stage of Divine union, we are given the ability to recognize the "tormentors" within, so that giving in to anger, resentment, hatred, or pettiness is no longer tolerable. In a sense, giving in to your negative impulses or failing to forgive others is no longer an option. We often feel mystery or wonderment at how figures such as Ramana Maharshi, Mother Teresa, or Francis of Assisi can radiate only love and compassion with no apparent thought for themselves, but this may not be so mysterious after all. Perhaps they could not be otherwise even if they wanted to, because it would simply be too painful for them. In the story about Ramana that I related earlier, it was clearly less painful for this saint to suffer a broken hip than to watch a squirrel being devoured by a dog when he had it in his power to help.

Near the end of Matthew's Gospel (25:31-40), Jesus talks of a final judgment in which the God "will separate people one from another as the shepherd separates sheep from goats." And what criterion will He use? Is it how well people have kept His commandments? How much they have repented their sins? How closely they have followed the laws of the church?

The Son of man, Jesus tells us, will welcome those whom the Father has blessed, saying, "For I was hungry and you gave me food, I was thirsty and you gave me drink, I was a stranger and you made me welcome, lacking clothes and you clothed me, sick and you visited me, in prison and you came to see me."

He says nothing about commandments, repentance, or church dogma. What Jesus counts as the highest criteria for salvation are essentially acts of service to others. It's no wonder this Scripture is so rarely quoted by Christian evangelists and church apologists. It makes no argument in favor of condemning homosexuality or fornication, attacking other religions, or requiring contributions to the building fund. It is purely about serving others, especially the less fortunate. As someone dwelling perpetually in the state of Divine union, Jesus clearly understood the primacy of compassionate service to others. What was his entire life and death, in fact, but the manifestation of precisely that service?

## EXERCISE: HOW CAN I HELP?

This exercise will be a little different from the others we have done so far. At the close of your next meditation and prayer time, take a few moments to ask God the question, "How can I be of service to You today?" In this case, don't expect an answer immediately; instead, listen for the answer however it may present itself in certain situations throughout the day. Allow your intuition to guide you, but be attentive, because the answer you receive may be the one you least want to hear. It could be an impulse to give money to a panhandler or someone you would normally avoid. I used to be dead set against giving money to beggars on the street because I was certain they were just going to drink it up, and I'd be contributing to their deaths. Then one day I got a very clear message from God that what the beggar did with my money was between him and God, but that how I responded to that person was between God and me. In some cases, the panhandler may need to be recognized as a human being. By stopping and talking to a homeless person for a few moments and listening to his tale of woe, you may be doing more for him than any amount of money. Money usually helps, though, and if the person is one of those unfortunates who rambles on incoherently, give the money anyway.

I caution you not to endanger yourself unnecessarily in carrying out this exercise. Be guided by your instincts whenever you are approached on the street. If the situation seems dangerous or doesn't feel right, cross the street or do what you need to avoid physical danger. I know of one spiritual teacher who, when he is giving a workshop in a city, goes running in the early morning with a $100 bill in his pocket, with the aim of giving it away to the first person he sees in need.

On a more mundane level, your act of service could be as simple as taking the time to talk to a friend or relative for whom you don't usually (or gladly) make time to talk. We all know someone in our lives who calls or drops by unexpectedly in the middle of the day as if they have nothing better to do. Well, maybe they don't—but, of course, *we* do! If you work at home, or are in the middle of cleaning or cooking, this can be especially irritating, especially when your friend has nothing but time to kill. For once, indulge this person gratefully. Focus your full attention on what he or she is saying. You don't need to "fix" anything; just being present with this person without constantly checking your watch is enough.

If you feel moved to be of service in a more consistent way, by all means follow through, whether that involves working with hospice or at a local soup kitchen or family rescue center in your town or city, or doing volunteer work of any sort. Time is a more precious commodity for some people than money, so giving up one day or night a week can be a huge sacrifice.

And don't forget the old maxim that charity begins at home. If your kids need more help with their homework, or have been bugging you to fix a broken toy or rearrange the furniture in their room, make time for it. The same obviously goes for your spouse or partner. A simple offer to help with the laundry or making dinner is not only an act of service, it may also do wonders for your relationship. Remember, in Divine union, everything is a manifestation of Divine love, and no manifestation is too small or insignificant.

# PART II

# THE WAYS OF PRAYER

# CHAPTER EIGHT

## Prayer in the Five Stages of Healing

aving examined in detail the five stages of healing, in this second half of this book I will explore with you some methods of prayer that will help speed up and intensify your progress through those stages. I will discuss the role of the chakras, or centers of psychospiritual consciousness derived from Eastern yoga, and their relationship to the stages of healing. I will demonstrate ways to invoke the spirit and power of holy men and women who have lived before us by imitating their approaches to prayer. We will explore the necessity for silence and solitude in our prayer life. You will learn a variety of ways to infuse the entirety of your everyday life with an awareness of the sacred. Finally, we will examine together the supreme necessity of forgiveness as a launching pad for genuine prayer.

Before we go any further, though, I would like to sketch briefly the ways in which the evolution of your personal prayer life may correspond to the five stages of healing that we discussed in so much detail in part I of this book. As you journey through those five stages, you will discover that the nature and quality of your prayer life changes accordingly. Once again, I want to stress that these changes are for the most part gradual and incremental and are not always clearly marked. As one stage of healing metamorphoses into the next, the different approaches to prayer characteristic of each stage tend to overlap and often to coexist. Learning to recognize the style of your prayer life may help you identify where you are in the stages of healing. But more significantly, it will help you spot the limitations in your approach to prayer and spur you to move on.

## Prayer in the Awakening Stage

During the long awakening stage of healing, prayer is not a priority. The dominant form of prayer at this stage is petition, or what I have referred to as the "gimme" prayer. We pray as if we were talking through a telephone on which sound travels in only one direction: from us to God. We aren't listening for any response other than the granting of our petition—and sooner rather than later. The limitations are clear, and I don't need to repeat here what I've already said about the nature of the awakening stage. Suffice it to add that we are not so much novices at prayer—we may well have been praying this way for decades, since early childhood in many cases—as we are immature. Just as we all know 40- and 50-year-olds who are emotionally immature despite the fact that they are functional individuals with jobs and families, so it is possible to have been praying all our lives and still be limited to asking God for favors. In fact, this is most often the case.

The good news is that once we get the message and are suitably inspired, we generally find it rather easy to move on to a more sophisticated and less egocentric level of prayer. This does not necessarily mean that we will never ask for God's help in prayer. In times of crisis or great stress, we may find it natural to ask our Father/Mother for support, for ourselves or a loved one. But after leaving the awakening stage, this should be the exception rather than the rule. Those who have made a study of the effects of petitionary prayer, like Dr. Larry Dossey, have determined that asking for favors for someone else is somewhat more effective than asking for something for yourself. So if you must ask, try doing it on behalf of a third party.

## Prayer in the Purification Stage

Once we have entered the purification stage, prayer begins to take on heightened importance. As this stage progresses, you may discover what I call prayers of affirmation. These are not affirmations in the conventional sense, but affirmative prayers that help enhance the positive feeling that all is well. To gain a deeper understanding of how prayers of affirmation function, however, we first need to discuss the nature and kinds of affirmations in general.

Some people say affirmations in an effort to make certain wishes come true—for example, "I am skinny," or "I am wealthy," or "I have resolved all my feelings of anger toward my parents." This kind of affirmation may have some value, but if we doubt its reality at all, we may block it on an unconscious level. If I am 100 pounds overweight, for instance, how many times can I say, "I am already my ideal weight" before some part of my conscious or unconscious mind says, "Are you kidding me?"

The most powerful form of affirmation in my experience is a statement of fact that is already true, such as "I am a child of God" or "God wants me to prosper and live life abundantly." These are true on a level of absolute reality, although they may not yet have manifested on the level of relative reality. Saying the affirmations can help these statements manifest in your life. You can form this kind of affirmation by taking some of the beautiful lines of Scripture and personalizing them, such as these paraphrases from the Sermon on the Mount in the Gospel of Matthew:

*I am the salt of the earth.*
*I am the light of the world.*

In the Old Testament Book of Joel, God says through the prophet Joel, "Let the weak say I am strong" (3:10b). With a little imagination, you can extend that to a whole litany of affirmative prayers based on the implied eternal truth that even the weakest among us is strong in the Lord:

*Let the poor say I am rich in the Lord.*
*Let the sick say I am healthy in the Lord.*
*Let the fearful say I am fearless in the Lord.*

In what was most likely its original Aramaic form, the Lord's Prayer consisted of a series of affirmations. As rendered by the various translations from the Greek that have come down to us, however, this marvelous prayer appears as merely a long string of petitions. (In my previous book, *The Healing Path of Prayer,* I discussed this prayer in great detail.) The phrase "Lead us not into temptation," for example, always confused and irritated me. Even as a Roman Catholic priest, I couldn't understand why we ought to beg God not to tempt us to do evil, as the translation implies. What kind of God would that be? (In fact, it's the anthropomorphic, punitive image of God with which many of us were raised.) What the original Aramaic actually means, however, is that God will never lead anyone to trust in external things. As beautiful as the physical world can be at times, we cannot focus entirely on material goods. I prefer to render this phrase from the Our Father more like this: "You preserve us from the temptations inherent in false appearances." Making it an affirmation heals and dissolves the bitterness that often accompanies the guilt we transfer to others as anger, and breaks the hold that negative past actions have on us.

The most arduous struggle we face during the purification stage of healing is with that element of the personality that wants to eliminate God from our lives, which is the ego. The ego can be a very effective part of one's survival mechanism. In most cases, it keeps you from doing certain things that could harm you, like picking a fight with somebody twice your size or constantly running red lights. The problem with the ego is that it mainly serves our physical survival; it may feel threatened by spiritual activities and so may concoct all sorts of reasons why they aren't worth our time and energy. Part of the goal of spiritual practice, after all, is to diminish certain aspects of the ego and allow us to embrace others without fear. The ego is always telling us to watch out for others, even those closest to us, because their needs may conflict with our need to survive. Your ego may tell you that even your spouse, your children, or your closest friends and associates represent a threat to your dominance, and so must be controlled, even though the opposite may be true.

Once the ego is transformed, however, it can be a powerful force for serving others. When you progress from "gimme" prayers to affirmation prayers, you have begun to surrender your ego to God in the sense that you are turning your life back over to the healing presence within you and are no longer attached to the results of your prayers. My mother would never pray to Thérèse of Lisieux, who upon dying had said that she would let fall from heaven a shower of roses, because my mother believed that "those roses always come with thorns." Surrender and trust are implied in affirmation. You don't have to beg God to send a new man or woman into your life. You trust that all is well exactly as it is because nothing can go wrong in your life when you let God direct you. When you pray in this fashion, you are underlining the affirmative feelings in your heart and soul.

## Prayer in the Illumination Stage

As you enter the illuminative stage of healing, you will experience not so much a change as an enhancement of your prayer life. By that I mean that you will continue to pray in the affirmative mode, having gotten out of the habit of continual petition. But other kinds of prayer will begin to enter your spiritual vocabulary as well, especially prayers of praise, thanksgiving, and worship. These prayers may take the form of a simple chant of Hallelujah, or of spontaneously dancing around your room and saying, "Thank you, God!" You may also feel drawn to spiritual groups in which such spontaneous forms of worship are openly accepted.

Our English word *worship* derives from an Anglo-Saxon root meaning "worth." During this stage, you begin to sense that life is worth living and that you yourself are worthy. As a result, you will feel possessed by a desire to thank somebody for this internal illumination and joy. Few of us, unfortunately, have ever been taught to look into a mirror and say "Thank you" to the image we see there. Loving oneself unconditionally tends to be frowned upon in our culture. Once you can recognize that the Divine presence is in you, however, you can speak to God by looking in a mirror and saying "Thank you" as if to God Himself.

When I was in this stage, I would sit in my chair in the morning and be overcome with gratitude for the beauty of nature. Watching the butterflies flutter outside my window some days, I could feel my heart and my whole energetic being coming alive with the same kinds of feelings that caused Hildegard of Bingen to write a symphony that is a prayer, or that moved David to write the Psalms, which are largely songs of praise. Since I don't compose music, I try instead to compose simple prayers of praise and thanksgiving. There is no need to feel self-conscious about this. You may not have the skill of a David or a Hildegard, but if you are feeling the illumination of God's love, how badly can you do?

One method you can try is to draw inspiration from some of the great hymns of praise that have been written over the ages. One of my favorites is the "Canticle of Brother Sun" by Francis of Assisi, which is an extended paean to God through the vehicle of nature and the elements:

*Most high, all-powerful, all good, O Lord!*
*All praise is yours, all glory, all honor*
*And all blessing.*
*To you alone, Most High, do they belong.*
*No mortal lips are worthy*
*To pronounce your name.*
*All praise be yours, my Lord, through all that you have made.*
*And first my Lord Brother Sun,*
*Who brings the day; and light you give to us through him.*
*How beautiful is he, how radiant in all his splendor!*
*Of you, Most High, he bears the likeness.*
*All praise be yours, my Lord, through Sister Moon and Stars;*
*In the heavens you have made them, bright*
*And precious and fair.*

*All praise be yours, my Lord, through Brothers Wind and Air,*
*And fair and stormy, all the weather's moods,*
*By which you cherish all that you have made.*
*All praise be yours, my lord, through Sister Water,*
*So useful, lowly, precious, and pure.*
*All praise be yours, my Lord, through Brother Fire,*
*Through whom you brighten up the night.*
*How beautiful is he, how gay! Full of power and strength.*
*All praise be yours, my Lord, through Sister Earth, our mother.*
*Who feeds us in her sovereignty and produces*
*Various fruits with colored flowers and herbs.*
*All praise be yours, my Lord, through those who grant pardon*
*For love of you; through those who endure*
*Sickness and trial.*
*Happy those who endure in peace,*
*By you, Most High, they will be crowned.*
*All praise be yours, my Lord, through Sister Death,*
*From whose embrace no mortal can escape.*
*Woe to those who die in mortal sin!*
*Happy those She finds doing your will!*
*The second death can do no harm to them.*
*Praise and bless my Lord, and give him thanks,*
*And serve him with great humility.*

## Prayer in the Dark Night

Before the fourth stage, or dark night of the soul, we have changed the form of our prayer utterances from petition to affirmation, praise, thanksgiving, and worship. Now we experience a change in substance as well as form, as we begin to move toward what some refer to as the prayer of the stillness or the prayer of the quiet. Often this occurs because we don't know what to say or are simply worn down by the emotional struggles of the dark night. By this time, we have given up trying to figure out everything rationally. As things continue to go wrong, out of exhaustion or despair, with our senses numbed, we take one last stab at prayer, and in that moment of wandering, or what Deepak Chopra refers to as "the gap" between thoughts, the answer comes in utter silence.

The overall progression in our prayer life through these first four stages represents a continual development of confidence and awareness. When we lack confidence and awareness, we have to beg for help—for health, money, material benefits—which is what prayers of petition do. As we gain more confidence, we learn to affirm that God is for us and not against us. We no longer have to ask; we have faith that what we need has already been provided, even if we don't yet see it. As a result, we feel the impulse to thank God, to praise and worship Him. Now in the fourth stage, in spite of our sense of abandonment and spiritual exhaustion, or perhaps because of it, we learn to be receptive; we begin to see that we receive the guidance we need without asking for it. We are learning to be quiet so that we can listen in utmost confidence of receiving whatever response God deems appropriate, which is the significance of the prayer of the stillness.

Yet none of this should be interpreted as meaning that we have abdicated our responsibility to act on whatever guidance we receive. This kind of listening for God's will is not a passive state, even if it might seem that way to the observer. Think of it instead as a state of alert receptivity and readiness to act, once we have clearly apprehended our "marching orders." In a subsequent chapter on silence and solitude, I will develop this idea in more detail.

### Prayer in Divine Union

When I was a parish priest, some of my parishioners would say to me, "I don't pray as much as I used to. My work is my prayer." Back then, I thought that was a cop-out, and in some cases it may well have been. But I have since come to realize that if we understand this idea properly, work can be the height of prayer. The Hindu tradition speaks of the four kinds of yoga as different roads to God. Sometimes called *margas,* or "paths," the yogas offer four distinct approaches to enlightenment, tailored to different temperaments and orientations, and none is considered better than the others. One of the four is *karma yoga,* the path of work or action. The aim of karma yoga is to get to God by doing good, but without attachment to the fruits of one's work. Selfless detachment in the act of doing is the karma yogi's ideal. This may apply to traditional spiritual acts such as ritual sacrifices or to the way the yogi performs the simplest daily actions.

Once you have reached the stage of Divine union, all your actions become acts of karma yoga, including daily routines such as brushing your teeth, the work you do for a living, and acts of consideration for others, like driving your kids to the mall when you might rather be home reading a good book. In fact, the issue of what you would "rather" be doing does not arise, because what you would rather do more than anything else is help those who need your help. This is what St. Paul means in his Second Letter to the Corinthians (1:3-4), when he writes that God is "the Father of mercies and the God of all comfort," adding (in somewhat convoluted language) that He "comforts us in all our affliction, so that we may be able to comfort those who are in any affliction, with the comfort with which we ourselves are comforted by God."

Having reached a state of continual union with God, even our sufferings are turned into a vehicle for helping others. This may help alleviate our puzzlement over the fact that great saints and mystics have been known to suffer terribly painful diseases at times. God said to Abraham, "I have blessed you so that you may be a blessing to others." Like Abraham, we become vehicles for God's grace, rather than mere recipients. We are passing on the world's spiritual riches rather than trying to possess them.

This all results from the change in our prayer, which has gone from being part of our life to being our entire life. If Mother Teresa had spent four hours a day in prayer and then sat at home the rest of the time, I wouldn't consider that a manifestation of Divine union. The compassionate work she did every other part of the day flowed out of her time of prayer, and was actually a continuation of that prayer. In that sense,

Divine union is the time during which all previous forms of prayer are subsumed into St. Paul's directive to "pray without ceasing." I may spend time in prayer and meditation in the morning, say my ejaculatory prayers throughout the day, and express gratitude at night. But in between, my prayer is "How may I serve today?" This becomes not so much a spoken prayer or even a mentally recited prayer as it is a state of consciousness.

Author Wayne Dyer tells a story about a radio announcer he knows in Phoenix who had Mother Teresa as a guest on his show. At the end of his interview, the man asked Mother Teresa how he could help her, suggesting that perhaps he could raise some money for her missionary activities. Mother Teresa said that if he really wanted to help, he should get up at four o'clock the next morning, go out into the streets of Phoenix, and find a lonely, homeless person and let him know that he is loved.

Dr. Jerry Jampolsky, who wrote *Love Is Letting Go of Fear*, said that after hearing Mother Teresa speak in Los Angeles one day, he drove with her to the airport. He told her that he would like to accompany her on her flight to Mexico City.

"Why?" she asked in her disarming way.

"Just to be in your presence and learn from you," Dr. Jampolsky responded. Mother Teresa told him that if wanted to learn from her, he should find out the price of a round-trip ticket from Los Angeles to Mexico City and give that money to the poor instead of traveling with her. He did, and it made a profound difference in his life.

From stories like these and from my own experience, I have concluded that the key prayer of Divine union is "How may I serve today?" Add to that the prayer of thanksgiving that can be expressed as simply as "Thank you, God," and you have all you need to know about this final stage of prayer.

# CHAPTER NINE

# The Chakras, Yoga, and the Stages of Prayer and Healing

Whether we refer to the five stages I have outlined as stages of healing, prayer, or enlightenment, the rational mind still has difficulty coming to grips with them. The stages must ultimately be experienced, which is why I have included so many prayers and spiritual exercises in this book to help you implement these teachings. But it also helps for the mind to have some rational understanding of how things work, or else why would we read books at all? We can learn a great deal from the different ways of organizing spiritual knowledge and energy worked out by traditions other than our own. Eastern mystics have been experiencing and studying the interrelationship of physical and spiritual energy for over 3,000 years, and what they have learned can help us understand how the stages of healing that I have been describing are organized on an energetic level.

I first learned in detail about the centers of psychospiritual consciousness known in the Hindu tradition as *chakras* during the years I spent giving workshops around the country with medical intuitive Caroline Myss (author of *Anatomy of the Spirit*). Through her books and workshops, Caroline has done as much as anyone to spread awareness and knowledge of the chakras in the West, describing fascinating correlations between the seven chakras, the seven Christian sacraments, and the ten *sefirot* of the Tree of Life in the Kabbalistic tradition of Judaism. My own understanding of these vital centers differs somewhat from hers, however, and it may be helpful to examine briefly how I view the chakras and their role in prayer and healing.

Like the stages of prayer and healing, the chakras represent a progression of spiritual knowledge and power. Although the seven chakras don't line up neatly with the five stages of prayer, they do share a similar arc throughout the course of our lives. By understanding the shape of this arc and the nature of the stages that make it up, you may be better able to navigate through those stages.

To understand the role of the chakras themselves, however, we first need to know a little about the Indian belief system out of which they sprang, including the practice of yoga. Most Westerners are familiar with hatha yoga, a series of physical exercises and stretching postures originally developed as just one step along the way to liberation (the Hindu equivalent of salvation). In their Scriptures, the Indian seers known as *rishis* described a complex system of subtle energy unknown to Western science. According to this system, the spinal column supports 72,000 *nadis*, or energy channels, through which *prana*, the life force, flows to the rest of the body. The most important nadi is the *sushumna*, which reaches from the base of the spine to the brain, and is complemented by two other nadis, called the *ida* and *pingala*. These two, which spiral around the central nadi from either side, control the flow of intellectual energy and physical-emotional energy, respectively. The three channels together look surprisingly like the caduceus, the winged rod entwined by two serpents that often serves as the symbol of the medical profession here in the West.

The purpose of yoga is to bring these energy fields into balance, internalizing and releasing the main flow of consciousness-energy from the base of the spinal column though the crown of the head. As originally developed and taught in India for thousands of years, yoga also aimed to purify the body and prepare it for the release of psychospiritual energy through the chakras. That energy is traditionally pictured as a coiled female serpent at the base of the spine, and the energy that is released is known as the *kundalini* (Sanskrit for "she who lies coiled").

There are many different kinds of yoga in India, but this particular path is known as *raja* ("royal") yoga, which has been described as "the way to God through psychophysical experiments." As presented by Patanjali in his *Yoga Sutra* (although the term "raja yoga" was created long after Patanjali), the premise of this path is that we are each composed of body, conscious mind, the subconscious, and Being Itself—what we in the West might call the presence of God within each of us. By mastering certain techniques for mind and body control, the yogi can experience the bliss of Being Itself that already exists within him. St. Paul meant much the same thing when he said, "I live, now not I, but Christ lives in me."

Patanjali provides eight steps, or sets of techniques, which are known as the "eight-armed yoga"; the first five govern external activities that pave the way for the last three, which concern the inner functions of the mind and spirit. The first two steps are called *yama* (moral restraints against harming, lying, stealing, sexual incontinence, and greed) and *niyama* (disciplines involving inner and outer purity, calmness or contentment, asceticism, Scripture study, and submission to God).

These are followed by the yoga postures themselves (*asanas*); breath control (*pranayama*); the withdrawal of the senses from their accustomed focus on external sense objects so that they may center on the inner plane (*pratyahara*); and concentration (*dharana*), focusing the mind on one thing as a prelude to entering deeper states of meditation. This is achieved through practices such as *tratakum* ("steady gaze"), fixing the eyes on the tip of the nose; a spot between the eyebrows; or a candle flame; or by concentrating the mind on the navel, the heart, or other areas of the body.

The seventh step is a form of intense meditation (*dyana*) that is intended to lead to the final stage, called *samadhi*, total absorption in the object of concentration. If that object is God, then this state amounts to union with God.

We are now ready to take a closer look at the chakras themselves, which follow a similar kind of progression, although the stages are not necessarily interchangeable with the steps of the yoga path. According to

# THE SEVEN CHAKRAS

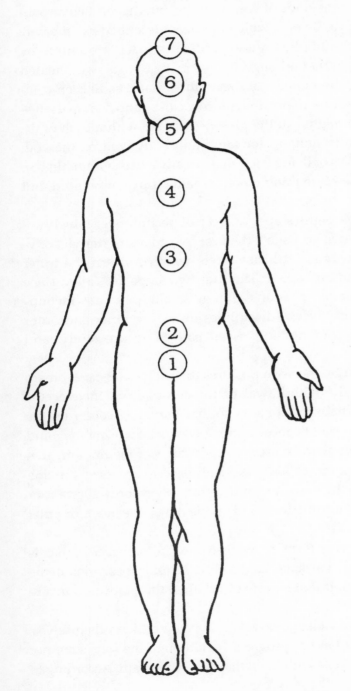

Seventh Chakra
(Crown)

Sixth Chakra
(Third Eye)

Fifth Chakra
(Throat)

Fourth Chakra
(Heart)

Third Chakra
(Solar Plexus)

Second Chakra
(Genitals)

First Chakra
(Root Chakra)

the Hindu Scriptures, our vital energy is contained in these seven centers of consciousness, which are not actually located in the physical body, but in the subtle bodies or energetic sheaths that surround it. The chakras do correspond, however, to certain areas of the physical body, beginning at the base of the spine and moving up to the crown of the head.

The chakras are usually pictured as circles (the Sanskrit word *chakra* means "wheel") arrayed along the spinal column in ascending order. The three lowest chakras, corresponding to the coccyx, genitals, and solar plexus, respectively, relate to our most material levels of consciousness: survival, sex, money, power, and self-esteem. The highest three chakras, corresponding to the throat, the pineal gland behind the forehead, and a space just above the crown, relate to our creativity, insight, and spiritual consciousness. Located between the lower and higher chakras is the fourth chakra, which corresponds to the heart and which serves as a bridge leading from lower to higher consciousness.

Through yoga, breath control, and meditation, Eastern practitioners have traditionally sought to cleanse the chakras in sequence from bottom to top. This purification of the body facilitates the flow of energy—called *prana* in India, *chi* in China, and *grace* in the Western Christian system—as a prelude to Divine union. Whether we are consciously aware of it or not, as we develop spiritually through our life on Earth, we move upward through the chakras, opening each energy center as we progress. We all begin our lives in the lowest chakra, fixated on survival, seeking enough nourishment to stay alive and grow. As we enter adolescence, our attention turns to sex, which begins to be a driving force in our lives, even if it is sometimes repressed. This is followed in quick succession by the drives for money, power, and self-esteem controlled by the second and third chakras.

The lower chakras also correspond to the kinds of prayer in which most of us engage early in our lives: begging and pleading for survival-oriented issues such as health, wealth, a mate, and control over our environment. The key to our spiritual development is the opening of the fourth, or heart, chakra. It is not an accident that the organ of the heart has long been associated with both profound love and compassionate concern for others. If we say that someone has a big heart, is tender-hearted, or speaks in a heartfelt way, we are describing a state of being that goes beyond mere romantic attachment.

Some people progress through this stage intuitively, perhaps through deep suffering or works of service directed to others out of the kindness of their own hearts. Most of us, however, need to spark our spiritual development through conscious practices and continual striving for awareness. Opening the heart is a process that can consume much of one's life, and many people fail to achieve this seminal breakthrough. Yet if we can open this chakra, our entire worldview begins to change. We no longer see ourselves as separate from the rest of humanity any more than we see our left hand as being separate from the rest of our body. The American Zen master Bernie Glassman uses the metaphor of the body graphically in his book *Bearing Witness*:

> My right hand won't attack my left hand unless there's an illness that makes the right hand think it's separate from the left. If there's a gash in my left leg and blood is spurting out, my hands don't say, "Too bad, let the leg take care of itself; we're too busy to take care of it right now." They don't talk about how my body is all one, they just function that way. If my stomach is hungry my right hand doesn't say, "I'm too busy to put food in the mouth."

The entire message of the Buddha could be boiled down to the insight that we are not separate, individual beings, and that the illusion of separateness is a misperception that lies at the root of all human suffering. Although the Buddha seemed to speak more to the human mind, and Jesus more to the human heart, their messages resonate with each other. If we see ourselves as not essentially separate from one another, then it follows that we will love our neighbors as ourselves. The secret to this insight, I believe, lies in opening the heart chakra, allowing the spiritual imperatives of the higher chakras to direct the material urges of the lower chakras. Once we do this, our systems are opened and allow the flow of Divine energy to proceed in us unimpeded.

The fifth, or throat, chakra relates to human will and creativity, and when opened and in balance, directs us to align our work and all our creative expressions with our spiritual mission on Earth. This doesn't necessarily mean that we quit our job as a farmer, construction worker, accountant, or rock singer because these occupations are somehow perceived as not "spiritual." It *does* mean that we strive to do work that harms nobody and to find the work that best harmonizes with God's will as we perceive it in our heart.

The sixth chakra, sometimes called the "third eye," directs our ability to combine intellectual insights with spiritual wisdom. When activated, it opens the way to the crown chakra, which is our point of communion with the Divine. The intellect, no matter how greatly endowed or highly developed, cannot reach its full capacity until the heart has opened. Without that vital connection, we get mad scientists, powerful despots, and brilliant but ruthless businessmen who represent a greater danger to the race than less intellectually empowered mortals.

The kinds of prayer I associate with the higher chakras are prayers of affirmation, which express our confidence that our will is in alignment with God's will; prayers of gratitude, which express thanks for everything in our life, the good with the bad; and prayers of praise, simple expressions of our human wonderment at God and His creation.

I don't want to strain the parallels between the seven chakras, the eight steps of Patanjali's yoga, and the five stages of prayer, yet they all follow a similar progression. The first two steps of yoga, for example, which represent the moral do's and don'ts, lay the foundation for the practices that come after. There is little point in pursuing complex yoga postures, breath control, and advanced meditation techniques if you continue to live an ethically impoverished life. Such conflicted behavior has been the downfall of any number of deluded spiritual masters of both East and West, who mistakenly believed that their spiritual attainments entitled them to special license. Like the awakening stage of healing, the moral practices and disciplines of yoga open the door to the next steps; in fact, they are prerequisites.

Just as the second stage of healing entails purifying ourselves through prayer, self-discipline, and other practices, yoga postures and breath control serve to purify the body and prepare it for the rigors of the kundalini experience, when that potential energy at the base of the spine becomes activated and rises through the spinal column. This extraordinary event entails a relatively rapid opening of all the chakras in succession, often accompanied by feelings of bliss, and has been documented in practitioners of Eastern and Western disciplines.

The illumination stage of prayer and healing, in which the practitioner receives certain graces or powers, calls to mind the powers of concentration and even psychic abilities, known in the Hindu tradition as *siddhis*, which develop in the devoted practitioner of yoga and meditation at a certain point. In both cases, these powers represent a potential distraction if one's ego is not firmly under control, which is why most masters warn their students to beware of such powers. It is also one reason for the rigorous purification built into both processes. Without appropriate preparation, the experience of disorientation when the kundalini rises can be profoundly discomfiting. In extreme cases, this rush of energy may be experienced as a psychotic break, or perceived as such by family and friends.

Lee Sannella, a medical doctor and an expert in kundalini experiences, has documented numerous cases of people being hospitalized or committed following such an intensive experience. He has sought to make the medical and psychiatric communities aware of such states so that they can learn to diagnose them properly. Even great spiritual masters can appear unbalanced or crazy to outside observers. In the Gospel of Mark, we read of an early incident in Christ's ministry, not long after his enlightenment in the River Jordan, when those who know him seem to think he has become mentally deranged: "And when his friends heard it, they went out to seize him, for they said, 'He's gone mad.' And the scribes who came down from Jerusalem said, 'He is possessed by Beelzebub. . . .' " (3:21)

I am not aware of an exact corollary of the dark night in the advanced meditation practices of yoga. Yet both Easterners and Westerners who have tried to follow the path of raja yoga have reported feeling lost or spiritually burnt out as they move into the deeper reaches of the path. One of the many ways in which the dark night has been described is to say that aspirants have left behind many of the most familiar guideposts in their journey toward God, but have not yet arrived at a place of feeling consoled by union with God. We tend to romanticize the yogis of the East as supremely deft and competent spiritual voyagers with great discipline, sailing from one blissful experience to the next. That may be partly true, and yet the spiritual literature of the East is filled with stories of long periods of aridity, of meditating for hours a day without seeming to progress at all, and of temptations and distractions so severe that the aspirant feels he will never achieve enlightenment.

When that final stage is reached, however, there can be little doubt about the parallels between Divine union as perceived in the Eastern and Western traditions. Once the seventh or crown chakra is opened, energy flows freely between the Divine and human levels. The love and compassion that suffuse the person who has reached this stage of spiritual development comes directly from the infinite reservoir of Divine love, and expresses itself as both a feeling of oneness with all humanity and a desire to serve in some way. So-called spiritual masters who have no service component to their ministries and are constantly soliciting funds from their followers, for example, or who do not radiate a feeling of love and compassion for their students and followers ought to be scrutinized very carefully. This does not mean that real masters may not challenge or "tweak" their students from time to time. Some Zen masters have even been known to whack their monks on the head at key moments as a way of getting them to "wake up," and the Western tradition has had its share of difficult saints. But if a clear current of love does not run underneath all of a teacher's actions, he probably has not achieved the realization he claims.

Many Christians question the whole idea of a relationship between traditional Western prayer and the yogic teachings and techniques derived from India and points East. Yet I have come to believe that labeling Christianity a Western tradition is somewhat misleading in the first place. Christianity spread rapidly though the West, but it developed in the Middle East and was influenced in its formative stages by other traditions prevalent there—most notably Judaism, but also

Zoroastrianism in nearby Persia, which derived from the same Indo-European peoples who helped to create Hinduism in India. I don't necessarily agree with those authors who say that Jesus went to India or Tibet to learn esoteric spiritual techniques. He didn't have to go anywhere to absorb Eastern wisdom, because he was living at the hub of the trade routes, where traveling monks, mystics, and sadhus crossed paths between Egypt and the Orient. The Essenes, who have been linked to Jesus by a number of reputable scholars, were among the first monastics of the Judeo-Christian tradition, practicing the kinds of asceticism, fasting, prayer, and meditation we associate with the early Buddhist monastics and wandering Hindu holy men. They eschewed violence and cruelty and professed communal love, strict celibacy, and often vegetarianism.

A spiritual order from around the same time known as the Therapeutae ("healers") practiced austerity and meditation as a way to heal themselves of the ills of worldliness. Located near Alexandria, Egypt, the Therapeutae were formed from the educated upper class of Egyptian Jews and admitted women to their congregation, although they also took vows of celibacy. Since they existed long before the birth of Jesus, they must be considered one of the principal models of early Christian monasticism, and may have directly influenced the beliefs of Jesus.

Even as Christianity spread to the West in succeeding centuries, its mystics have maintained a connection to the same meditative and esoteric practices that underlie the mystical traditions of all the world's great religions. Following these practices intuitively, they often achieved inner openings similar to those described by Eastern masters. Although Western mystics did not use the same terminology, they seem to have recognized stages similar to those represented by the seven chakras and the eight arms of yoga. When Teresa of Ávila and John of the Cross described their spiritual journeys in the *Interior Castle* and *The Ascent of Mt. Carmel*, respectively, they were talking of very similar progressions.

In his book *The Divine Romance: Teresa of Ávila's Narrative Theology*, Joseph F. Chorpenning, O.S.F.S., describes how Teresa mapped out for the sisters of her Order of Discalced (Barefoot) Carmelites a plan for spiritual growth based largely on her inner experiences. She modeled her ascent to oneness with God upon a journey in which one passes through the seven rooms of God's heavenly mansion, based on the Scripture: "In my Father's house there are many places to live" (John, 14:2). By augmenting Father Chorpenning's lucid encapsulation of Teresa's map with my own interpretation of it based on my personal journey, I have developed the following blueprint.

In room one, Teresa says, we remember who we truly are. We had forgotten that we were created in the image of God, but through prayer and meditation we discover that we can reclaim our true identity as Spirit. Teresa warns us about the shadow side of this room, however, saying that one must be on guard against misguided zeal, which causes one slowly to abandon one's love for other people. That rings true for me, because I was a fairly loving person until I entered the early stages of purification, and then, as I have taken pains to point out, my zeal turned gradually to self-righteousness. In my lust for God-realization, I forgot about the primary commandment to love others as ourselves.

In room two, according to Teresa, we are called to ascend, or to move away from attachments to worldly matters such as business affairs and to develop a system of spiritual priorities. The call away from attachments comes in the form of cues—those intuitions or hunches I described when talking about the illumination stage of healing. These cues may arise as a result of the war waged within us in the lower three chakras that control the drive for survival, money, sex, and power. The cues take many forms, such as a realization that money isn't everything, or that when you were in a loving relationship but lacked money you were happier than at times when you had money but no love in your life.

In the third room, we conquer the obstacles to ascending—those feelings of separation, loneliness, and alienation that will hold us back if we give in to them. Teresa advises us to keep in mind that such feelings invariably accompany the ascent, and that we should be patient and realize that they will pass in time. We develop patience—the key to faith—through the virtue of love, for faith grows only when we also have love. Although Teresa believes that penance and fasting are helpful, she warns us to be on guard against doing anything that might harm our health. The shadow lurking in this room, for her, is the kind of overzealousness that leads us to forget to love ourselves, just as in the previous room we might forget to love others.

In her warnings against doing harm to our bodies, Teresa perhaps unconsciously echoes the Buddha's principle of the Middle Way. When the Buddha set out on his life's quest to solve the dilemma of human suffering, he began by practicing the radical asceticism of the Indian yogis of his time, nearly starving himself to death in the process. After six years of extreme self-abnegation, he came to the conclusion that asceticism in and of itself was not the answer. No matter how much he fasted, he eventually had to replenish his body so that he could continue traveling and learning. Moreover, he saw that the logical conclusion of denying the physical body is death. But the principles of reincarnation in which he believed dictated that he would return in another body and be forced to repeat the process ad infinitum. During his last, life-threatening fast, the Buddha realized that enlightenment could be reached only through the vessel of the body, and that there was a limit to how much deprivation his body could safely endure. And so he abandoned the extreme asceticism he had been practicing in favor of what he termed a Middle Way between devotion to pleasures of the senses and complete denial of them. Accepting a bowl of rice and milk that was offered him, he ate and his strength began to return; only then did he undertake the meditation that led to his enlightenment. Although it is unlikely that Teresa had read about the Buddha, she intuitively understood that harming the body amounts to a roadblock on the path to spiritual wisdom.

Teresa also warned against allowing reason to have too much control of our lives, choosing rather to surrender that control into the hands of God. I want to add a word of caution here, however. The Bible talks in several places about the war between flesh and the devil, or flesh and spirit, but the use of the word *flesh* in those contexts is misleading. "Flesh" was a convenient shorthand that many translators used to mean "the things of this world," but today it has an unfortunate negative connotation of carnal pleasure and sexuality. A better rendition might be "mind" or "logic" or "ego." "Ego" in this context is a useful survival mechanism, which is essential to life but can at times militate against spiritual practice. Yet even Scripture does not tell us to abandon ego or logic totally, rather to prioritize so that reason is under the control of spirit, just as, in the classic metaphor from the *Upanishads*, the fiery chariot horses of the senses are controlled by the charioteer.

And so, although we do need to learn to surrender and, in the words of the popular saying, to "let go and let God," we do not give up our critical faculty altogether. This is especially true when it comes to choosing a living teacher or spiritual master. It may be one thing to give yourself up unconditionally to Jesus, or Allah, or the Buddha; but giving yourself up unconditionally to human teachers who may present themselves as conduits to Jesus, Allah, or the Buddha requires much more circumspection. No matter how charismatic a teacher may seem or how inspired his teachings may be, you still have to maintain some objective standards. If a guru asks you to do something that goes against your instincts or your moral code—like turning over large sums of money, submitting sexually, or agreeing not to communicate with your parents or loved ones—run, don't walk, to the nearest exit. A genuine spiritual master needs nothing from you, not your love or even your compliance, and certainly not your money or your body.

In the fourth room, Teresa tells us that we enter the energy of the "prayer of the quiet." This is the technique I have already discussed of learning to sit quietly and listen to God. In Aramaic, the word for *prayer* comes from a root that means "to set a trap." The idea behind prayer as Jesus taught it is to set your mind like a trap to catch the voice of God as it appears in your heart. Silence and solitude, as we will see in a subsequent chapter, are prerequisites to progressing on the path.

By the time we get to the fifth room, Teresa says, we can begin more fully to encounter heaven on Earth, experiencing the union of wills between us and God. Here she uses the image of the silkworm, who constructs a cocoon, dies, and emerges as a beautiful butterfly, signifying rebirth, resurrection, new life, the ascent from darkness into light. This is somewhat parallel to the beginning of the dark night, because here we are learning to exchange the Have-Do-Be Principle for the Be-Do-Have Principle, as discussed earlier.

So far the journey has been back to oneness, to remembering that we are Spirit. In the sixth room of Teresa's paradigm, we become more aware of the immediate presence of God and of being in His presence increasingly. Teresa likens this stage to a betrothal, during which one begins to spend much more time in the presence of the beloved. As a result, we begin to feel the fruit of our commitment in the form of raptures that God sends the soul, blissful moments in which He reveals secrets about heaven. I find some of that sense of wonder in the Book of Revelation or Apocalypse. Many Christians emphasize the scary, doom-laden aspects of this last book of the New Testament, but I also find all kinds of delightful descriptions there of rapturous states, as in chapter 19: "Then I heard what seemed to be the voice of a great multitude, like the sound of many waters and like the sound of many thunderpeals."

In the Old Testament Book of Jeremiah (33:3), God says through the prophet, "Call to me and I will answer you, and I will tell you great and secret things that you have never known before." When I first read that, I equated it with the spiritual insights and intuitions that I was just beginning to receive. Likewise, when God tells Solomon to ask for anything he wants, including riches and long life, Solomon asks instead for the wisdom to lead his people. God then tells Solomon that because he asked for wisdom, He will also give him those other things.

I want to emphasize once again the often mundane nature of the "secrets" and "wisdom" that God reveals to us. It can be as simple as picking up the phone to call a friend and mentioning that you are looking for work or for a place to stay. The friend then happens to mention something that solves your problem without even realizing it. At certain times, our lives seem to be blessed with events that we like to call "happy coincidences" or strokes of luck, but which Jung referred to as synchronicity. In this room or stage of healing, these experiences of rapture and the secrets of heaven increase our desire for union with God. Teresa warns us here, however, to be on our guard against ridicule or praise. We may find that certain people who hear of our experiences attack them as ludicrous, or even as frauds or delusions. Others may try to make more of the experiences than they really are, in extreme cases inducing in us delusions of spiritual grandeur. Both scenarios are equally dangerous.

Finally, in the seventh room, says Teresa, the Divine romance comes to completion, and the soul is permanently united with God, never to be separated again. Since I believe that we are never separated from God entirely, I would prefer to say that here we become aware for the first time with full force that we have *always* been united with God. Many Buddhist teachers like to say that we are all already perfect Buddhas, but we just don't realize it. The only difference between enlightened beings and the rest of us, they say, is that the enlightened ones *know* they are buddhas, whereas we are merely hoping it might be true. To put that insight into Christian terms, the difference between Jesus and the rest of us is that Jesus *knew* he was Divine.

The knowledge that you are eternally united with the Divine does not mean that you never have another problem or crisis, but rather that your knowing allows you to proceed in trust that God's will is at work in everything that happens to you. You no longer feel torn between doing what is right and what is best for you, because the two are one and the same thing. This Divine marriage then produces good works fortified by prayer, just as the final stage of healing manifests as the compassionate desire to serve others.

John of the Cross, a contemporary of Teresa who knew her personally, describes a similar process of ascent in stages. Rather than breaking down his description into discrete steps as I have done with Teresa, let me quote the excellent summary of John's insights presented by Wayne Simsic in his book *Praying with John of the Cross*, which rather eloquently and organically recapitulates everything I've been trying to say:

> John's own experience of longing for love taught him about the ladder of love. For sincere seekers, the ascent goes something like this. The hunger for love draws the seeker to search for it. The heart grows restless, and one realizes that the created world will never completely satisfy the yearning. Then the seeker sacrifices willingly in answer to the call of love and lets go of attachments to things. The seeker becomes even more restless and forgets his or her own self and concentrates on the burning desire for God. On the final steps of the

ladder, nothing deters the longings of love, and the person swiftly and boldly moves toward union.

John invites us to embrace the process as grace calls us to it. God extends the promise of union with infinite love to those who persevere in the ascent. The process will cost us our attachments, compulsions, addictions, and even our life. But the culmination of the ascent is union with God who is love.

## EXERCISE: AWAKENING THE HEART CENTER

Hilda Charlton, whom I mentioned earlier in discussing negative spiritual energies, is someone who learned quite effectively to harness the spiritual insights of both the East and West. On the same night that she won her struggle with the evil forces, an Ascended Master named Hilarion taught her about the chakras and gave her an exercise designed to awaken the heart chakra. "Develop love by training the mind to think loving thoughts," he told her. "It is sad to find today so many human beings with their heart centers atrophied."

Hilarion then instructed Hilda to meditate on the heart chakra by visualizing it as "a great white light sending forth rays of Divine love to the world, blessing all. With every inhaled breath, strongly will that a mighty current of love may fill your heart from the Divine Source itself. As you retain the breath for a few moments, affirm strongly, believe sincerely, and feel intensely: 'I am filled and thrilled with the power of love.' As you exhale the breath, visualize the whole universe overflowing with Divine love from your purified heart."

He then advised her to practice this meditation as often as possible during the day, sending her love blessings out to everyone with whom she interacted. I can't emphasize that advice strongly enough. My own experience has been that new spiritual exercises rarely bear fruit immediately. That would be like expecting an afternoon at the gym after years of inactivity to result in bulging muscles and vastly increased stamina. Exercise, whether mental, physical, or spiritual, just doesn't work that way. What we generally experience instead is what I would call the "breakthrough and plateau effect." After sticking with certain prayers or exercises for a good while, you may experience a gradual or in some cases a sudden shift in perception as the exercises take hold. You may then remain at that plateau for some time before breaking through to the next level.

Hilda Charlton's comments on her own experience with the heart center exercise are classic in that regard. For several months, she did the exercise prescribed for her religiously, breathing in love and breathing out love, but nothing happened. Still, she kept on.

One day I was out for a walk in the woods and sat down thinking, *What a farce—love in and love out! More like nothing in and nothing out! What is the use of going on with this pretense?* I closed my eyes and took a breath, and wham! My heart center in the middle of my chest seemed to open up and love poured like a torrential stream. . . .

I loved the world and all in it, the good and the evil. The pendulum came to a stop and remained balanced. I closed my eyes. The Master's face appeared and he smiled his approval. He was pleased. I walked back quietly through the park. Strangers smiled at me and said, "Hello," then stopped and looked embarrassed, as if to say, "Why did I do that?" I glanced back over my shoulder and I saw that they had stopped and were staring at me. I felt like dancing, but controlled myself. I thought, *It is true. Love is the controlling force of the universe.*

Try doing the meditation and repeating the affirmation: "I am filled and thrilled with the power of love" at least once a day. But keep in mind that you can repeat the affirmation itself any time, even without going through the whole visualization. Riding a bus, waiting on line at the bank, shopping for groceries, or driving the kids to Little League, repeat it silently and believe it. Especially when you feel challenged by a situation or when someone is pushing your buttons, take a deep breath and repeat it to yourself. At the very least, this will give you a chance to regroup and refocus your mind on what really matters.

## EXERCISE: LETTING THE LIGHT OF GOD
## SHINE THROUGH THE CHAKRAS

Because energy often gets stuck on various levels of our being, mainly due to our fears, we need to cleanse those energy systems within us known as chakras, or centers of consciousness. At the first Pentecost, fifty days after the Resurrection, the light-energy of God not only hovered over the heads of the followers of Jesus gathered in the upper room, but the radiance of God began to move through them from the seventh chakra, or energy system, down through the sixth, fifth, fourth, third, second, and first chakras. Before Pentecost, the disciples had been paralyzed by fear, afraid to go outside, but after that encounter with God, they became fearless. They allowed the Divine presence to move through every part of their being, healing them of fear. An observer schooled in Eastern mystical practice might say that they all experienced a spontaneous kundalini release that cleansed them of their fears and instilled certain powers within them.

Begin by taking three deep breaths, then continue to breathe normally, allowing the peace of God to touch you. Keep your inner focus on the presence of God within you. Let yourself bring Pentecost to this present moment and allow that flame and energy of God to begin at the seventh chakra, just above the crown of the head, and move through your whole being as I describe the fears that are lodged in each of your centers of consciousness. Just let those fears be touched by the light of God to allow them to be dissolved. Be aware of the presence of God over your head, and sense that Divine presence releasing its light, its love, its mercy. In the seventh chakra, the two most prominent fears of every human being are the fear of knowing yourself and the fear of spiritual growth, which ultimately means a fear of God. We fear that achieving union with God will mean our personal dissolution, when in fact it means our complete realization. But since we have difficulty conceptualizing complete God-realization, we are afraid. Allow the light to pass through your seventh energy system and be aware of the presence of God removing this fear. There is nothing to be afraid of. Fear not.

Now the light uncovers the darkness of fears lodged in the sixth energy system. In that level of existence lie the fear of self-examination, the fear of one's own intuitive skills, the fear of being open to the ideas of others, and fear in the form of jealousy and insecurity. Now let this light pass within, cleansing the sixth energy system and releasing these fears into the light of the Holy Spirit.

As the light of God moves down through the fifth center of consciousness, it uncovers the fear of self-assertion, creativity, expressing one's needs, feelings, and opinions. Here lies the fear of expressing grief and hurt, and the fear of saying "I'm sorry," which also afflicts the most powerful among us, especially politicians. As this light of God moves down through the energy system and heals our fears, it also touches and heals the physical illnesses that evolve from those fears.

Next, the Spirit of God moves down through the fourth energy system. Here lies the stuck energy of the fear of showing affection; fear of loneliness; and the fears resulting in guilt, resentment, and a judgmental attitude. This is where we are rigid and inflexible. As the light of God passes through this center, God is putting us back into harmony with ourselves, taking the fragmented pieces and putting them all back together again so that we may truly experience the abundant life.

The light or Spirit of God continues its journey through your energy system, moving down to the third level. Here it encounters the fear of failure, of intimidation, of assuming responsibility for needs, the fear of being criticized, of not living up to another's expectation—all of which result so often in depression and despair. Wherever the light of God touches, love is replacing fear.

Now the light of God is moving through the second energy center. This is where feelings of inadequacy, especially in the area of sexuality, reside. Here, also, are the fears that accompany feelings of low or negative self-worth and the fear of honesty in personal relationships. As the presence of God moves through your energy system, be aware of what is going on in your body. Sense whether flexibility is replacing rigidity. See if a sense of peace is not overcoming you.

At last, the light of God enters the first energy system, where it shines on the fear that you won't be able to provide the necessities of life for yourself and your family. Here you see the world as a threatening place against which you are unable to protect yourself. Here also lies the fear of abandonment and separation that make you feel that there is no place you can call home. Let the Spirit of God move unhindered, because with this healing from the inside out comes a great sense of empowerment.

Now, Lord, we thank you because we experience the light of your love and presence moving within us. For some of us, this is our first deep experience that you truly love us and that your love is not based on what we do or fail to do. You love us because we *are*. In that awareness we experience a tremendous sense of peace, and out of that peace flows the energy of joy that makes life worth living. Spirit of God, thank you for your presence, your Divine light, your Divine love. The answer to everything is simply love. We call it healing, but it is just the love of God, the presence of God.

In the Old Testament, God told the spiritual leaders to bless the people in a specific way. When these words are spoken, a very powerful energy is released. The power of this blessing acts as the medicine of God to touch and restore us, because they are the words of God:

*May the good Lord bless and keep you. May He let his face to shine upon you and be gracious unto you. May the Lord turn his face toward you, be generous and gracious unto you, and grant you peace, meaning completeness and wholeness in every area of your life. God bless you.*

# CHAPTER TEN

# Praying in the Energy of the Saints

My family on my mother's side is Polish, and when I was growing up, they transmitted to me the belief that it was perfectly normal and natural to talk to the "other side"—meaning the spirits of departed relatives—and to expect to get a response. My mother's father was very psychic, although he never claimed to have any special ability in this department. One night at dinner I watched him as he suddenly stopped eating and stared into the air above us, then put his head down solemnly. When we asked him what was wrong, he said simply, "My mother just died in Poland."

We sat there in silence, not knowing what to say to him, but a few weeks later a letter came from the Old Country informing him that she had died on precisely that day. When our parish priest heard about this, he told my grandfather that he had to stop communicating with the other side or the priest would refuse to give him absolution. I asked my grandfather what he would do the next time he went to confession. "I'll lie," he said. He had no intention of pretending that he did not communicate with spirits beyond the veil.

I have since read many accounts of similar experiences upon the death of a loved one, but my family seemed to have them all the time. As a young child, I remember seeing a male relative and hearing him speak to me. When I told my mother, she assured me that there was nobody else in the house. Later it came out from my description that this was a relative who had died.

When I was in my teens, my mother often said that prayer is talking to God, the Blessed Mother, or the saints, and hearing them talk to you. At the time, this seemed like a natural extension of talking with my dead relatives. If it is true that some people can communicate with departed spirits, I wondered, does that mean that the spirits of saints and holy people are in our midst and available to help us? I had no answer for this question then. As I grew older, I always experienced a remarkable movement of energy whenever I prayed or sang the litany of the saints. At certain times throughout my life, in fact, I have been attracted to particular saints and holy people without knowing much about them or understanding exactly why I was drawn to them. It didn't matter if the saint was Christian, Hindu, Muslim, or Jewish; or European, Asian, or Indian. I use the term *saint* here generically to refer to mystics of any faith, including Christians who have not actually been canonized, such as Padre Pio, Sister Faustina, and Thomas Merton.

As a result of my attraction to these saints, I came to believe that when you understand how a particular mystic prayed, and you then pray in that same energy—that is, using their words, prayer forms, and attitudes—healing forces begin to enter your life. You may even be drawn to a particular saint because on an intuitive level you know that you need that saint's energy to heal some aspect of yourself physically, mentally, emotionally, or spiritually.

The best metaphor I can think of to explain this phenomenon is that of the painter, writer, or musician who consciously evokes a previous artist whom he admires and who has influenced his own work. The poet T. S. Eliot created the phrase *objective correlative* to refer to a conscious evocation of another writer's work inserted into one's own with the intention of calling to the reader's mind the particular flavor, essence, and energy of that writer's words. Eliot used this technique freely throughout his own work, most notably in "The Waste Land," the famous 1920 poem in which he evokes works as disparate as the poems of Baudelaire, the Fire Sermon of the Buddha, the Gospels, and the *Upanishads*. Likewise,

Claude Debussy, the great French Impressionist composer from the late 19th and early 20th century, wrote a beautiful piece called *The Tomb of Couperin*, which was his evocation of the early-18th-century French harpsichordist and baroque composer François Couperin.

Artists evoke the work of their predecessors partly in homage to them and partly because the aesthetic energy of those artists' work, when summoned consciously, enhances their own aesthetic powers. The same thing is true on both levels when applied to what I call praying in the energy of the saints. We are paying homage to Hildegard of Bingen, Thérèse of Lisieux, Padre Pio, or Yogananda by praying in their fashion, but we are also consciously evoking their spiritual energy. Just as aspiring artists study the works of their greatest predecessors, we can draw inspiration and energy from those who have gone before us on the spiritual path.

Perhaps my earliest attraction to any saint was to Thérèse, whose "Little Way," as she called her path of childlike simplicity and ordinariness, appealed to me when I was quite young. Thérèse believed that you didn't have to perform extraordinary or heroic acts, but needed only to have trust in God. As a troubled teenager, I called on Thérèse to help me, and when I did, I was able to go to sleep without worry. When I later read in Thérèse's writings that she liked to use visualization in her prayers, as I do, this deepened my attraction to her. But the connection was already there.

Around the same time that I went to see that psychiatrist when I was struggling with suicidal thoughts after my mother died, I also happened to start reading the devotional book *Praying with Thérèse of Lisieux*, by Joseph Schmidt. One section described Thérèse's desire to commit suicide and her struggle against that impulse. Realizing that this holy woman to whom I had felt such a strong connection since the age of 17 had also contemplated suicide was a great comfort to me. Although I had started taking the antidepressant medication the shrink prescribed, I took it for just a few days—not nearly enough time for it to have had any effect on my psychological state. Talking with the doctor about my feelings of anger toward my father and others in my life probably did much more to help me at that time. But I can't rule out the synergistic effect that reading about St. Thérèse's own struggles with suicidal feelings had in snapping me out of my self-destructive funk. Afterwards, I felt closer to her than ever.

On some occasions, I have felt an attraction for a spiritual being based only on a picture. When I first saw a photograph of Padre Pio, for example, something in his eyes captivated me. I had never heard of him, but I immediately knew that the energetic essence emanating from that face was something I wanted in my life on a daily basis. These attractions are not necessarily based on likes and dislikes or logical reasons. Even after I had read about Padre Pio's life, I felt no interest in his struggles with the "Devil" and no desire for the stigmata, the marks of Christ's wounds from the crucifixion that mysteriously appeared on Pio's own body, as they have on Francis of Assisi and other saints. I was impressed by Pio's ability to read hearts, but more than anything, I was fascinated by the fact that he was a person who prayed so naturally that his whole life had become continual prayer. I had always instinctively known that we didn't need prayer books to commune with God, yet I felt guilty whenever I tried to pray on my own. Like most Catholics of my age, I had been taught to say only prescribed prayers such as the Hail Mary or the Apostles' Creed. So when I read that Padre Pio simply talked to Jesus or Francis of Assisi as naturally as he would with anyone living, that resonated with me and began a lifelong relationship with his spirit. This experience also deepened my curiosity about whether the saints were present for us in some way that transcended time and space.

Not long after becoming aware of Padre Pio, I came across a book by Matthew Fox dedicated to the work of Meister Eckhart, the medieval German mystic who has long been ignored by the institutional church. Johannes Eckhart (1260–1328) was a Dominican monk who earned a master's of theology degree in Paris and thereafter was known as Meister Eckhart. Eckhart's teachings today are ranked with those of the great mystics of the world, but in his own time, despite having presided over 50 monasteries and 9 convents in Northern Europe, his mystical sermons got him in trouble with the church. Among other things, he used the term *Godhead* to refer to the kind of impersonal, transcendent

Absolute the Hindus call Brahman, as distinguished from God as the personal creator of the universe. This kind of thinking disturbed the Church, and Eckhart was tried several times for heresy. He was finally found guilty, and a papal bull, or edict, was issued against him, but he was never actually punished since he'd had the foresight to pass over shortly before the bull was published.

Reading Fox's book *Meditations with Meister Eckhart*, I discovered a passage that electrified me:

> Whatever I want to express in its truest meaning must emerge from within me and pass through an inner form. It cannot come from outside to the inside but must emerge from within. Now, [the Gospel of] John says "Bear fruit that remains" (15:16). But what is it that remains? It is that which is inborn in me that remains. The work that is with or outside or above the artist must become the work that is in her, taking form within her. In other words, to understand one's vocation as an artist, we should interpret the verse, "The Holy Spirit shall come upon you" (Luke 1:35) to mean: "The Holy Spirit shall come from within you."

As I read those words, I recalled a passage from the Book of Acts in which Paul says of the Lord, "In him we live and move and have our being." To my mind, this meant "I live in the energy of the Holy Spirit." If we are living in God, and the saints who have passed over are also in God, and we are all one, I reasoned, then the saints must still be here with us on Earth. They may be functioning on the other side of the veil, on the spiritual plane, but they are nonetheless right here among us and not dwelling somewhere "up there" or "out there" in heaven.

Eckhart writes:

> God created all things in such a way that they are not outside Himself, as ignorant people falsely imagine. Rather all creatures flow outward, but nonetheless remain within God. God created all things this way: not that they might stand outside of God, nor alongside God, nor beyond God, but that they come into God, and receive God, and

dwell in God. For this reason, everything that is, is bathed in God,
is enveloped by God, who is round about us all, enveloping us.
Everything that is in God is God.

Eckhart's perception confirmed my suspicion that the saints live right beside us, except that they vibrate at a different energetic frequency. Just as radio and television signals from hundreds of different sources all co-exist in the air around us by occupying different frequencies, so do the spirits of saints who have chosen to work with us here on earth. When St. Thérèse was ill, she admonished those around her, "When I die, do not cry for me, for I will spend my heaven on earth doing good." She intuitively knew that her spirit would continue working on the earth plane, helping us with her spiritual energy from the other side of the veil.

This awareness wasn't unique to Thérèse. I believe that all the true saints from all the great traditions—at least, those who so choose—continue to be in contact with us after they die, functioning in a universe parallel with our physical one. Mahayana Buddhism has long had the tradition of the *bodhisattva*, the fully realized human being who puts off his own nirvana or bliss to remain on the Earth plane and help bring all other sentient beings to enlightenment. And the Western esoteric tradition has its Ascended Masters, like those about whom Hilda Charlton wrote, who also remain in contact with the Earth plane to help us with their wisdom.

I have become convinced that by praying as these saints, mystics, and spiritual masters prayed, we not only pay homage to them and invoke their energy, but in a sense we draw them to us and actively engage their help in our spiritual unfoldment. As I was still working on the material for this chapter, I received an unexpected confirmation of my theory. A clairvoyant who attended one of my workshops later sent me sketches of several figures whom she claimed to have seen near me as I taught, prayed, and led healing sessions. I might have dismissed her drawings as fanciful if I had not recognized among them the figures of Padre Pio, Sister Faustina, and the late Cardinal Bernardin, to all of whom I have felt closely connected for some time.

**Blessed Sister Faustina**

Died in 1938.
Polish mystic who gave us the Prayer of Mercy.

**Padre Pio**

Died in 1968.
Italian monk and stigmatist.

**Saint Martin de Porres**

Died in 1639.
A Dominican brother of mixed race who ministered to the poor.

**Joseph Cardinal Bernardin**

Died in 1996.
Archbishop of Chicago who used his own experience of terminal cancer
to work with the dying.

We have no idea what **Jesus of Nazareth** looked like, but when I saw this drawing, I immediately thought it reflected the Jesus I know in my heart.

*The artist who created the drawings in this chapter was born in Germany in 1929 and now lives in California. Ever since childhood, she has been able to sense or see the subtle energies around people. Without any formal training, and modest by nature, she prefers to remain anonymous. Her sensitivity allows her to see the guardian angels, guides, or saints who are around a person. Especially in meditation groups, she sees the faces of others in the room change as their guides come forth to be with those in meditation or prayer. Sometimes the appearance of the "faces" quickly changes, like a Rolodex file of photos, and some have costumes from other time periods. The guide's face seems to replace the face of the person who is meditating or doing healing work, to work through the healer, or to help from the other side of the veil.*

*At one point in her life, the artist sensed or saw the "stuff," for lack of a better term, in which we all exist. It was like glittering layers of cotton wool, laced with golden patterns resembling intricate snowflake designs made of light. This, she assumes, may be both the energies and the information network around us. She believes that "all we ever take with us to the other side is the love we have given to others while here." Perhaps those on the other side are more present than we have previously recognized.*

*While attending one of my seminars, the artist saw or sensed some figures surrounding me. She went home and sketched the pictures displayed here. During the seminar, I felt my guides were there, but on such a subtle level that I did not even think about it. I had only a faint feeling in my heart. When the drawings arrived in the mail a few weeks after the seminar, I recognized the faces she had drawn as guides who I have sensed were with me for some time. The woman who drew these portraits did not know that I intuitively felt connected with these specific saints, and claimed not to have heard of any of them, including Cardinal Bernardin.*

While being alert to our attraction to saints and mystics who have passed over, we would do well to pay attention to certain aspects of their identity and character. The woman now known as Blessed Sister Faustina died in 1938, around the time I was born, but I didn't know very much about her until a friend showed me excerpts from Faustina's diary. I learned that Faustina had belonged to a convent of the Congregation of Sisters of Our Lady of Mercy in Cracow, Poland. Born Helen Kowalska, she came from a poor farming family and had only three years of basic schooling. Seven years before her death, she experienced a vision of Jesus, clothed in a white garment, which she described in her diary:

> One hand was raised in blessing, the other was touching the garment at the breast. From the opening in the garment at the breast came forth two large rays, one red, and the other pale. In silence I gazed intently at the Lord; my soul was overwhelmed with fear, but also with great joy. After a while, Jesus said to me, "Paint an image according to the pattern you see, with the inscription: Jesus, I trust in You."

On another occasion, the spirit of Jesus explained the vision to Sister Faustina in this way:

> The pale ray stands for the Water that makes souls righteous; the red ray stands for the Blood that is the life of souls. These two rays issued forth from the depths of my most tender mercy at that time when my agonizing heart was opened by a lance on the cross.

Perhaps because of my Polish roots, I was drawn immediately to Faustina. I do believe that the genetic and ethnic inheritance that is part of our DNA coding is significant in a positive way. For whatever reason we choose to be incarnated in a particular family, ethnic background is part of that decision, and so we may feel drawn to at least one saint or holy person who reflects our own heritage. I felt closer to the Polish side of my family growing up, and that part of the family seemed to have much more of a mystical bent. So I was fascinated to read in Faustina's diary that she loved to dance the polka, as I did, and that she could bilocate, as Padre Pio could.

But in the end, what most attracted me to Faustina was her devotional prayer life, especially the prayer of mercy that she composed in response to her vision of Jesus. In my heart I wanted to be an embodiment of love and mercy, and I knew very clearly that I was far from it at the time I first encountered Faustina. As I said her prayer over and over, however, whenever I came to the part where she agrees to "take on the most toilsome task that belongs to others" or to help even those who will take advantage of her kindness, I would cringe in fear. Only after I had passed through the five stages of healing was I able to accept that kind of unconditional openheartedness and realize that this is what genuine devotion moves one to feel.

Faustina stressed the primacy of mercy; the attribute of God she emphasized most was not that He loves us but that He is merciful—a meaningful distinction. We can use the word *love* to mean many different things: romantic attachment, admiration, filial respect, and even our attraction to certain foods. But mercy is far more specific, implying a compassionate forgiveness based on unconditional love. When I first read her prayer, I immediately felt that it had a healing quality like few other prayers I had ever come across. I mentioned at the beginning of this book that when people ask me for the best way to pray to be healed, I say, "Pray for others." Odd as it sounds, that is the message I got from Faustina. She promulgated a version of the rosary that she called the Divine Mercy chaplet, which she said was given to her in a vision by Jesus with the intention that it was to be prayed over people who are dying, to release an energy of grace that would carry them happily to the other side.

Faustina also prayed the chaplet for people on the other side who were stuck in what we used to call purgatory. On the "Our Father" beads, she would say "Heavenly Father, I offer you the body and blood, soul and divinity of your dearly beloved Son, our Lord, Jesus Christ." On the "Hail Mary" beads, she prayed, "For the sake of his sorrowful passion, have mercy on us and on the whole world." Faustina said that on occasion she found herself in the presence of a dying person, pray-

he Divine Mercy chaplet on her knees, and yet invisible to the per-
because she had bilocated there. She often saw dark shadows about
e people that dissolved as she prayed for them, easing their transi-
into death.

### Sister Faustina's Prayer

*O Lord God, as many times as I breathe, as many times as my heart beats,
as many times as my blood pulsates through my body, so many times do I
want to glorify your mercy, your presence, your light. I want to be completely transformed into your light and mercy and to be your living reflection,
your living energy, O Lord. May the greatest of all Divine attributes, that
of your unlimited mercy, pass through my heart and body to my neighbor.*

*Help me, O Lord, that my eyes may be merciful, so that I may never sus-
pect or judge others by appearance.*

*Help me, O Lord, that my ears may be merciful, so that I may give heed to
my neighbors' needs and not be indifferent to their pains and moaning.*

*Help me, O Lord, that my tongue may be merciful, so that I should never speak
negatively of my neighbor but have a word of comfort and forgiveness for all.*

*Help me, O Lord, that my hands may be merciful and filled with good
deeds, so that I may even take on the most toilsome task that belongs to others.*

*Help me, O Lord, that my feet may be merciful, so that I may hurry to
assist my neighbor who is in need.*

*Help me, O Lord, that my heart may be merciful, so that I myself may feel
the sufferings of my neighbor, thereby refusing my heart to no one, even those
who will take advantage of my kindness. And I will lock myself up in the
most merciful heart of Jesus. I will bear my own suffering in silence. May
your mercy, O Lord, rest upon me.*

*You yourself command me to exercise the three degrees of mercy. The first:
the act of mercy, of whatever kind. The second: the word of mercy—if I cannot carry out a work of mercy, I will assist by my words. The third: prayer—
if I cannot show mercy by deeds or words, I can always do so by prayer. My
prayer reaches out even there where I cannot reach out physically.*

## Getting to Know the Saints

I highly recommend familiarizing yourself with some of the holy men and women of the great traditions as a way of building up a vocabulary of spiritual voices to help counter the negative energies or elementals that surround us. I would advise steering clear of pious, institutional books like the various lives of the saints, however. Either read their original works, or avail yourself of any of the fine compilations of their writings available in bookstores and libraries. One commentary on the saints that I do find useful and enlightening, however, is Hilda Charlton's *Saints Alive*. Hilda was born in London and came to the U.S. as a young child early in the 20th century. A modern dancer by profession, she traveled to India in the late 1940s and remained there for 15 years, studying with Eastern masters such as Sri Nityananda and Sathya Sai Baba, as well as with the Ascended Masters on the inner plane. Raised by agnostic parents, Hilda was able to incorporate these teachings with what she later learned of Christian mystics, and for many years before her death she instructed audiences in New York City about her discoveries. *Saints Alive* is a compilation of these lectures about holy figures as diverse as Jesus, Sai Baba, Joan of Arc, Thérèse of Lisieux, J. Krishnamurti, St. Martin de Porres, Sri Ramakrishna, and St. Colette, along with some unexpected figures we might not normally think of as saints, such as Pericles of Athens and George Washington Carver. This work is also available as a set of audiocassettes that includes picture cards of each individual that you can carry with you or place on your home altar. (See the bibliography.)

Some years ago, I was delighted to come across a series of books entitled *Companions for the Journey* that offered to help readers do precisely what I have been talking about. Each book in this series is devoted to a Christian mystic who had made a spiritual impact on society, with titles including *Praying with Catherine of Siena, Praying with Francis of Assisi, Praying with Thomas Merton*, and *Praying with Dorothy Day*. After a brief biography, each book intersperses excerpts from the mystic's writings and prayers with reflections and meditations by the author designed to help the reader pray in the essence or spirit of that mystic. A similar series of books including titles such as *Meditations with*

*Hildegard of Bingen* and *Meditations with Meister Eckhart* presents mainly excerpts from the work of these mystics, preceded by brief biographical and critical sketches.

Although all these books are relatively slim, they are packed with invaluable material to help jump-start your prayer life. Until I read Matthew Fox's book about Hildegard of Bingen, for example, I had little idea of who she was or why I should care about her, even though she is a canonized saint of the Catholic church. Once I began to read some of her prayers and poems to the Holy Spirit, however, I was immediately struck by her respect for the Spirit, and I felt a powerful connection to her. Hildegard had a vision in which she saw herself among the disciples when the Holy Spirit descended on them at the first Pentecost. Here was a 12th-century woman daring to count herself among Christ's first (male) disciples, and something in me took heart from her courage. I realized that we don't have to cave in to hierarchy and authority, and that soothed a part of my psyche that still needed healing.

I later discovered a book by two German doctors who are using Hildegard's medical prescriptions, including crystals and herbs, to treat their patients. I realized that there was a connection between Hildegard's relationship with the Holy Spirit and her holistic approach to healing. It was wintertime, and I had a fire going in my fireplace as I read a meditation in which she likened the Holy Spirit to "an unquenchable fire" that "sparks all worth, awakes all goodness, ignites speech, enflames humankind." I knew that this could not be coincidence but must represent a communication from the other side. That experience led me deeper into prayer and communion with the Holy Spirit than anything else had ever done.

I have since grown close to Hildegard because of her love and understanding of the Holy Spirit—the feminine aspect of the face of God, the energy of love, tenderness, compassion, and kindness that heals. When I read her meditations and prayers to the Holy Spirit, my whole body began to vibrate. This wasn't merely a mental or emotional reaction; I could actually begin to feel aspects of my being come alive, aspects that seemed to have been dead for some time. Here is an example of her work:

*Fiery Spirit,*
*fount of courage,*
*life within life,*
*of all that has being!*
. . . . . . . . . . . . . . .
*O sacred breath, O blazing*
*love, O savor in the breast and balm*
*flooding the heart with*
*the fragrance of good,*
*O limpid mirror of God*
*who leads wanderers*
*home and hunts out the lost.*
. . . . . . . . . . . . . . . . . . . .
*O current of power permeating all*
*in the heights upon the earth and*
*in all deeps:*
*You bind and gather*
*all people together.*

*Out of you cloud*
*come streaming, winds*
*take wing from you, dashing*
*rain against stone;*
*and ever-fresh springs*
*well from you, washing*
*the evergreen globe.*

*O teacher of those who know,*
*a joy to the wise*
*is the breath of Sophia.*
*Praise then be yours!*
*You are the song of praise,*
*the delight of life,*
*a hope and a potent honor*
*granting garlands of light.*

("Sequence for the Holy Spirit" from *Symphonia*, translated by Barbara Newman, in *Praying with Hildegard of Bingen* by Gloria Durka.)

In a similar book, *Meditations with Hildegard of Bingen*, by Gabriele Uhlein, I read other hymns to the Spirit that poured from Hildegard's enflamed heart of devotion:

*Who is the Holy Spirit?*
*The Holy Spirit is a Burning Spirit.*
*It kindles*
*the hearts of humankind. . . .*

*Holy Spirit is*
*Life-giving-life,*
*all movement.*
*Root of all being.*
*Purifier of all impurity.*
*Absolver of all faults.*
*Balm of all wounds.*
*Radiant life, worthy of all praise,*
*The Holy Spirit resurrects and awakens*
*everything that is.*
. . . . . . . . . . . . . .
*O Holy Spirit,*
*Fiery Comforter Spirit*
*Life of the life of all creatures,*
*Holy are you,*
*you that give existence*
*to all form.*
*Holy are you,*
*you that cleanse deep hurt.*
*Fire of love,*
*breath of all holiness,*
*you are so delicious to our hearts.*
*You infuse our hearts deeply with*
*the good smell of virtue.*

These words of Hildegard called my attention to the passage in *A Course in Miracles* that says that the Holy Spirit is the only therapist we need. Just meditating on Hildegard's words is enough to release a healing energy that emanates from the Spirit itself at the center of our being, touching all levels of our life with truth, joy, peace, love, and the presence of God.

We have already spoken about John of the Cross's poem *The Dark Night of the Soul*. In *Praying with John of the Cross*, author Wayne Simsic presents another of John's mystical poems, *The Living Flame of Love*:

*O living flame of love*
*That tenderly wounds my soul*
*In its deepest center! Since*
*Now you are not oppressive,*
*Now Consummate! If it be your will:*
*Tear through the veil of this sweet encounter!*

*O lamps of fire!*
*In whose splendors*
*The deep caverns of feeling,*
*Once obscure and blind,*
*Now give forth so rarely, so exquisitely,*
*Both warmth and light to their beloved.*

Thomas Merton's attraction to silence and solitude has resonated with me from my earliest days in the seminary. Merton not only went from being an essentially agnostic youth to becoming a Trappist monk, but he also developed an affinity for Eastern religions, especially Zen, about which he wrote knowledgeably in books such as *Mystics and Zen Masters*. Traveling throughout Asia, he met the Dalai Lama and many other figures from Buddhist and Taoist culture and published his own translation of Taoist poems. Alongside his interest in the world's religions, and a sense of political awareness that led him to protest the Vietnam War and to write about Gandhi's teachings on nonviolence, Merton valued silence and solitude. This combination of respect for other spiritual traditions and a love of silence continues to attract me to Thomas Merton and to move me to pray in his energy. *Praying with Thomas Merton* contains these two extracts from Merton's 1956 book *The Sign of Jonas*:

> So much do I love this solitude that when I walk out along the road to the old barns that stand alone, far from the new buildings, delight begins to overpower me from head to foot and peace smiles even in the marrow of my bones.

> When your tongue is silent, you can rest in the silence of the forest. When your imagination is silent, the forest speaks to you, tells you of its unreality and of the Reality of God. But when your mind is silent, then the forest suddenly becomes magnificently real and blazes transparently with the Reality of God. . . . This is prayer and this is glory!

In another place, Merton writes:

> My life is a listening. His [God's] is a speaking. My salvation is to hear and respond. For this my life must be silent. If our life is poured out in useless words, we will never hear anything, will never become anything.

Merton's understanding of silence as a state of receptivity to God's word exactly parallels my own beliefs. Some mornings I will read passages like these from Merton's works and sit silently, waiting for one or more words to come forth from the page, words such as *solitude, delight,* or *Reality.* I may repeat one of them over and over, letting it float in my consciousness until my mind again falls silent.

Try that with these two passages, and if you feel an attraction for them, pick up a copy of this book or any of Merton's. He also wrote a small but outstanding book called *Contemplative Prayer,* which offers a lucid analysis of the history of Christian prayer, but his more poetic works may make more suitable devotional reading.

Around 1988, I was led to the works of Paramahansa Yogananda, the Indian-born founder of the Self-Realization Fellowship of Los

Angeles. Yogananda was a remarkable mystic who achieved a high level of realization through yoga, but who was also conversant with the sacred Scriptures of Christianity and many other religions. He was able to see the mystical truths underlying the Gospels and the Hebrew Bible so succinctly that his comments on them often opened my own eyes to things I hadn't seen there myself. Yogananda's works, especially *Autobiography of a Yogi* and *Divine Romance*, inspired me at a very deep level because of his understanding of God as pure energy. He believed that we can know beyond the shadow of a doubt that this energy is present in the core of life because we are made in the image of divinity. In his autobiography, Yogananda applies his pluralistic understanding of Scripture to the famous verse from the beginning of the Book of Genesis (1:3), "Let there be light! And there was light." He writes:

> In the creation of the universe, God's first command brought into being the structural essential: light. On the beams of this immaterial medium occur all divine manifestations. Devotees of every age testify to the appearance of God as flame and light. "His eyes were as a flame of fire," St. John tells us, ". . . and his countenance was as the sun shineth in his strength" (Revelation 1:14-16).

Passages such as this one not only helped me to reconnect with Christian Scripture in a new way, but also led me to focus on the nature of God as light-energy, something that has influenced my life and my prayers ever since.

Sri Daya Mata was chosen by Yogananda to assume leadership of the Self-Realization Fellowship following his death in 1952. In *Enter the Quiet Heart*, she demonstrates the truth that there is only one religion—the religion of love. "God is attracted to the compassionate heart," she writes. "He comes to that pure-sighted devotee who relates to Him as the one hidden within every form. Think of each person as none other than the Lord himself wearing a disguise to see how you will react."

Here, Sri Daya Mata reminds me of Mother Teresa of Calcutta, who said that she looks for the face of Jesus in every person with whom she comes in contact. Mother Teresa's philosophy was based on the premise that she wanted to present a loving God through the form she knew best, which was Jesus the Christ. She has also stated in her writings, however, that her major concern both in her teaching and in serving the poorest of the poor was to model Christlike behavior, so that the Hindu would become a better Hindu; the Christian, a better Christian; the Jew, a better Jew; and the Muslim, a better Muslim.

### How I Pray in the Energy of the Saints

When we pray in the energy of the saints, not only do we make contact with those Divine beings on the other side of the veil, but the spirit of that being is attracted to us in turn. The mystic to whom I feel the closest bond is Francesco Forgione, the Capuchin monk who lived in San Giovanni Rotundo, Italy, and is better known as Padre Pio. My attraction to Pio goes back 20 years to when I saw his photograph on the cover of a book and was first drawn to him. I subsequently began to feel his presence around me in a profound way without knowing why. Today I know with all my heart that Pio has been guiding me through my work of healing and prayer, because his entire life and being were constructed around prayer and healing. Pio not only prayed powerfully, he also made powerful statements about prayers, some of which appear in the book *Padre Pio of Pietrelcina* by Alberto D'Apolito:

> One seeks God in books; one finds him in prayer. If today one no longer believes, a lack of prayer must be blamed. . . . The more we pray, the more our faith grows and we find God. You children do not ever neglect prayer; pray often during the day. Do also a bit of meditation; you will find and see God. . . . Prayer is the bread and the life of the soul, the breath of the heart, our recollected and prolonged encounter with God.

When I am asked how I pray, I sometimes say that I pray like Padre Pio did, based on what he has written. That is true perhaps not so much of specific techniques as of the feeling or spirit of his prayer, which he himself described as quoted in the same book:

> My usual manner of prayer is this: I no sooner begin to pray than my soul becomes enveloped in a peace and tranquility that words cannot describe. The senses become inactive. . . . I suddenly feel a touch of our Lord in a most penetrating and sweet manner in the depths of my soul. . . . I'm obliged to shed tears of sorrow and love. In prayer, my soul seems to be completely lost in God. On other occasions, I'm utterly in love with God and it seems to me that I must die. Time flies and there is never sufficient time for prayer.

Inspired by Padre Pio and other holy men and women to whose prayer energy I have felt attracted at various stages in my life, I have developed an approach to daily prayer that works very well for me. I offer it here as an example of the possibilities inherent in this powerful mode of prayer. I don't expect readers to follow all of it, but to use it for inspiration and to see what ideas it may spark within their own imaginations.

On arising and preparing myself for prayer and meditation, I sometimes light a candle to help focus my attention. I also have a number of small, portable fountains throughout my house, and the bubbling of that water brings me to the conscious awareness that balance and harmony are a part of my spiritual wiring. I don't have to focus on that, because it becomes a part of me as my unconscious hears the bubbling of that water.

I begin most mornings with the Prayer of St. Francis. This lovely prayer sets my focus and aligns my energy with the will of God by reminding me that when we pray, we must eventually move beyond praying for things and learn to surrender our hearts to the perfect will of God.

*Lord, make me a channel of your peace.*
*Where there is hatred, let me sow love;*
*where there is injury, pardon;*
*where there is doubt, faith;*
*where there is despair, hope;*
*where there is darkness, light;*
*and where there is sadness, joy.*

*O, Lord, grant that I may not so much*
*seek to be consoled as to console;*
*to be understood as to understand;*
*to be loved as to love;*
*for it is in giving that we receive;*
*it is in pardoning that we are pardoned,*
*and it is in dying that we are*
*born to eternal life.*

When I pray or ponder this prayer, I'm usually sitting in my office area looking outside, where I have a flower garden, a bird bath, and the statue of St. Francis. Then I close my eyes and allow the energy of that prayer and that statue to bring me into a focus on the light of God within. I become aware of my breath, and I allow myself to breathe through my heart chakra rather than through my nose or mouth. To do this, I relax in the awareness that the Divine energy of God emanates from the part of our being we call the heart or the heart center. This area, especially in Catholic and Orthodox Christianity, is represented by the images of the Sacred Heart of Jesus or the Immaculate Heart of Mary. Allowing the breath of God to move through me, I gently lay my jaw upon my heart area with the intention of breathing through the heart. As I breathe in, I think of the opening of the St. Francis prayer, "Make me a channel of your peace." I pick out the word *peace,* breathing it in and out, and as I do so, I become aware that I live by the breath of God.

I allow God's breath to fill me, doing nothing else, no guided imagery, experiencing this prayer and allowing that energy from the form of St. Francis to move through me. This part of my opening devotional can last 20 or 30 minutes, because I allow the Spirit to take over and guide me through this time of communion with God.

From this point on, I connect with the energy of Padre Pio in praying the novena that he prayed every day. It's not a true novena, the traditional Catholic prayer form that is said for nine days; Pio said it every day of his life for those who were seeking his guidance. (See appendix.) I know that his energy is guiding me to help all the people who have asked for my prayers that particular day or who will be asking.

I use Catholic prayer beads—not in a traditional manner, but in a creative way that allows the Spirit to take me into a deeper awareness of God by pronouncing the names of God. I may say something like "God, I love you so much. Lord, reveal your continual love for me. Let my eyes be filled with your love. Let my heart be filled with your love." I may finger the beads, taking only one word as an attribute of God's personality that I want to emanate from my personality, perhaps love or peace or gratitude. I may take the words *omnipotent, all-powerful, all-knowing,* and *everywhere present,* and allow the Spirit to teach me on an inner level through experience that I also emanate these qualities of God, this wisdom of God. I know that I am not God, but I am an incarnation of the Holy Spirit. On the beads I may remind myself that I am God's peace, God's light to a dark world.

This usually leads to some forms or acts of gratitude and praise of God, which Hindus refer to as *bhajans,* devotional prayers. I then express gratitude and sit in the stillness, listening for the voice of God. This is often when I get inspiration for my books or talks. Thoughts will come to me about a subject or a phrase that I want to impart or allow God to impart to others. The next day I may bring that particular thought into my consciousness and let it build from there, waiting again for God to provide guidance.

Being a follower of Jesus, I like to say the ancient prayer of the name of Jesus, sometimes referred to as the Jesus Prayer, because it is a very simple form: "Lord Jesus Christ, have mercy on me, a sinner." I may pray it on the beads, but I simplify it: "Lord Jesus, mercy. Lord Jesus, mercy." I don't say it in a begging or pleading way, but as an invocation to let his mercy flow and let me experience his mercy, and to let others experience his mercy flowing through me.

From here I usually move on to what I call spiritual reading. I may open a Scripture from any of the world's religious traditions, or I may take a spiritual book like the teachings of Yogananda, Jesus, or a particular saint or enlightened master. I allow myself to be guided to a section or a phrase that on a spiritual level will empower me. Sensing the movement of the Spirit and the energy of the empowerment, I then rest with that until I feel that my prayer time or devotional time is over. The important task at this point is to allow that teaching or those thoughts that have come from the Spirit to manifest throughout that particular day. I try not to do this in some programmatic way, as if to say, "Okay, Ron, you'd better pay attention to mercy today." But I do form the intention to be aware of this characteristic when the appropriate moments arrive during the course of the day.

I generally close my morning sitting with a brief prayer of gratitude that I improvise each day, because I have no trouble thinking of different things to be thankful for.

## *Praying in the Energy of Jesus: A New Approach to the Our Father*

When Jesus gave us the Lord's Prayer, he never intended for us to rattle it off without being aware of its deeper truths. Each phrase and sentence within it contains a particular seed of wisdom on which we are to meditate to extract its essence. In my last book, *The Healing Path of Prayer,* I wrote at length about the implications contained in the original Aramaic language in which Jesus actually spoke these words. Here I prefer to present the Our Father in the manner in which I meditate on the traditional version, in the hope that this will help others be more fully open to the Spirit who teaches us to pray in the energy of Jesus. When I lead the Lord's Prayer at one of my workshops, I usually begin by saying the traditional form of the prayer as it appears in most English Bibles:

*Our Father, who art in heaven, hallowed be Thy Name. Thy kingdom come. Thy will be done on earth as it is in heaven. Give us this day our daily bread, and forgive us our trespasses as we forgive those who trespass against us. Lead us not into temptation, but deliver us from evil. For Thine is the kingdom, and the power, and the glory, for ever and ever. Amen.*

I then go on to interpret the Our Father in the following manner:

*Our Father, you who love us and care for us, who are unbounded and unlimited in your love for us, who are our true Daddy, you alone are God, Creator of all that exists.*

*Your Name be held holy, sacred, consecrated. May we use it only in prayer and not profane it in any way, nor adulterate its power by using it casually or in anger. May your Name be understood as Healer, Shepherd, Lord, Adonai, Yahweh, Protector, Guide, All-Wise, All-Knowing, Counselor, and Everywhere Present. When we call upon your Name in reverence, you are present, your peace fills us, and your love surrounds us. Your joy becomes our strength. Your Name becomes our healing balm.*

*As we hallow your Name, a soft, warm light begins to glow within us as your Holy Spirit tells us you are here.*

*May your kingdom come, a kingdom where love and peace reign supreme because you, God, are our authority, our Lord, and our King. Your authority is the power of this kingdom; it has no end and is never exhausted. It reigns wherever people are filled with your Holy Spirit of mercy, love, justice, and compassion.*

*Yes, we can boldly and knowingly pray, "Our Father, Who art in heaven, hallowed be Thy Name. Your kingdom come. Your will be done!" Your wonderful "will" for your children is that they choose life and blessing. Yet they often choose death and cursing. You've called your children to abandon complaining and bitterness lest they receive the same fate as the Israelites, who wandered in circles for forty years because they chose cursing and complaining instead of blessing and praise.*

*Yes, Father, we know your will: "You shall love the Lord your God. You shall love yourself as your neighbor." That is your will on Earth as it is in heaven, on the material plane as in the spiritual realm. We shall express that love through our desire to help the afflicted, heal the sick, build the family of God.*

*Loving Father/Mother, you give us this day our total daily sustenance, all the good that we need to have our lives extended both materially and spiritually, and for this we give you thanks. Father, we pray for physical, emotional, and spiritual bread to feed our total being. We know that you give it all to us for we are you children, whom you love.*

*Father in heaven, forgive us our mistakes as we forgive those who err against us. We confess before you our guilt, knowing that we sometimes obstruct the growth of your Kingdom. We so often reject your desire for us to love and do not behave like your children. We confess before you: how often we fail to speak the word that could bring peace. How often we keep silent when a word could have resolved the conflict. How often we butt in and hinder reconciliation.*

*How often we seek to justify ourselves, thinking to free ourselves of guilt but only clouding the issue. How often we forget our misdeeds, hoping you will forget as well, Lord. How often we become hopeless, thinking there is no way to be rid of our habitual mistakes.*

*We ask that you forgive us our mistakes. We name them before you as your Holy spirit directs in order that you may wipe them out. We know that you have tied your forgiveness to our willingness to forgive others. Father, help us to forgive. Our Father, who art in heaven, forgive us our trespasses, as we forgive those who trespass against us, through Jesus Christ, our Lord.*

*Father, you do not lead us into temptation. We know you don't lay snares for us or desire to trap us in some error, so that we might fall headlong into disaster. That is not a picture of a loving Father, surely not of you.*

*We know that you are our fortress in time of trial and attack and we are protected. You deliver us from evil. Your children must realize that "evil" is "live" backwards, and living backwards entails so many negative things: fear of life, of people, of what others will think; tension and anxiety; the stress that comes when we forget you and your presence in our lives; pain, especially emotional pain that we cause to come into the lives of others and that will eventually come back upon us; hate, jealousy, and envy, which are all signs of fear.*

*You deliver us from evil if we will but look to you.*

*O Father, such joy fills me as I understand these words, reflect upon them and affirm them. Knowing this, my heart is filled with praise, worship, and adoration as I tell you: For yours is the kingdom, and the power, and the glory, now and forever. So be it. Amen.*

# CHAPTER ELEVEN

# Silence and Solitude

*"Behold my beloved, I have shown you the power of silence,*
*how thoroughly it heals and how fully pleasing it is to God."*
— St. Anthony the Great

The idea of withdrawing into silence and solitude as a spiritual path seems to be as old as the history of religion. The *rishis* who composed the ancients Vedas of India over 4,000 years ago are said to have received their knowledge while in deep meditative trances, for which some measure of silence and solitude was clearly necessary. The Buddha himself is believed to have learned at least two different kinds of silent meditation from the wandering monks and ascetics of his time (the sixth century B.C.). In Egypt and Palestine, as we have seen, a tradition of Jewish monastic communities preceded the birth of Christ, from the Therapeutae of Egypt to the Essenes in the Dead Sea region.

But in third-century Egypt, a number of early Christian men and women developed what was to become the basis for the great monastic traditions of medieval Europe, Greece, and Russia. St. Anthony, considered by many to be the first Christian monk, was born around the year 251 in central Egypt to a family of peasant farmers. At the age of 18, one day in church he heard the passage from the Gospel of Matthew (19:21) in which Jesus tells the rich young man who asks what he must do to be saved, "Go, sell what you own and give your money to the poor and come follow me." Anthony took the words to heart and began to practice asceticism under the guidance of a recluse who lived nearby. We don't know who the recluse was, or whether he might more properly be considered the first Christian monk.

In 285, Anthony withdrew into the desert and lived there for 20 years in solitude. During that time, he was subjected to many psychological and spiritual trials that have become the stuff of legend and the subject of some famous paintings. He emerged from these conflicts victoriously, but his success was due not to disciplines of asceticism or willpower, but to learning in the solitude and silence how to surrender to God. Anthony gave up his solitude for five years to act as spiritual mentor to a group of like-minded souls who had gathered near him, but then returned to solitude, traveling only rarely until his death in 356.

In his book *The Way of the Heart*, Henri Nouwen writes of St. Anthony, "When he emerged from his solitude, people recognized in him the qualities of an authentic 'healthy' man, whole in body, mind, and soul. They flocked to him for healing, comfort and direction." That says something profound about the healing power of solitude and silence. At a time when the average life expectancy was somewhere between 30 and 40, Anthony lived to be 105.

Following the example of Anthony and others, including Pachomius, men and women of diverse backgrounds began moving into the deserts of Egypt and Syria to experience the presence of God by stripping themselves of everything and entering into a radical aloneness with the Divine. Referred to as *nyptic*, meaning "serene and wise," they practiced *apathia*, or transcending the passions through continual prayer. Kyriacos Markides writes about this practice in *Riding with the Lion*:

> The early Christian mystics believed that the passions associated with the ego obstructed the full expression of the Spirit within. They thought they could silence the passions through various forms of *askesis*, or "exercise," by subjugating the body to all forms of deprivations, such as food, sleep, sex, and bodily comforts of all sorts. It was

believed that these forms of spiritual exercises—or bodily mortifications, depending on how you want to look at it—would render the practitioner a vessel for the power and grace of the Holy Spirit. All that, of course, was done within the context of Paul's injunction of ceaseless prayer.

But what exactly does Paul's famous statement mean? The 19th-century Eastern Orthodox classic, *The Way of a Pilgrim*, written by an anonymous Russian peasant, begins as the author is attending a church liturgy one Sunday and hears the admonition of St. Paul in his Letter to the Thessalonians to "pray without ceasing." Puzzled by the Scripture, the narrator goes on a journey and visits many preachers, asking what Paul might have meant by this startling statement. He is treated to numerous sermons *about* prayer, but at first no one is able to tell him how to go about actually praying continually.

Finally, the pilgrim comes across a *starets*, a Russian holy man and spiritual counselor, who tells him about the prayer that doesn't cease, based on the teachings of the *Philokalia*. From the Greek for "Love of Spiritual Beauty," the *Philokalia* contains mystical and ascetical writings of 25 Eastern Orthodox masters collected over 11 centuries, including detailed instructions on the art of continual interior prayer. One master, St. Symeon the new theologian (949–1022), offers very specific directions:

> Sit down alone and in silence. Lower your head, shut your eyes, breathe out gently, and imagine yourself looking into your own heart. Carry your mind, that is, your thoughts, from your head to your heart. As you breathe out, say "Lord Jesus Christ, have mercy on me." Say it moving your lips gently, or simply say it in your mind. Try to put all other thoughts aside. Be calm, be patient, and repeat the process very frequently.

The starets advises the pilgrim to repeat the prayer throughout the day, and to return and report on his progress. Finding work in the garden of a nearby peasant, the narrator does so, but begins to feel bored and sleepy from the constant repetition. The starets then advises him to use a rosary and to say the prayer exactly 3,000 times a day. When he has accomplished that daunting feat, he is then told to repeat the prayer 6,000 times a day, then 12,000 times, and finally as often as possible. This is very difficult for the pilgrim, but over time the prayer moves from his head to his heart, and he begins to feel the loving warmth that emanates from praying the name of Jesus. One morning, after months of continual prayer, the pilgrim wakes up and discovers that the prayer of the name of Jesus is already on his lips. By assiduous practice, he has arrived at the point where he is able to say the prayer even in his sleep. Indeed, he can no longer live without it.

> I grew so used to the prayer that I went on with it all the time. In the end I felt it going on of its own accord within my mind and in the depths of my heart, without any urging on my part. Not only when I was awake, but even during sleep, just the same thing went on. Nothing broke into it, and it never stopped even for a single moment, whatever I might be doing. My soul was always giving thanks to God and my heart melted away with unceasing happiness.

This prayer, known variously as the "Prayer of the Heart" or the "Jesus prayer," now forms an important basis for much of Eastern Orthodox spirituality. Yet the practice of its continual repetition carries clear echoes of the Hindu practice of *mantra yoga* or *japa*, the continual repetition of the name of God or some holy phrase such as *Om Nama Shivaya* ("Om! Praise be to Shiva!"), often with the help of a rosary. Other traditions, notably Buddhism, Zoroastrianism, and Sufism, place great emphasis on praying, singing, and chanting the names of God in their own languages. Sufis practice saying the 99 Beautiful Names of Allah for hours on end, until they are virtually saying the names under their breath without conscious effort. They also spend hours in a combination of chant and physical movement called *zhikr*, an Arabic word that means "remembrance" (of God). The idea in both cases is the same as the Prayer of the Heart: to find ways to focus on the presence of God so continually that, in fact, one's prayer never ceases—that is, it becomes "continuous" rather than "continual."

We no longer have to go into the desert to practice desert spirituality, however, nor do we need to enter a monastery, ashram, or convent. We can experience desert spirituality where we live by practicing the Prayer of the Heart. Solitude and silence can help one enter such a state of constant, almost subconscious awareness of the Divine. This does not necessarily mean withdrawing from society and becoming a wandering mendicant. You can begin by practicing brief periods of silence throughout the day, during meditation or while traveling to and from work. The solitude of which I speak is a state of mind and grace wherein the old self dies and the new self, the essence of Spirit, is born. In his book *The Orthodox Way*, the Greek archimandrite (bishop) Kallistos Ware writes:

> "Know yourself" means "know yourself as God-sourced, Godrooted; know yourself in God." From the viewpoint of the Orthodox spiritual tradition it should be emphasized that we shall not discover this, our true self "according to the image," except through a death to our false and fallen self. "He who loses his life for my sake shall find it" (Matt. 16:25): only the one who sees his false self for what it is and rejects it, will be able to discern his true self, the self that God sees. Underlining this distinction between the false self and the true, St. Varsanuphius enjoins: "Forget yourself and know yourself."

Dying to the self is a slow process that is aided immeasurably by regular periods of withdrawal from all the elements that distract us from genuine awareness. And so we would all do well, while remaining engaged in our social structure of family, jobs, and friendships, to absent ourselves for a time each day from other people, television, radio, telephones, especially cellular telephones, and allow ourselves to be in the presence of God—to listen attentively and hear God speak to our hearts the great love that He has for us. In solitude, we don't have to do anything; we need only to be.

This level of prayer usually occurs in one who is passing through the dark night of the soul, which can also be thought of as the dark night of the senses. That is the stage, you will recall, in which we need to confront our own demons, our shadow side. Perhaps for this very reason, many of us are mortally afraid of silence and solitude. When we remove ourselves for a time both from the external noise of society and its electronic environment, and from the persistent chatter of the mind, we begin to glimpse the shadow in our lower selves, which may not be a welcome sight. And yet in facing squarely those darker aspects of our nature, and giving them over to the light of the Spirit to dissolve, we can then cross the bridge of the fourth chakra—the chakra of love, compassion, and forgiveness—and enter the realm of higher spiritual consciousness.

The paradox of solitude is that, by entering it utterly alone and accepting our aloneness, we are able to experience more clearly that we are not at all alone, because God is with us. In some cases, the past that we have buried is so overwhelming that, when it springs into consciousness during our desert spirituality experience, we could be crushed if we did not know down deep that God has never abandoned us. In those memorable words of the Gospel, Jesus tells us, "Behold, I am with you always, even until the end of time." He knew that the Christ consciousness would always be available to each of us whenever we call on it. But until we remove ourselves at least temporarily from the clutter and noise of society, we do not have the chance to experience its presence.

We might compare our state before entering the place of solitude to a patient preparing for a heart transplant. Our human heart, which has been weakened through the years by the negative energy of jealousy, resentment, bitterness, and a reluctance to forgive, and our vital arteries, which have been clogged with selfishness, loneliness, and grief, are about to be replaced by a new heart and arteries cleansed by the fire of the Holy Spirit. When we face our own demons and encounter God in the silence and solitude, our heart is strengthened and infused with the compassion of God. We are then better able to help others, to read their hearts and become one with them in their grief and sorrow; as a result we can offer them comfort and consolation, as St. Paul remarked in his Second Letter to the Corinthians quoted earlier.

The many mystics of various religious traditions in one way or another have declared that without solitude, it is virtually impossible to embark on a spiritual path. In solitude we make room for God in our lives; in solitude we give God our attention. This is what Jesus meant when he said, "When you pray, go to your private room. Shut the door behind you and pray to your Father who is in that secret place." In solitude we come to know the Holy Spirit, who is helping us even in the midst of our sufferings. We come to know peace; we come to know joy even in the midst of sadness.

Scholars generally agree that the Gospel of Mark is the first of the four gospels to be written and the one on which both Matthew and Luke based their accounts. And the first chapter of Mark is absolutely action-packed. Beginning with John the Baptist preaching and baptizing in the River Jordan, it narrates in rapid succession the baptism of Jesus, his enlightenment, the forty days of solitude and temptation in the desert, the arrest of John, and the beginning of the ministry of Jesus. In the same brief chapter, Jesus calls his disciples, teaches in the synagogue, begins healing the sick and casting out demons. But the line that caught my attention years ago was verse 35, following the Master's first public healings. "Early in the morning, long before it was dawn, Jesus got up and left the house where he was staying and went off to a place of solitude and there was absorbed in prayer."

That verse changed my life, because it suggested that the healing work of Jesus was inextricably linked to his discipline of solitude and silence. If I imitated him in that way, I realized, each day would flow out of my being and I would be guided according to the Spirit of God. I later learned that the world's mystics have long held that the most valuable time for prayer and meditation is the hours just before dawn. Starting my day with the practice of silence and solitude, which means not being alone but being alone with God, I began to get hunches about what I was to do that day. As I learned to do this each morning, it generated tremendous energy that seemed to appear out of nowhere to guide me through the day. Later in the day, that energy stopped, as if to tell me that the day was over and it was time to relax.

According to Mark, as Jesus is meditating, the disciples seek him out, saying, "Everyone has been searching for you." Unfazed, Jesus announces that it's time to move on and preach in the next town, where he promptly heals a leper. Again, the connection between prayer in solitude and healing in public was made clear to me.

Let's look more closely now at one of the events that Mark crammed into the first few verses of his gospel, and that later turned up in the fourth chapter of Matthew. Immediately after his spiritual opening in the River Jordan, Jesus goes into the desert, where he is led by the Holy Spirit for 40 days and nights and is tempted by Satan. As we have seen, the word *satan* originally meant a roadblock or obstacle put in one's path by God. In this case, the obstacle appears to be the temptation to use the psychic and telekinetic powers generated by advanced spiritual practice for one's own comfort and glorification—like so many accomplished but ultimately deluded gurus of East and West who have been tested and found wanting in our own time.

First, Jesus is tempted to satisfy his desire for food by changing stones into loaves of bread. Jesus replies that it is more important to realize that we can be fed by every word that comes from the mouth of God. Satan then takes Jesus to the roof of the Temple in Jerusalem and suggests that he jump off and prove that he is a child of God by calling on the angels to protect him. Jesus responds that it is foolish to put God to the test. Finally, Jesus is taken to the peak of a high mountain and shown every nation in the world. "If you bow down and worship me," Satan says, "I'll give you all of this." Jesus tells Satan to be gone, because only God is to be worshiped.

When examined, each of the temptations sounds like an appeal to the ego of Jesus: to use his spiritual powers to feed his material needs, his grandiosity, and his desire for power. On a more mundane level, we can think of the temptations as those negative thoughts or elementals that enter our lives and keep us from experiencing God. Jesus replies to all three temptations in a very positive way, causing these negative thoughts to dissolve, because his focus remains on the presence of God.

What is offered in these temptations is not necessarily wrong in and of itself: sustenance, angelic protection, and leadership over nations. That only makes the temptations more insidious, because the goal of spiritual practice is union with God. If material well-being, protection, and power follow from that, so be it. But to use one's spiritual powers to obtain these material goals is a form of self-delusion. Fueled by the energy engendered in solitude and silence, Jesus sees the potential delusion and responds by affirming that God is the source of his identity. As he will later say, "Seek first the kingdom of God, and everything else will be added to you."

We should also note that the temptations are part of the spiritual path. When we begin to withdraw our attention from the things of the world even briefly and temporarily, our ego immediately throws up roadblocks and tries to call us back to our old ways. The stories told by saints and mystics like Padre Pio of being attacked by demons can be seen as a manifestation of ego and the negative elementals trying to prevent them from moving toward God. Yet it is only in silence and solitude that we have the strength to overcome these "temptations" of ego and negativity, because silence is our communion time with God. As it says in the Book of Psalms, "Be still and know that I am God." Without being silent, one cannot begin to know God. There is a difference between knowing God and knowing *about* God. In stillness, we begin to experience the Presence even if we may not be able to explain or understand it.

In the last parish I served as a Roman Catholic priest, I developed the discipline of meditating in silence and solitude prior to any service, mass, teaching, or preaching. I would then proceed to the stage area or pulpit and allow the message to flow through me from the Spirit, a practice that I still follow to this day. During one Sunday mass at the end of the Gospel, as I was gathering my thoughts to start preaching the sermon that normally comes at that point in the service, I distinctly heard a voice within me that I recognized as God saying to me, "Not today. Just call the people to silence—no music, no nothing. Just be silent in my presence and I will speak to them."

Needless to say, this startled me. Being a man not of few words but of many, I sometimes find it difficult to remain quiet, especially when an audience is sitting in front of me. I did not know how to approach this subject with the people. They had gotten themselves comfortably seated following the Gospel reading and were waiting for me to speak. I opened my mouth, no doubt looking a bit flustered, and said, "I've got good news or bad news, depending on what your perception is. I feel down deep within myself that I am not to speak to you today, that God wishes to do that. And God speaks best through the silence."

My congregation had been with me long enough that they never knew what to expect from me anyway, so they were not overly surprised by this latest message. People often came as guests to my church for various reasons, however, and I could look out over an audience on Sunday and recognize faces I had not seen before. On this particular Sunday, a whole row of newcomers was seated directly in front of the pulpit. After I gave my brief message, I very nervously took my seat in the altar area and allowed the church to grow completely quiet. One minute of silence seemed to last an hour. After all the praying and singing that had preceded it, the sudden quiet did seem deafening. I thought of that wonderful passage in the Old Testament Book of First Kings (19:11-12) where Elijah the prophet stands on a mountain seeking God.

> And behold, the Lord passed by, and a great strong wind rent the mountains, and broke in pieces the rocks before the Lord, but the Lord was not in the wind; and after the wind, an earthquake, but the Lord was not in the earthquake; and after the earthquake a fire, but the Lord was not in the fire; and after the fire a still small voice.

God is in the quiet, in the still small voice within each of us, if we are quiet enough to hear it, and this was the experience I was about to have with my congregation. To this day I do not know how long we were in the silence. It might have been 25 or 30 minutes, because that's what it felt like. More likely just four or five minutes had gone by when I began to hear sobbing in the audience. Looking up, I noticed a man in the row of strangers in front of me weeping quietly. The silence seemed to magnify everything as his body began to convulse and he started to weep out loud, almost hysterically. Soon others joined him, and the weeping grew louder and went on for another ten minutes or so. Then I was guided by the inner voice, which said, "Now have them sing a very quiet worship song in honor of my presence."

I realized that God was leading the worship and the prayer time. He always does that, of course, but I was never so consciously aware of it before. My pianist and organist and the choir began to move softly into a simple chorus called "Hallelujah," which comes from two Hebrew words that literally mean "to celebrate God." And that's exactly what began to happen. The chorus continued on that one word for ten minutes before we moved on to other forms of worship. I could feel the exhilaration and the movement of energy throughout the congregation during the rest of the service. That experience demonstrated to me once and for all the power that emanates from the silence. Not only do powerful words that uplift and heal the spirit come from the silence, but the silence itself can heal and elevate people's spirits.

When the Gospel of John refers to the Word becoming flesh, it is talking about the experience of power manifesting in our world when it comes from that place of silence, of communion with God. Unfortunately, we have all but forgotten how to listen today, or even how to be still and quiet. The increase in speed brought on by the electronic environment has meant a concomitant increase in noise. From TVs and radios left blasting idly in the background to the constant hum of the computer and the roar of jets overhead, we have a difficult job to find silence anywhere. Even our religious services are noisy, as I can attest. The healer Kathryn Kuhlman once said that people have mistaken noise for the power of the Holy Spirit, and I see that often in Christian church services that seem more geared for entertainment than inspiration.

To counteract this trend, I try to make the heart of all my healing retreats the practice of the discipline of silence. That way people can begin to sense the importance of living in relationships based on stillness and solitude. Before we speak, we listen. Before we counsel or teach, we listen. As we have seen, for many people prayer is nothing more than speaking to God or at God. For others it is largely an intellectual pursuit, in which they spend time thinking about God, trying to figure out who and what God is and the best way to appease God or get Him to answer their prayers. Perhaps because we live in the information age, we have come to believe that if we have enough intellectual data on a subject, we can master it. When we realize that no amount of information brings us closer to an intimate knowledge of God, a profound frustration sets in.

Silence helps us reduce and neutralize the constant humming of the mind and allows us to penetrate more deeply into the heart of prayer. The Russian mystic and recluse Theophan describes the Prayer of the Heart this way: "To pray is to descend with the mind into the heart and there to stand before the face of the Lord, ever-present, all-seeing within you."[1] This concept is central to the understanding of prayer as seen by the early Desert Fathers and Mothers. When we speak of the heart in this particular matter, we mean that source of all physical, emotional, intellectual, volitional, and moral energies. From a spiritual viewpoint, we could say that the heart is the central organ for our unique personal life. In his book *The Way of the Heart*, Henri Nouwen writes:

> The Prayer of the Heart is a prayer that directs itself to God from the
> center of the person and thus affects the whole of our humanness. . . .
> The Desert Fathers in their sayings point us toward a very holistic
> view of prayer. They pull us away from our intellectualizing practices
> in which God becomes one of the many problems we have to address.
> They show us that real prayer penetrates through the marrow of our
> soul and leaves nothing untouched. The Prayer of the Heart is a prayer
> that does not allow us to limit our relationship with God.

When the Desert Father Macarius was asked how one should pray, Nouwen adds:

> The old man said there is no need at all to make long discourses. It
> is enough to stretch out one's hand and say "'Lord, as you will and as
> you know, have mercy." And if the conflict grows fiercer, say "Lord,
> help." He knows very well what we need and He shows us his mercy.

Here we can learn something from the Zen masters, for whom silence was often the most eloquent answer to a student's question. Of

---

[1] *The Art of Prayer: An Orthodox Anthology*, edited by Timothy Ware. London: Faber and Faber, 1966.

course, one must say something at times, but often our approach to prayer could benefit from the artistic truism "Less is more." When I was in parochial school, the nuns taught us to stay in connection with God through simple, short prayers called ejaculations. We need not express ourselves in fancy words, they said, but in the simple phrases of a trusting child that bring the greatest experience of God into our lives. Here are some examples:

*Jesus, help.*
*Mercy, Lord.*
*Lord, I long to love you with all my heart.*
*Let me feel your love, O Lord.*
*O God, come to my assistance.*
*Lord, mercy.*
*The Lord is my shepherd.*

Like the Jesus prayer, these brief phrases are enough to activate the Spirit within us and make God's presence visible wherever we go and to whomever we speak.

## Praying in Silence and Solitude

If you don't already have a sacred space in your home, find a spot where you can be alone in silence for at least 30 minutes. Be sure the phone is disconnected or the volume is turned off on your answering machine, and that you will not be disturbed. In preparation for my own prayer time in silence and solitude, I like to begin with the prayer of Cardinal Newman. John Henry Newman (1801–90), who came from a British family with Evangelical sympathies, was active in the Anglican Church before becoming a Roman Catholic in 1845. His prayer is now said daily by Mother Teresa's Missionaries of Charity. What appeals to me most about it is the clear evocation of the Christ as light-energy that shines through us as we make ourselves yielded vessels for God's work. You may personalize the prayer by substituting the singular pronoun for the plural. Recall that Jesus, like all enlightened masters, is for everyone. You need not follow the Christian religion to say these prayers:

> Dear Jesus, help us (me) to spread your fragrance everywhere we (I) go. Flood our souls with your spirit and life. Penetrate and possess our whole being so utterly that our lives may only be a radiance of yours. Shine through us, and be so in us, that every soul we come in contact with may feel your presence in our soul. Let them look up and see no longer us but only Jesus! Stay with us, and then we shall begin to shine as you shine; so to share as to be a light to others; the light, O Jesus, will be all from you, none of it will be ours; it will be you, shining on others through us. Let us preach you without preaching, not by words but by our example, by the catching force, the sympathetic influence of what we do, the evident fullness of the love our hearts bear to you.

After saying this prayer, lapse into silence and follow your breathing. You do not need to exaggerate the sound of your breathing, but inhale and exhale so that it is inaudible. When you are comfortable with this, begin to say the Prayer of the Heart silently. As you inhale, say mentally "Lord Jesus Christ"; and as you exhale, say, "Have mercy on me." Actually breathe the words into your heart on the inhale, and send them out into the universe on the exhale, as if you were filtering the prayer through your heart. Visualize your heart being filled with the white light of Divine love as you breathe your prayer. Continue this for as long as you can. Above all, be patient with yourself; there is no need to hurry this exercise.

# CHAPTER TWELVE

# Invoking the Sacred

*T*oward the end of *The Way of a Pilgrim*, the narrator, having mastered the Prayer of the Heart, sings its praises to everyone with whom he comes in contact. When the educated magistrate with whom he is staying professes ignorance of this practice, the pilgrim reads him a passage from the *Philokalia*:

> One must learn to call upon the name of God, more even than breathing—at all times, in all places, in every kind of occupation. The Apostle [Paul] says, "'Pray without ceasing.'" That is, he teaches men to have the remembrance of God in all times and places and circumstances. If you are making something, you must call to mind the Creator of all things; if you see the light, remember the Giver of it; if you see the heavens and the earth and the sea and all that is in them, wonder and praise the Maker of them. If you put on your clothes, recall Whose gift they are and thank Him Who provides for your life. In short, let every action be a cause of your remembering and praising God, and lo! you will be praying without ceasing and therein your soul will always rejoice.

I could not have encapsulated any better the goal of integrating prayer into every aspect of your daily life. What that passage makes clear, moreover, is that prayer need not mean the repetition of words or phrases, even of the beautifully simple Jesus prayer. As I have been saying, prayer is awareness—of God, of gratitude, of every element that makes up our life.

Clearly, introducing silence and solitude into your prayer life as we explored in the previous chapter will help move you along the spiritual path. But since most of us are not likely to be able to incorporate more than brief periods of silence or solitude into our lives, we need to explore other ways of expanding prayerfulness to cover more and more of our daily existence. This is a process I call "Invoking the Sacred," based on the title of a workshop that Caroline Myss and I give every year. It means finding room for the sacred in everyday life, from creating a sacred space in your home to using small sacred objects to help you pray wherever you may be. Invoking the sacred also means discovering different ways to pray, ways that may seem a bit unusual to those of us who grew up saying the standard Christian and Jewish prayers our parents taught us. Prayer comes in so many forms that I hesitate to recommend one way to invoke the sacred. I will try instead to offer you a wide range of approaches from which I hope you will choose those with which you resonate most joyfully.

To begin with, prayer means developing an attitude of gratitude. People who are sour on life have never learned to be grateful, and so they see only the darkest side of life. If you have a heart filled with fear, then you will see a world characterized by fear. If you have a heart filled with love, then you will perceive the world as a loving, secure place in which to dwell. It's up to you how you view life, just as it's up to you to learn how to integrate this sacred element of prayer into your life and make it part of your daily rituals.

If you feel that rituals are not important, I suggest that you take another look at what rituals actually are. During the 20th century, rituals acquired a bad name based on the perception that they are meaningless formulas characterized by rote repetition. And yet we live by rituals, from brushing our teeth in the morning to folding our eyeglasses and putting them on the night table before turning out the light to go to sleep. Kissing your mate on entering your home in the evening can be a meaningless gesture devoid of feeling or it can be an uplifting affirmation, depending on the intention behind the act. Likewise, a daily ritual of prayer or veneration can be pointless if done perfunctorily with no awareness of what the act implies. But it can also be a way of charging your spiritual batteries and elevating the intensity of feeling behind all your daily actions. It's up to each of us to put back the meaning in these simple gestures.

Margot Anand defines rituals as "prayer in action." Of themselves, they are neither good nor bad, but when used appropriately, they can become carriers of Divine energy. Take, for instance, the sacramental rituals of Christianity. The sacraments are rites that once were vital but that have become largely drained of their energy; they need to be made practical so that we can have an everyday mystical experience. In *The Healing Path of Prayer*, I sought to give the sacraments back to the people, because these rituals were never intended to be for the exclusive control of a caste of ordained priests. As I showed in that book, we can break our own bread among friends and have it be a communion ritual of great power, as it was among the first Christians who gathered in each other's homes to celebrate their faith. You can put blessed oil or blessed water into your bathtub and take a baptismal bath that will be a healing and energizing bath for you. You can consecrate your work each day for the glory of God.

The sacraments work because they are conduits of energy. Most religious traditions utilize water and oil in their rituals because these substances are the two greatest natural conductors of electricity. When a prayer is said over water or oil, as it is in some of the sacraments and other rituals from the Eastern Orthodox church, the breath of the Divine in the one who is praying comes forth and infuses that item in a way that it was not infused before the prayer.

A relatively simple way of bringing the dimension of the sacred back into all areas of life is to revive the practice of saying a blessing before meals. By that I don't mean speeding through some formula you learned in grammar school. Instead, raise your hands over the dinner table and say something as simple as "Thank you, God," or any other words that come to you. Once again, the intention and the feeling behind the ritual is far more significant than following a preexisting formula.

In line with making prayer a constant element in your daily life, you can learn to bring the sacred with you wherever you go. To make the sacred portable, you might try creating a small version of what in the American Indian tradition is known as a medicine bundle, a collection of objects sacred to the individual's worship of the Great Spirit. When a bird or animal appeared in a vision as a messenger of the Great Spirit, for instance, the skin of the animal had to be secured as a medium through which its power could be realized. That skin, along with certain medicinal herbs and other elements vital to the life of the Indian people, are all carried in the medicine bundle.

Rabbi Zalman Schacter-Shalomi once told of being at a spiritual conference held at a downtown hotel in a big city and going up to the roof early one morning to perform his prayer rituals. As he stood there in his prayer shawl and other ritual garments, praying and reading his sacred texts, he noticed in a nearby corner of the same roof a Native American teacher who was at the same conference. The man had his medicine bundle spread out before him and was performing a ritual that seemed as mysterious to the rabbi as his must have seemed to the Indian. And yet the fact that both men had sought this literal and symbolic high ground, perhaps the quietest area in the entire building, to commune with the Divine, was not lost on Schacter-Shalomi.

My version of the medicine bundle is a small silver rosary case, in which I carry certain objects that bear a special significance for me. I have a gold medal of Padre Pio along with a small circular picture of him with a piece of blessed cloth that was touched to his tomb. The picture has inscribed on it Pio's prayer: "Don't waste energy on things that generate worry, anxiety, and anguish. Only one thing is necessary: Lift up your spirit and love God." Also in my bundle is a small crucifix with tiny fragments of bone from St. Francis and St. Clare. (Whether they are authentic relics or not hardly matters to me.) Whenever I'm away from home, which is quite often these days, my little rosary case with these sacred objects helps me to keep my conscious awareness focused on the reality that I am one with the Divine energy that flows through Padre Pio but comes from God. With this constant reminder, I'm able to stop numerous times throughout the day for a minute or two to remind myself that I am one with God. I am open to the love of God. I am a channel of God's love and peace, and for this I am grateful.

The ancient Chinese science known as *feng shui* consists of choosing auspicious sites and layouts for buildings, graves, or the furniture in your home. The idea behind feng shui is that vital energy, or *ch'i*, flows along invisible lines in the earth, and man-made structures must be properly placed to maximize its power and promote health. We might say that this is an Eastern method of creating a sacred place to experience the abundance of blessings that are always available to the individual who is tuned in to the sacred. You can, of course, hire someone adept in feng shui to help you plan the layout of your home. Without taking quite so precise and scientific an approach, however, you can also place small water fountains, chimes, or images of nature in strategic locations in your home. When you hear a chime or the bubbling of water or see an image of natural beauty as you go about your day, you will find it natural to think of God.

Perhaps the most helpful addition you can make to your home is a place where you can focus your sacred energy on a regular basis. If you are fortunate enough to have a spare room that can be set aside for use as an altar area or shrine room, that is ideal. Where space is at a premium, a corner of a bedroom or other room will do fine. And if the only place where you can have silence and solitude is your bathroom, that's all right, too. The altar itself can be as simple as a wide board supported by a few bricks, just large enough to place images or statues of the Deity, saints, and holy people of whatever traditions appeal to you. In Eastern traditions, it is common to include pictures of one's spiritual teacher or teachers, and perhaps their teachers as well. If for religious or personal reasons, images of the Divine are not appropriate, you might focus your altar around a rock, a leaf, a water fountain, or an empty space.

Whatever else you place on the altar is up to your own imagination and creativity. In many parts of Asia, it is customary to have pictures or remembrances of one's parents and grandparents. In some Buddhist shrines, offering bowls are placed before the sacred images, to be replenished daily with offerings representing each of the senses: food (rice or fruit), water, incense, candles, flowers, bells or finger cymbals, and so forth. It isn't necessary to be that elaborate, but if you do like candles, incense, or flowers, why not make use of them? Part of your daily sacred practice can include the care of the shrine room, replacement of flowers and other offerings, lighting of candles, and other devotional duties.

You can use your shrine room for sitting meditation, chanting, visualizations, and other practices. If you choose to repeat mantras or brief prayers like the Jesus prayer, some form of prayer beads may be helpful. You can use Catholic rosary beads of ivory, crystal, or plastic; a Hindu mala of 108 prayer beads made from rudraksha or tulasi berries; a Buddhist mala made of lotus seeds; or Sufi prayer beads for reciting the 99 Beautiful Names of Allah. If you come from the Catholic tradition as I do, you don't have to pray the rosary the way you were taught; you can use each bead to repeat a sacred name, an affirmation, or a simple word like *love, peace, mercy,* or *one.* There are many different avenues to follow, so be creative. Prayer is not about memorizing forms and repeating them mindlessly; prayer is heart-to-heart communion with God.

There are many other uses for a home altar, as I learned the hard way. I was on vacation in Southern California with my friend Paul and my mother visiting relatives, when we were joined by a couple of dear friends from Illinois, Phil and Cathy. I thought it would be fun to take my guests to see Universal Studios in the brand new silver Ford Crown Victoria that I had recently bought. As we were driving there, I had a very distinct intuition not to take a particular freeway, but I ignored the presentiment because I thought this freeway would be quicker, and it didn't seem to be as busy as the others. Sure enough, though, as we were approaching Los Angeles, we came over the crest of a hill and were greeted by the sight of an endless row of red taillights in front of us as traffic came to an abrupt standstill. My annoyance at the inevitable delay this signaled quickly turned to apprehension, as Paul, who was driving, struggled to stop our car in time to avoid rear-ending the car in front of us.

I was grateful that we were able to stop in time, and said out loud that I hoped everybody behind us could stop, too. We were on the inside lane, next to the wall that separates the eastbound and westbound lanes of the freeway. I looked behind us to see everyone stopping and I relaxed—until I heard the screeching brakes of a tractor-trailer three lanes to our right and realized that there was nothing between our car and this massive semi but empty road. I could see the truck's tires smoking as it skidded sideways and careened right at us, and I quietly whispered, "Oh Jesus." I braced myself as the truck screeched and howled and finally slammed us broadside, bounced off, fishtailing, and hit us again. My car was crushed, all the windows shattered, and I watched with a kind of dumb fascination as our front right tire broke off the axle from the force of the impact, rolled up the front windshield and over the roof, and hit the car behind us. The only one who wasn't hurt in the collision was Paul; the rest of us were pretty badly battered, although, miraculously, nobody was seriously injured.

I had very little immediate recall of what happened as we were waiting for the rescue people to arrive, because I was so disconsolate at the loss of my car and was in a lot of physical pain besides. The rescue squad had to pull us out through the shattered windows because none of the doors would open, and when we got to the hospital and the nurses took off my clothing, they found glass in my underwear and socks. I was in tremendous pain, and all I could think of was the idiot who had been driving the semi and failed to stop in time. Then the doctor informed me that although I had no broken bones, the pain from my bruised ribs would be worse than if I *had* broken a bone, and might persist over the next six months. I began to hate the doctor even more than the truck driver.

After I was released, I decided to cut my vacation short and rent a car to drive back home to Illinois with my mother. The whole time Paul was driving, I was lying in the back seat nursing my bruised ribs and my resentment at my bad fortune. I knew in my heart that I was supposed to forgive, but I just thought, *No!* There is no way I can forgive such lunacy on the part of that truck driver. I began feeling very sorry for myself, which was enough of a mistake, but I compounded it by listening to what everyone was telling me. My car was only six weeks old, and they all said I would never get the full price back from the insurance company, nor would my insurance pay for the cost of the rental car. With each negative thought I took in, my resentment and bitterness grew. I reminded God what good work I did for Him, and asked Him how He could do this to me, but I received no answer.

When I didn't hear back from the California Highway Patrol about the accident report I needed for my insurance company, I called them and learned that they had somehow misplaced all their records of the accident. Now I hated the Highway Patrol more than the doctor and the trucker. I kept transferring my hatred and unforgiveness and growing more confused and bitter in the process. Next I called my insurance agent, who told me not to worry about the report, although he sounded dubious about the possibility of my getting a "full deal," meaning the cost of a new car replacement. I quickly added him to my emotional hit list.

Thoroughly depressed by now, I went to see a dear friend of mine who was a minister in the Assembly of God church. After I unburdened myself of my tale of woe, including my mounting anger at the driver who had crashed into us, Bill smiled serenely. "Ron," he said, "there is something I feel you need to do that will really help you in this situation."

I sat up and paid attention, because Bill is one of the few people I know whose life works for him. "You need to make a blessing altar," he said.

"A blessing altar?" I was listening, but I wasn't taking it in.

"Yes," Bill said. "It can be as simple as one of those little TV trays, and you just put it in a corner of your room." He paused while I digested this bizarre notion.

"I heard that you had the photos from the car wreck," he continued.

"Yeah," I said, "you should see my poor new car!"

"Put those on the blessing table," Bill said. "And any other reports that you have about the accident, any memories that you can write down, any mementos of the accident—put them all on the blessing table. And then put a picture of Jesus there, look at it, and begin to forgive this driver."

*For once,* I thought, *Bill has it all wrong.* But just to be a good friend, I went through the motions. I set up the table and put the items on it that he suggested, and then I sat down and looked at it all. It did not create any feeling of healing energy or forgiveness within me. *Okay,* I thought, *let me do this right.* Bill had said to start by drawing a mental picture of the truck driver and saying "I forgive you." So I looked at the pictures and tried to visualize the man who had hit us, without much luck. I saw the semi coming at me, and I started my practice of saying, "I forgive you." This went on for about five minutes, with me saying, "I forgive you, damn it, I forgive you."

The embarrassing thing is that at this time I was making my living as a Catholic priest and spiritual healer. Healings of the most wondrous sorts were happening to people all around me. Yet here I had been in an accident, was still in pain, and was unable to heal myself. What would people think of the healer? This went on for two or three days, and I was feeling more and more down on myself. Maybe it was my embarrassment that made me stay with it, but by the fourth day, something surprising happened. I genuinely began to feel that I could forgive this situation and I could forgive the driver who had injured me and totaled my car. So I simply said, "God, help me. Give me the willingness to forgive."

And in that moment, a picture came into my mind of the accident as clear as if I were reliving it again. But this time I saw all the things I either didn't see or couldn't remember having seen at the time. For the first time I saw the driver of the truck quite clearly, watched him get out of the cab of his own damaged vehicle, crying hysterically, "Oh my God! Is anyone hurt?" He was a big, strong guy who must have weighed 250 pounds, and he was sick with worry about *us!* He didn't seem at all concerned that his big rig, which was probably his main source of livelihood, was also in pretty bad shape. In that moment, I realized that the accident wasn't this man's fault. He had done the best he could. He had tried to stop and then had tried to help us in every way he could. When that thought came to me, something broke in my heart, and I felt compassion pour through me. At that moment, I was able to say, "I do forgive you," and I meant it.

I also began to see other things, some of which I had been only vaguely aware of at the time. Many people had stopped to help us up until the time the police and the ambulances arrived. As we were lying there, one man came up and took pictures of my car with a Polaroid so I would have a record to show the insurance company. He offered to take our baggage from the trunk and hold it for us at his office. Then he gave his name and address to the officers at the scene and told us exactly where we could come and pick up our things. Complete strangers had been wonderful to us, but I'd had no place in my heart to register thanks for their help. I also realized, as if for the first time, that although my car was destroyed, none of us was killed or even seriously injured. Cathy, who had been sitting in the back seat with her husband, Phil, had been taken on a stretcher to the hospital. Fortunately, her x-rays had revealed no internal injuries—but they also showed that she was pregnant, which she hadn't even known. (Eight months later, she gave birth to twins.)

As I saw all of this at my altar that day, I wept. My sense of release and relief was so great that I no longer worried about my car, my pains, the insurance, or anything else. Within 24 hours, the California Highway Department called and told me that they had found the accident report, which they forwarded to the insurance company. Then my insurance agent called and told me how much they would reimburse me for the car, an amount that was $1,000 more than what I had paid for it. He also informed me that they would reimburse me for the rental car and the hotels I had stayed at on my way home. Some people actually believe in coincidences, but after something like that happens, I no longer can. I believe with all of my heart that it was the act of forgiveness that made everything else begin to flow back to me.

Ever since that day years ago, I've kept an altar of some kind in my home. Nothing so dramatic has happened since, but I now have a place to come every day, to bring my troubles and frustrations along with my joy and satisfaction. Mainly, I have a quiet place to pray whenever I need it. Just sitting down in front of my altar changes my state of mind and helps me invoke the sacred in my own life.

There are other ways to sanctify your home, like placing sacred images where you may see them in the course of the day and be reminded of the Divine. These don't have to be ostentatious crucifixes or statues, but can be as basic as a small image of a saint or spiritual teacher you admire, such as Sai Baba, Mother Teresa, Francis of Assisi, or Ramana Maharshi. Some people feel funny putting up holy pictures in their home. Yet it has long been common to see pictures of political or military heroes such as Eisenhower, John F. Kennedy, or Martin Luther King Jr. in American homes, or so why not a spiritual hero? You also have plenty of great religious artwork to choose from, such as Rembrandt's *Head of Christ*, medieval paintings of saints and madonnas, and Russian and Greek icons. The art market being what it is today, nobody will fault you for hanging a reproduction.

You can also make a sacred place of your bedroom. Margot Anand, who has made an extensive firsthand study of the practices of Tantric sexuality as a path to the Divine, suggests creating a sacred area devoted to your most intimate relationship with your spouse or partner. You can assemble objects to delight all the senses: scented candles and aromatic oils, your favorite music, special clothing, and what Anand calls "power objects": feathers, stones, crystals or any beautiful things to which you feel drawn. She also suggests creating rituals with your partner to intensify the joy in this very significant act. At the times you have set aside for lovemaking, you can use all these objects to create a sense of the sacred, and at the same time heighten your pleasurable sensations.

Moving outside of the home, you can begin by going to your church, mosque, temple, or synagogue, but be aware that it is not the only place where you can meet God and experience the sacred. If you really want to grow in your understanding of sacredness and the inclusiveness of the Divine will of God, after you go to the house of worship of your own tradition, visit one that you've never been to before. If you're a Catholic, for instance, that could mean going to a Protestant or Eastern Orthodox church. But don't stop there. Next Saturday, go to a Jewish temple; the following week, visit a Hindu temple or a Muslim mosque. If you feel uncomfortable about going to the home of another religion, don't let fear or awkwardness defeat you. If you know someone of that faith, ask them to take you along. If not, try to call the head of the congregation in advance and ask if they would mind your coming. Nobody has turned me down yet.

You can also ask what customs you'll need to observe so that you'll feel comfortable. At a mosque, for instance, you'll be expected to remove your shoes in the anteroom. At a Jewish temple, men will need hats or yarmulkes, and in most Orthodox and Conservative temples, women will be seated separately, as they will in most mosques. If you want to know more, try reading any of the excellent books on comparative religion or world Scripture currently available. Better yet, you can consult a recently published reference work designed for this very situation. *How to Be a Perfect Stranger: A Guide to Etiquette in Other People's Religious Ceremonies* collects information on what to do and not to do, provided by authorities of a wide range of religions, including all the major traditions and many smaller Christian sects (see the bibliography).

I can think of several reasons why most people feel uncomfortable going to the sacred place of another religion. Leading the list is the fear that God will punish you for abandoning Him and going to that "other place." Does that mean that if a Hindu comes to your church or synagogue service, Shiva will punish him, too? And what if you went to a mosque? That's a tough one, since Muslims actually worship the same God as Christians and Jews. They call Him by His Arabic name, Allah (which means "the God"), but He is identified as the God of Abraham and Isaac—who also happen to be revered as prophets by Islam. Do you really believe that God listens only to Christian prayers?

The other chief reason is fear that members of another religion will be hostile or will laugh or sneer if you do the wrong thing. All I can suggest is to reverse roles and imagine seeing an Indian family, say, come into your church and sit in the last row during a service. Would you assume that they are there to mock your religion, or would you feel good that they felt welcome? If you are the kind of person who emanates openness and respect, that won't be lost on others. If you create sacred space in your own life, not only will you breathe in the sacred, but you will also exhale the sacred to all the people who come within your energy field. They will sense why you're there, and will respond accordingly.

I am not suggesting that we minimize the differences between religions. Although these distinctions exist mainly at the surface, they are real and should be acknowledged. Judaism, Islam, and many Protestant denominations reject the use of statues or personal images of any kind, whereas Roman Catholics, Orthodox Christians, Hindus, Taoists, and most Buddhists revere a wide range of visual images in all forms. This is a sore point that has led to bloodshed in past centuries. That is lamentable, and yet all religions do use some kind of visual imagery. Islamic mosques, for instance, are often decorated with the most beautiful calligraphic renderings of Arabic verses from the Quran, as well as delicate abstract arabesques and other designs. Some Jews use images of the Tetragrammaton, the four Hebrew consonants that make up the name of God (Yahweh), as a visual basis for meditation. Although there is no magic in images on their own, I do believe that, like prayer rituals, the energy of what they depict can be transmitted through them. Jesus with arms outstretched, his sacred heart blazing for everyone, does project an energy of love that can inspire us. If you focus on a statute or painting of Quanyin, the Chinese goddess of mercy, you can begin to experience the energy of mercy flowing into you.

Teresa of Ávila was once asked to define what prayer meant to her. "Prayer," she said, "is when I look at God, and God looks at me. I talk to God, and God talks to me. I love God, and God loves me." That brief but lovely statement can also be applied to invoking the sacred. It means putting all of your attention and focus on the sacredness of life itself. It means looking at God and talking to God in all situations throughout the day. Above all, it means finding creative ways to express your love for God in unexpected places, knowing that God is forever expressing his love for you, whether you are consciously aware of it or not. Invoking the sacred is simply a way of making that awareness more conscious.

## EXERCISE: INVOKING THE SACRED THROUGHOUT THE DAY

This exercise is an outline that can be revised on a daily basis. It's helpful to begin with some kind of ritual, which can be a simple physical action such as lighting a candle. I like to play music, either classical or jazz or chant, and light incense, a scented candle, or an aromatherapy atomizer. It's helpful to activate as many of the senses as you can to help invoke the sacred. You may choose a picture of a saint and use the image instead of or along with the candle flame to stimulate your visual sense.

Take three deep breaths and focus on the candle flame as the light of God, and through the motion of your breath, bring that light into your heart chakra. Close your eyes and begin to place your attention on your heart center and the light burning there that represents the fire of God. Now call upon a name of God that suits you personally and gives you a feeling of uplift when you think, speak, or chant that name. Express your gratitude by saying, "Thank you, God."

At certain times throughout the day, as you are grooming yourself in the morning, going to work, cleaning the house, or making dinner, bring that name into consciousness again. You don't have to say a prayer, just repeat the name so that its energy vibration continues to resonate within you. If you have a particular object in your house that symbolically reminds you of God—a crystal, rock, or seashell, or a religious medal, mala, or chaplet—put it in your pocket or purse to take with you. Anytime during the day when you open your purse or reach in your pocket, touch the object and once again bring the name into consciousness for a few moments. Recognize the presence of that energy, and then go on with the day.

At the end of day, as you prepare for sleep, bring the name of God into consciousness again and offer thanks. Then go to sleep with the assurance that this presence is always with you. At night I put my focus on the feminine aspect of God, either through a picture of Mary or my statue of Quanyin, because I like being comforted by preparing to go to sleep in the arms of the Divine feminine.

The following day, repeat the procedure using a different name of God or some sacred being.

# CHAPTER THIRTEEN

## *Forgiveness— Prerequisite to Prayer*

*I* have long believed that Jesus meant what he said when he told his disciples, "Whoever says to this mountain, 'Be taken up and cast into the sea,' and does not doubt in his heart, but believes that what he says will come to pass, it will be done for him" (Mark 11:23-24). The faith Jesus is talking about here is the faith that results in healing. But the verses that follow are even more significant.

"Whatever you ask in prayer, you will receive if you have faith," Jesus says, inexorably linking prayer with the ability to heal and produce miracles. Then he adds one crucial condition, which is often overlooked: "Whenever you stand praying, forgive, if you have anything against anyone; so that your Father also who is in heaven will forgive you your trespasses."

Jesus is clearly saying that forgiveness is a prerequisite to authentic prayer. We shouldn't even attempt to pray if we are harboring negative thoughts and feelings in our hearts; otherwise, our prayers will be no more than words. In fact, our negative thoughts and lack of forgiveness short-circuit and neutralize our prayers. Although the Biblical passage may seem to imply that God will withhold forgiveness, this is not the case. Forgiveness, like a radio broadcast signal, is always transmitted by God; our negativity acts like a tall mountain blocking His forgiveness from getting through to us.

I have already described how my deep feelings of resentment and anger toward my father were part of an emotional complex that was preventing me from progressing spiritually. An important first step in overcoming my anger would have been to forgive my father, and yet I had trouble doing that for many years. Finally, when I was about 40 and my father was dying of cirrhosis of the liver, the legacy of years of alcoholism, I went to visit him in the hospital with my mother. He was in a coma when we arrived, yet as we sat by his bedside, we could see his body going through mild convulsions, rising and falling involuntarily. After watching this for a while, I decided to pray over him and put my hand on him, quietly asking the convulsions to stop, which they did—much to the surprise of the medical people who witnessed this.

The next evening, when I was alone with him in the room, I felt that the time had come to try to bring some closure to our relationship. As he lay there completely still, I began to speak to him as if he were awake. "Dad," I said, "I do love you, and I forgive you."

To my amazement, he opened his eyes, looked at me and said, "And I forgive you."

I was completely stunned, not so much by his coming out of the coma as by what he had said. My mother arrived soon afterwards, and I chose not to discuss what had just happened. We stayed in his room for a while, but as there was no further change in my father's condition, the staff suggested that we go home for the night. We lived only ten minutes away, but shortly after we got home, the hospital called to tell us that my father had died.

For the next few days, I tried to make sense of what my father had said to me. I had assumed all along that I was the injured party in this relationship, and had clung assiduously to my victim status. What, then, was I to think of my father's forgiveness of me? After some reflection, I had to acknowledge my own bitterly judgmental attitude toward him in the last years of his life, as his drinking became progressively heavier and more destructive. Moreover, his statement of forgiveness brought me to the realization that I also had to forgive myself for my own anger and resentment toward him, of which, until then, I had been barely conscious. Over those painful years, I had begun to rage at others the same way he had done with me, and I was well aware of how abusive I myself had become. So along with making peace with my father, I had to make peace with myself for having begun to resemble him in such a disconcerting fashion.

Writing about his mother's death, the Catholic author Henri Nouwen said that our last great gift to humanity is the manner in which we die. By that he meant that we can die leaving everyone feeling angry and guilty about how we have treated them, and vice versa, or we can make peace with those near to us and do what we can to neutralize the negative emotions and elementals that may have been generated in our relationships. If we can do that, we are granting them a boon of liberation from their own feelings of inadequacy. When Pope John XXIII lay dying and someone close to him was fretting that he wasn't doing enough to help the pontiff, John turned to him and said, "Don't worry. I've got my bags packed and I'm ready to go."

What the dying pope had said is true on a practical level, too. Some people work hard to put their affairs in order before they die and make sure that their heirs and loved ones won't have to wade through piles of papers or fight over their inheritance; others leave nothing but loose ends, and those they leave behind have to clean up their mess for them. That confused legacy is often a manifestation of unresolved feelings of anger and disappointment on the part of the dying parent. Years after my father died, I came to see that his act of virtually unconscious forgiveness—I believe it was his living spirit speaking through his comatose body—was his last great gift to me. He truly set me loose from whatever bonds of guilt still held us in mutual confinement. What remained was for me to acknowledge and understand his gift, and then to follow through by forgiving myself for my own shortcomings.

Someone once said that the only mistakes we make in life are the ones we don't learn from. All the rest are absolutely essential steps on our path to wisdom and spiritual healing. In that regard, forgiving others begins with forgiving ourselves. Until we see our mistakes as useful parts of the healing process, and forgive ourselves for them, we cannot move on to forgiving others for what we perceive as their harming us. This requires making use of what I have previously described as Witness consciousness, getting outside of ourselves and observing our actions with some emotional detachment. That is admittedly harder than it sounds, and it means first understanding something of the nature of forgiveness, and why forgiveness—of both ourselves and others—is so essential to healing.

Each of us has come into the world in love. We are perfect as we are created by God, who is love, light, and Spirit. But through the course of time, the beautiful, radiant light and love and Spirit within us become clouded by feelings of resentment and bitterness that result from our perceived slights at others' hands, and the attendant guilt and shame at our own responses to those acts. As a result, we are unable to demonstrate the essence of our being, which is love, peace, and joy, and so we don't experience the abundance that life has in store for us.

To change this sorry state of affairs, we have to learn how to forgive, which means getting rid of the negative emotions we have accumulated and which have become destructive elementals of guilt, shame, and resentment. Making a frontal attack on our guilt, shame, and resentment, however, is usually less effective than going into meditation and allowing Spirit to peel them away a layer at a time, like an onion. Think of forgiveness as a release or a letting go, rather than a caving in or condoning of another's faults. In the Scriptures, we find many references to forgiveness, such as Luke 6:37, "Forgive and you shall be forgiven." I would like you to substitute the words *let loose, let go, drop* for the word *forgive*. "Forgive and you shall be forgiven" becomes "When you let loose, you will be let loose."

In his Letter to the Ephesians (4:32), Paul writes, "Be tenderhearted and forgiving to one another, as God in Christ forgave you." In that particular sentence, the word *forgiving* means "gracious," an important distinction, because forgiving others doesn't have the emotional impact that being gracious carries. So be gracious to one another as God, for Christ's sake, has been gracious to you. The Lord's Prayer (Matthew, 6:12) asks God to "forgive us our trespasses as we forgive those who trespass against us." Here you can see this as letting go of the bonds of guilt and shame that bind others to you as God releases the cords of your own guilt. If you begin to shift your perception this way, forgiveness will not seem like such an arduous chore. Nor does it mean that you are condoning the poor behavior of another person. You are instead attempting to arrive at a point where you don't judge others so that you will not be judged.

Changing your perceptions in this fashion takes time and patience. If you finish reading this book and you are not perfectly whole, don't get anxious and think you've missed the point or failed again. Forgiveness is a process, and it requires constant awareness. With each day, you can begin to feel lighter and more at peace, and can more readily experience the presence of God. At the end of this chapter, I will provide some brief exercises to help facilitate the process of forgiveness.

In the Gospel of Matthew (18:21-35), we read that the disciple Peter came to Jesus and asked him, "Lord, how many times shall I forgive my brother when he sins against me?" Peter then proposes an answer to his own question by adding, "As many as seven times?" He no doubt thinks that he is being rather generous here, and maybe looking for a pat on the head from the Master.

Jesus answers, "I tell you not seven times, but seventy-seven times," which some ancient sources give as the even higher figure of "seventy-times-seven times." It helps here to keep in mind the relatively low numerical framework of an age when the entire population of the earth could probably have been counted in seven figures. When the ancient Chinese wanted to indicate everything in creation, they referred to "the ten thousand things," where today we would speak of "millions of things," or "a gazillion things." Seventy-seven times or seventy-times-seven times would have been Jesus's way of indicating an infinite number.

What Jesus means is that we need to learn how to release anger on a daily basis. I don't think he was implying that we should never be angry. There is such a thing as righteous anger, as Jesus himself apparently exhibited at the sight of the money-changers in the Temple (although if we are not careful, righteous anger rather easily degenerates into self-righteousness). Sometimes we have to get this kind of anger out of our systems—at least, I do. We need to learn to be aware of the times we feel bitter or resentful, however, especially when those feelings persist toward the same person. The first thing most marriage or relationship counselors tell you is not to let the sun go down on an argument, especially when bitter or hurtful words were spoken. It may not always be possible to resolve every argument so quickly, and my practical experience is that sometimes fatigue takes over before you do get a chance to heal a fight with a loved one, but you had better not let it go another day.

After Jesus tells Peter how continual his forgiveness must be, he relates a parable in which he likens the kingdom of heaven to a king who wants to settle accounts with his servants. "When he began the settlement, a man was brought to him who owed him 10,000 talents." Here again, Jesus is using exaggerated figures for effect. The talent is an ancient measure of weight in the Middle East, and that much gold would be worth over $60 million by today's standards. Since the man is obviously not able to pay, the master orders that he and his wife and children and all that he has be sold to repay the debt, a horrifying price in human terms.

> So the servant fell on his knees, imploring him, "Lord, be patient with me, and I will pay back everything." The servant's master took pity on him, canceled the debt, and let him go.

This is an astonishing act of forgiveness, considering the amount owed—virtually the price of an entire kingdom—which is probably what Jesus wanted his listeners to think. What overwhelming mercy! What a generous master! But no sooner is the servant released than he goes out and comes upon one of his fellow servants, who owes him a hundred denarii. This is a sum equivalent today to a couple of hundred dollars. The newly reprieved servant wastes no time in collecting his own debt:

> And seizing him by the throat he said, "Pay what you owe." His fellow servant fell to his knees and begged him, "Please be patient with me, and I will pay you back." But the man refused and went off and had him

thrown into prison until he could pay the debt. When the other servants saw what had happened, they were greatly distressed and went and told their master everything.

Then the master called the servant in and said to him, "You wicked servant. I forgave you all of that debt because you begged me to. Shouldn't you have had mercy on your fellow servant, just as I had on you?" In anger, his master turned him over to the tormentors to be tortured until he should pay back all he owed. This is how my heavenly Father will treat each of you unless you forgive your brother or your sister from your heart.

Let me emphasize that this is a parable, and that God the Father does not torture people because they are unforgiving. He doesn't have to, in fact, since unforgiveness leads to its own torment, as I found out following my accident on the freeway. To understand what "tormentors" means today, we have to ask ourselves how we feel when we are angry with someone. What begins to happen immediately? In my case, I suffer a loss of appetite, can't think straight, and feel confused. Anger is a form of intense stress, and the first thing that happens when we are under stress is that our intelligence is reduced by half. When we are consumed with bitterness and resentment, every part of our being becomes angry and we impose that anger on others. The "tormentors" enter our lives the instant negativity occurs.

It is perfectly legitimate to ask, "If I am going to practice the spiritual principle of forgiveness, what's in it for me?" That may sound blasphemous, but if I'm going to discipline myself, I want to know what the pay-off is. In this case, if I learn forgiveness, I begin to eliminate the tormentors from my life. I don't like it when I can't think straight, because then I cannot read or pray or relate to other people. So for that reason alone, I find it well worth the effort to contain my anger.

There is another reason for containing anger. Every judgment we make sets in motion a kind of domino effect. We could say, based on our earlier discussion, that judging another person calls forth or reinforces the elemental of unforgiveness. The moment you judge, you begin to blame. Once blaming has begun, the door is opened to vengeance. We are becoming a nation of victims because we are practicing judgment, blame, and vengeance—all forms of anger. We have lost sight of what forgiveness actually means. We think that if we forgive someone who has harmed us, we are condoning his reprehensible behavior. We don't want to let go of our judgment, so we cling to the blame.

This attitude is so ingrained in our society that when Caroline Myss discussed the dangers of identifying yourself by your victim status in an interview in *Yoga Journal* a couple of years ago, letters flooded in to the editor from outraged therapists and clients alike. They had misinterpreted her remarks to mean that she was "blaming the victim," whereas all she had said was that it was unhealthy for people continually to think of themselves as victims of incest, discrimination, or alcoholic parents, so that they always have someone to blame. Although support groups are helpful to such people, they place little emphasis on the need for forgiveness.

Forgiveness means letting go of blame and negative self-identification, but it also means releasing the urge to focus our negative feelings on someone else, even someone we feel entitled to despise, such as a serial killer, terrorist, Nazi war criminal, or someone like Saddam Hussein. And it is probably easier to forgive all of those people than the driver who cuts us off in traffic or beats us to that parking space we had our eye on. In all cases, you can say to God, "I let these people go from my thoughts, and I release them into your light. I will no longer give them power to wreck my day or my life. I am going to take my power back, but I do ask mercy. I am going to put on the mind of Christ and look at these situations the way God does."

Some years ago I had to stop watching the nightly news, because whenever I did watch, I found myself immediately going into a pattern of judgment-blame-tension. *Somebody ought to kill that guy,* I'd think, watching the latest villain. Long after the news was over, I would harp on the matter to other people, and I might carry that anger over into my personal relationships. I had to get away from the news for several months, but when I came back (because I did want to know what was happening in the world around me), I began to witness myself watching the news. As I took in the latest report of murder or rape or abandoned children, I would ask myself, *Am I making a judgment? Am I blaming? Am I feeling vengeful?* I still knew all those acts were horrible crimes and that we as a society have to do whatever we can to prevent them. But focusing our hatred on the perpetrators will not prevent crime; it might actually provoke aggressive impulses in ourselves.

After witnessing myself during newscasts for some time, I came to the conclusion that I could trust God to handle these awful people. If I released these people and situations into His light, God would handle them. Rather than ignore evil, we can choose to put it into the light, which is another way of saying putting it into God's hands so that you and God become one. You align your will with God's will, and you begin to hear the voice of God in your spirit directing what you do.

If you live in the past, bound and chained by your thoughts of the past, you are the one being harmed; the poison is poured into you, and the objects of your scorn may not even know that you hate them. In the Gospel of Matthew (9:2), Jesus says to the paralytic, "Be of good cheer, your sins are forgiven." By "forgiven," he meant released, sent away. You can't be happy or experience joy and peace if you keep holding on to your past mistakes.

If you want to develop into a whole person in whom body, mind, soul, will, and emotion are in harmony, then you have to learn to develop a love consciousness. The best way to do that is to meditate on God as unconditional love. We have by and large been brought up with the belief that God is a conditional lover and that He has prerequisites to His love. If we keep the commandments, if we belong to His church (assuming we can figure out which one that may be), if we observe the sacraments, *then* God will love us.

Emmet Fox wrote something years ago that made a deep impression on me when I first read it:

> Love is by far the most important thing of all. It is the Golden Gate of Paradise. Pray for the understanding of love, and meditate upon it daily. It casts out fear. It is the fulfilling of the Law. It covers a multitude of sins. Love is absolutely invincible.

There is no difficulty that enough love will not conquer; no disease that enough love will not heal; no door that enough love will not open; no gulf that enough love will not bridge; no wall that enough love will not throw down; no sin that enough love will not redeem.

It makes no difference how deeply seated may be the trouble, how hopeless the outlook, how muddled the tangle, how great the mistake; a sufficient realization of love will dissolve it and will dissolve it all. If only you could love enough, you would be the happiest and most powerful being in the world.

So we begin by taking our anger into meditation each day, mindful that that's essentially a long-range goal. It takes time to be e      and we have to wait until our next meditation to work on it.      we do in the very moment that anger is most explosive an    To start, we can practice Witness consciousness as a v   some perspective on the situation. But if you feel una    from the passion of the moment and want to do so   instead of cursing the person who has set you off, or    that allowed this awful thing to happen to you, I sugge   forth a blessing. This may make it easier for you to see    what it is: two characters in a drama that *you* can di   you're being phony if you don't feel like blessing    moment; you can say the blessing with the *intention* of me   any other habit, the habit of blessing is learned slowly, but   power with repetition. It can become a positive elementa   tioned reflex that builds with time and repetition. After pra   long enough, you actually *will* mean it when you bless some   has just offended or upset you.

## EXERCISE: LOVING KINDNESS

You can strengthen the positive elemental created by blessing by taking it into your meditation. Practice seeing the faces of people who have offended or hurt you in some way, either the previous day or many years ago—

the parent who mistreated you, the lover who left you, the boss who fired you. See them bathed in white light and toss in your hurt and angry feelings; let them all dissolve together in the light of the Holy Spirit.

If you are so inclined, you can learn the practice known as *metta*, or loving kindness meditation, in which you bless all the people in your life—good, bad, and neutral. If you want to study this in detail, I recommend any of the books or tapes on the subject by Sharon Salzberg, Thich Nhat Hanh, Joseph Goldstein, or Jack Kornfield, but I will give you enough of the basics now to get you started.

Loving kindness meditation is derived from an ancient Buddhist text and is meant to direct blessings in expanding circles of inclusiveness, beginning with yourself and working outward to take in your teachers, loved ones, friends, and enemies. Begin by focusing on yourself, not worrying about weighing your good and bad aspects, but accepting all of you, especially the God-essence that is the Spirit within you. Then think or say the following:

*May I be safe from inner and outer harm.*
*May I be happy and free.*
*May I be healthy and strong.*
*May I be able to care for myself joyfully.*
*May I be filled with loving kindness.*

Next, visualize a spiritual teacher or teachers who have helped you along the path. Say or think the same phrases, substituting the second person pronoun: "May you be safe from inner and outer harm," etc. Then visualize those near and dear to you—spouse, parents, children, friends, business associates, members of your spiritual congregation—and issue the same series of blessings. Next, bless those people with whom you interact neutrally, such as people at the store, the gym, or at work toward whom you have no strong feelings one way or the other. From there, make the great leap and move on to your enemies, people with whom you have difficulty, or who you know wish you ill. At this level, take special care that you visualize your enemies in the same kind of light that you used for your teachers and loved ones. They are also God's children, and by blessing them you are blessing yourself.

As several teachers have pointed out, these people who push our buttons and cause us grief can ultimately be the ones who teach us more about ourselves and about compassion than anyone else. Finally, visualize people in different parts of the world who are completely unknown to you, especially in those places that may be suffering most intensely at the moment. This may be the time to take those disturbing images from the evening news and bring them into the light, wishing the best to those who are suffering and who are inflicting suffering on others.

The Buddhist text on which this practice is based, known as the *Sutra of Kindness* (*Metta-sutta*), reads in part:

> Even as a mother watches over and protects her child, her only child, so with a boundless mind should one cherish all living beings, radiating friendliness over the entire world, above, below, and all around without limit. So let one cultivate a boundless good will toward the entire world, uncramped, free from ill-will or enmity.

### Love, Fear, and the False Self

By combining meditation and blessing every day, you will get to the point where you will be able much more readily to stop wasting energy in difficult situations, quiet yourself for a moment, and see God's light around you and the other person involved in any confrontation. Then you can put the situation into the light and say, "I bless this situation. I bless this person. God bless him, also."

We have been taught to believe that the opposite of love is hate, but as anyone who has studied *A Course in Miracles* knows by now, the opposite of love is fear. From fear come all the other negative emotions, just as all the positive emotions proceed from love. The contest between love and fear is perhaps the most difficult conflict we face in our lives. How well we resolve it is a good indication of how high we will be able to climb on the spiritual ladder. Love and fear sound terribly abstract, however, and we would do well to identify the key components of our nature that correlate most closely with these abstract emotions. To my mind, love corresponds to spirit, the most God-identified aspect of our nature, and fear corresponds to ego, our most survival-oriented aspect. Seen from this perspective, the conflict between love and fear comes down to a clash between spirit and ego (in Biblical terms, spirit and flesh).

In the seventh century, the Prophet Muhammad struggled for many years to bring to life the new spiritual path known as Islam in the Arabian peninsula, including many armed clashes with fellow Arabs who opposed him. After finally defeating the military forces arrayed against him and marching victoriously into Mecca, Muhammad is said to have uttered the words, "We have returned from the lesser jihad to the greater jihad." The Arabic word *jihad*, often poorly translated as "holy war," literally means "struggle" or "exertion." When asked by his followers what he meant by the "greater jihad," the Prophet replied, "Struggle against the lower self." By the lower self, he implied the forces of the ego, which, as we are seeing, is dominated by the emotion of fear. The ego is a great survival mechanism honed over millions of years of evolution. It is designed to keep us alive and "on top," but is not necessarily concerned with advancing us on the spiritual path that will lead to eternal survival.

In its role as promoter of physical survival, the ego often takes the expedient of removing God from our lives. That is why I like to say that the letters e-g-o stand for "easing God out," because recognizing His presence may lead us to go against the principles of self-preservation. In his book *New Seeds of Contemplation*, Thomas Merton writes of the ego,

> My false and private self is the one who wants to exist outside the reach of God's will and God's love—outside of reality and outside of life. And such a self cannot help but be an illusion.
>
> We are not very good at recognizing illusions, least of all the ones we cherish about ourselves. . . . For most of the people in the world, there is no greater subjective reality than this false sense of theirs, which cannot exist. A life devoted to the cult of this shadow is what is called a life of sin.

Merton's perception of the "false and private self" as sheer illusion reflects Vedantic and Buddhist concepts of the limited self or ego as essentially a misperception on our part. The great Indian sage Shankara illustrated this form of illusion with the image of someone who, seeing a tree branch lying on the ground, mistakes it for a snake and is filled with fear. It is *avidya*, or ignorance, he wrote, that fosters our illusion that we are our body and our limited ego.

By contrast, Spirit is always urging us to follow the path of love that leads inexorably to God, and for this reason is often inconvenient. We may be dying to eat breakfast and get to work in the morning, for example, but we know we ought to spend some time with God. Spirit insists on taking time to meditate when ego would just like to feed the body and start earning money.

Spiritual healing, then, is a matter of experiencing the light and love of God's spirit in any area of our life that is still in darkness. By "darkness," I mean the part of our life that hurts, which is most likely to be the part that we have not yet had the courage to face. Spiritual healing also means unlearning the myth that God is out to get you, the old religious misconception that God looks at your sins and wants to punish you. That image is clearly based on *human* emotion, not Divine—which is to say, it is based on fear. Parents who are afraid that their child will not measure up and are just out to make life difficult will wait for the child to slip up and then invent some wonderfully cruel punishment.

Twelve-Step Programs have helped many people rescue the part of their lives that is in darkness. According to the fifth step in the credo of those programs, you agree to admit honestly what your faults are to yourself, to God, and to one other person. We often attempt to get around this idea by confessing directly to God. Although communicating our sorrow to God in prayer can be helpful, it may not satisfy the human need for psychological confirmation. Even in sacramental churches, where you confess to God through the person of the priest, you don't necessarily have to face your feelings. You may get some sense of relief from confessing feelings of anger or hatred, but psychologically you have not come to terms with those feelings, and so the hate stays in.

The original establishment of the Christian churches had a better concept of confession. In those early communities, you walked up to a person you trusted and expressed your failings. Over time, the church changed this approach, creating the confessional with a wall separating priest and confessor. That wall immediately invalidated the whole process, because the only way you can feel good about yourself is to be able to tell your deepest secret to someone who will show you love and acceptance no matter what you confess. You need to see the other person's expression, to see him take in what you fear is so horrible without being horrified.

The Twelve-Step Programs refer to this process as "validation," because as you unburden yourself of your worst self-image, and the person you are telling just nods her head and says, "Yeah," you realize that you won't be carted away to the dungeon for reprobates and psycho-killers. You are telling this terrible secret of which you are ashamed to someone who might even have a tender smile on her face, as if to say, "I know what that's like." You can almost feel the shame fly out of you because someone has validated you, and at that moment you begin to feel the power coming back into your life. You begin to feel that, as much as a human can, you can take control of your life again. This is what we all need.

To be validated means to be accepted for the spirit that you are, not the fallible mind and body that you appear to be. When you are not validated, you become, in a sense, an invalid. The two terms come from the same Latin and French roots meaning "not strong." We can trace a lot of our physical problems to the fact that we have become so invalidated that we feel unworthy—so what's the use of trying? Eventually "what's the use?" can take the form of a hip problem, a foot problem, a heart problem, a circulatory problem, or an immune system problem.

## EXERCISE: FINDING A CONFESSOR

This will not be like most of the other exercises we have been doing throughout the book. You can't set aside half an hour and sit down and do what I am suggesting, although you may find it helpful to bring this exercise into your meditation. If you have not already established a daily prayer and meditation time for yourself, then do set aside some time to begin this process.

The aim is to find a person or persons to whom you can express your deepest needs and feelings, secure in the knowledge that they will not judge you, blame you, or condemn you. If you are romantically inclined, you may think that your spouse or lover is the ideal person, but that is not always the case. Especially if your relationship is relatively new or has been through trying times of late, you may do better to choose someone else. Remember that if you do choose to confide in someone with whom you live, and they respond in a negative way to your revelation, it may create more problems than it solves. A best friend, parent, or sibling with whom you feel especially close is often the wiser choice. If possible, a very small circle of people with whom you share spiritual practice may also be good. If you are fortunate enough to be able to afford individual or group therapy, that is another obvious choice for unburdening yourself.

How do you choose the right person in whom to confide? That's a chance you take, one of life's many risks, but don't make it a life or death issue. If you select the wrong person, then you move on to the next choice. In choosing, rely on your intuition. Once again, you don't know until you take the risk, and the fear of not knowing can stop you from taking it, like a Catch-22 of the soul. Keep in mind that there is no such thing as risk-free living, and to tell yourself otherwise is a form of self-delusion.

Once you have set your mind on someone, ask if he or she would be willing to hear something that has been troubling you for a long time. If your choice is an appropriate one, the person will be grateful for the opportunity to help you. (If not, keep looking.) Then get together and tell your story. Go into your Witness consciousness and watch yourself as you are talking. Observe your emotional response when you are able to tell your worst side to someone who responds with equanimity. Be sure to tell whoever you have chosen that you do not expect or want them to "fix" your problem or suggest possible solutions, unless you decide to ask specifically for such help. All you need at this point is openness and acceptance.

## The Intuitive Risk

Forgiveness and risk are connected in many essential ways. Often when we resist forgiving someone, we are thinking that it is a risk that won't pay off. *I'll forgive that person for treating me badly, and then he'll be one up on me.* It's a little like the cold-war fear of unilateral disarmament: On a rational level, the fear seems warranted, but it ultimately leads to a paralyzing sense of distrust. To progress along the spiritual path, you will have to let go of such fears and learn to take a risk in certain situations.

The previous exercise is a good example. Yet when we take a risk and follow our intuition, and the hunch proves not to be right, the first thing we often do is to judge ourselves for having taken the risk. We blame ourselves for having a bad outcome, then wreak vengeance on ourselves by saying, "I'm not ever going to do *that* again!" What we forget is that on a spiritual level, our intuition is the voice of God. So how can the voice of God be wrong, you ask? For one thing, we should be humble enough to accept the possibility that we heard wrong. That may sound like a cop-out, but with all the noise and chatter flying around in our minds, we don't always allow a clear intuition to come through unfiltered. If you try to listen to a signal from a radio with poor reception, you'll hear a lot of static and maybe get a garbled message. With time and training, however, two things will happen. First, you'll acquire the knack of reading the signal through the static. At the same time, you may learn how to tune your receiver and maybe clean up the internal elements so that the static is diminished. In a rough way, that is what daily prayer and meditation do for your mental processes. They help clear the air so that the voice of your intuition becomes louder and clearer.

When Jesus said that unless you become as little children, you cannot enter the kingdom of God, he wasn't talking only about the positive attributes of little children, their joy, spontaneity, and resilience. He also had to mean their negative qualities, their immaturity, rebelliousness, and stubbornness. Let's not forget that under certain circumstances, rebelliousness and stubbornness can serve us well, as long as we control the negative energy that they can evoke. A survey of the world's great creative artists, inventors, and political activists will remind us how often these innovators had to rebel against the status quo and had to persist in the face of great opposition. Edison, van Gogh, and Martin Luther King, Jr., could all be considered stubborn and rebellious, but what would the world look like without them? By definition, a visionary is someone who has a vision of something nobody else at the time can see.

So when thoughts and hunches come to you, don't be afraid to test them. Along with the possibility that they may occasionally be off the mark, you also need to keep in mind that they don't necessarily always work out right away. In the interim, you may once again be tempted to blame yourself for taking a risk that didn't pay off. I'm in a position in my life where I could look back and consider my 25 years in the institutional priesthood a terrible waste of time. I know, however, that it was necessary for me to go through those 25 years to be able to get where I am today.

After I had been in the priesthood for about 17 years, I got an impulse to leave and go out on my own. For reasons not quite clear to me at the time, I decided to stay another eight years. I often joke that I wanted to get the retirement party or gold watch for 25 years of service. But the truth is that I hadn't acquired the necessary "escape velocity" to leave the institutional priesthood and establish my own orbit as a healer. If being a priest means being someone who ministers to the needs of his congregation and helps them to heal themselves, then I still consider myself a priest, although not a Roman Catholic clergyman. I feel infinitely freer to help people while still pursuing my own spiritual liberation than I ever could have if I had stayed within the confines of the institutional church. Yet it took me all those years to sever the ties.

Why do we continue to cling to our belief systems after they have stopped working for us? There may be a psychological payoff in being able to blame the people who taught us those faulty systems, once again making ourselves the hapless victims: "I was taught this way, and I don't know anything else." But we are the only ones who will pay the penalty if we continue to lash out at others and blame them for our situation. In my case, I felt trapped in the priesthood, largely out of fear of disappointing my mother if I left. I was also afraid of living on my own without the safety net of the parish and the diocese paying all my bills. The more frustrated I felt by my situation, the more I would lash out at those around me, and my bitterness only made my condition more painful. What I actually needed to do was to change the situation itself.

Both our spiritual and our material survival may, in fact, depend on our ability to maneuver deftly through changing times. Marshall McLuhan, who wrote so brilliantly about media in the 1960s and '70s but has been largely overlooked since, liked to point out the lesson contained in Edgar Allan Poe's short story entitled "A Descent into the Maelstrom." In that story, a fishing boat has been caught up in an enormous whirlpool hundreds of yards in diameter off the coast of Norway, along with other boats and flotsam of various sizes and shapes. The narrator, one of three brothers manning the boat, focuses his powers of perception on the debris trapped in the giant vortex. He notices that cylindrical objects are being sucked into the deadly maelstrom much more slowly than objects of any other shape, including the fishing smack to which he and his brothers are clinging. Having observed this, the narrator lashes himself to a wooden cask and throws himself from the ship into the raging waters. His strategy works, and he stays afloat high up in the maelstrom even as the ship with his brothers still clinging to its timbers is sucked under. In time, the whirlpool subsides, and he is rescued by a passing boat.

McLuhan argued that to survive, as individuals and as a race, we must keep a constant eye on the changing nature of the world around us and adapt as we go. Although this may require action that appears risky—as Poe's narrator had to summon the courage to jump from the "security" of his ship into the apparently more perilous waters—the potential for survival outweighs the risk. McLuhan was speaking specifically of the enormous changes wrought on us by technology and the electronic media, but his advice applies to many other areas of life.

When I was going to school, the prevalent career strategy was to land a job with a big company and hold on to that job until you died.

That was security—fringe benefits, pension, the works. Where I grew up in Central Illinois, if you didn't have any special professional skills, you were left with only two or three choices. You could work at Westclox, you could be a telephone operator, or, if you earned a college degree, you could teach. Illinois Bell had a major center in Peru-LaSalle, and Westclox employed thousands of people in a large building that dominated the twin cities. The building is still there on Route 6, but there is no more Westclox, and there are precious few telephone operators anymore, for that matter.

I lived across the street from the Westclox building, and the day was frequently disturbed by the screaming sirens of an ambulance pulling up to take away another person with a heart attack. They were trying to stick with it until they died, and unfortunately, they started dying in their 40s. Today we realize that we may hold four or five different jobs or careers during our lifetime. We may have to learn new skills along the way, like working with computers. We can't count on company pensions because we may not be with any one company long enough; even health care is problematical. The belief system that worked—or didn't work, as the case may be—when I was growing up, certainly doesn't work anymore.

When Westclox went under and the phone company started using computers and voice synthesizers in place of operators to handle most of the workload, people around here had to use their imagination and intellect to find new jobs, and it was a difficult scramble. So it is when we encounter a terminal illness or some other difficulty that turns our so-called normal life upside down. Fortunately, you don't need to wait for a crisis to initiate change in your life; you can start now.

Again, forgiveness plays a key role. As I grew up, I had to release myself continually from the thought patterns that I had inherited from my parents and grandparents. I needed to get to the point where I thought, *That might have been well and good for them, but it's not for me.* Then I had to forgive myself for breaking with a parental tradition, and, as it were, being unfaithful to them. You could say that my final act of disloyalty to the tribe was leaving the Catholic priesthood. I did what I needed to do—not for my physical survival, but for my spiritual survival. It turned out that I prevailed materially as well, but that wasn't my primary goal. If I had remained a Roman Catholic priest, tied to a diocese for life, I might have been assured of a pension and a bed in an old priests' home somewhere out among the cornfields. But I might also have died from boredom and frustration before I could retire, because I wouldn't have been free to do my healing work the way I need to do. And who knows? The way the church is going these days, there may not have been much of a pension for me by the time I was ready to retire anyway.

Sometimes we express the wish to let God take over our lives. If you do this—and I think it is a good thing—just be sure that you are not actually wishing that God will change your life without any effort on your part. You may long for change and yet be afraid that if you do follow your intuition, the world will say you're crazy. In that case, you will be tempted to stay put and try to make nice and let everything come to you. But it never does, and you may die just as bored and frustrated as I would have been had I stayed in the institutional priesthood.

That desire to stay put and wait for God to do everything can be the voice of fear speaking. Having grown up with an alcoholic father, I know a little about the disease. It isn't so much that alcoholics don't want to change, as that they have become comfortable with what they know. They have learned how to handle the sleepless nights and the rages and binges, excruciating as they are, but they don't know how they will handle going without a drink all day long. That unknown is more terrifying than the physical and material suffering that their drinking incurs. The same is true for workaholism or any other addiction. You may know that the addiction is killing part of your soul, but you don't know how to change. We fantasize that predictability is going to breed a peaceful life for us, but it doesn't.

I began this chapter by saying that we need to forgive others and ourselves, because that lets us move on. It also keeps us healthy, mentally and physically. In explaining the manifest happiness and good health of his monks, the Buddha once said, "They do not repent the past, nor do they brood over the future. They live in the present. Therefore, they are radiant. By brooding over the future and repenting the past, fools dry up like green reeds cut down."

Sometimes it seems that our whole life is lived thinking about the past, projecting into the future, and missing the present moment. We may think that we are in the present, but when we say that, often our body is here while our psyche and spirit are still plugged into the past. We have to learn through the ongoing practice of forgiveness—forgiveness of ourselves and others—to bring our energy forward from the past and back from the future to the present moment, which is where God dwells.

### *Two Exercises for Self-Forgiveness*

#### Exercise 1: Accepting Yourself

These two exercises can be done separately or sequentially. You may find it helpful to tape-record this visualization beforehand so that you can keep your eyes closed throughout, although you may also choose to read one portion at a time, then close your eyes and visualize that part. If the sound of your own voice distracts you, ask a friend to tape it for you, being careful to speak slowly and clearly.

In this guided visualization, we are going to enter into a dimension of becoming more aware of what forgiveness means on the practical, psychological, and spiritual level—learning how to release ourselves from the past so that we will be able to release others. Your focus here ought to be on learning to forgive yourself, to release yourself from past shame, guilt, or whatever is keeping you from living a full life as God intended. If you feel troubled at any point in the meditation, you may take three deep breaths. Because Jesus is my spiritual master, I will use his name in this exercise. But if you feel more comfortable substituting God, the Buddha, Mother Mary, or any other male or female saint or manifestation of the Divine, please do so. Choose now whom you will encounter during this visualization, and then proceed.

Close your eyes and go to your favorite spot, which can be a room in your home where you feel safe, a lake, alongside a gently rushing stream, or near the ocean as the surf is pounding the shore. It could be under a tree, especially in autumn as the leaves are brightly colored and starting to fall. The season can be summer if you prefer, and you may be in a meadow lying on your back, looking into the blue sky and watching white, billowing clouds float by. Go there now in your spirit and settle in, enjoying the look and feel and even the smell of your favorite spot.

If you have a hard time visualizing or creating an image, just relax and allow the feeling to touch you. Using your senses, feel a cool breeze or the warmth of the sun, smell the flowers or salt air, or perhaps the wood burning in your fireplace, depending on where you are. If you are out walking on the leaves, hear them crunching under your feet.

As you relax, whether you are walking, sitting, or lying down, imagine that Jesus is coming along and is going to walk with you, sit beside you, or lie down alongside you. What is important right now is that you see the look on his face. He is delighted to be in your presence. It doesn't matter who you are or what you have done, because he is with you in this present moment. I want you to relax and feel the love he has for you pouring out of his heart and into your heart, into your inner being. You might picture it as a warm, pulsating, golden light emanating from the heart of Jesus directly into your heart, and then spreading throughout your whole body. Feel the peace of this moment. Allow the joy, as much as is possible right now, to fill you fully.

Now see or feel yourself in this same spot, but sitting up. Jesus is seated alongside you and he puts his arm around your shoulder. Listen to him speak to you. "I love you," he says. "I'm so glad you're here. I wanted to spend time with you. You are a beautiful person. I want you to live an abundant life."

Just accept what Jesus is saying. As much as you can right now, accept the idea of living your life abundantly. Don't do anything but accept that love now. Let it sink in and suffuse your body and soul with its warmth. Tell Jesus in your own words that you are grateful for what he has told you and what he has given you today.

Then slowly open your eyes and come back to the present moment, realizing that you are always free to return to your favorite spot and speak to Jesus anytime you feel the need or desire to do so.

## Exercise 2: Forgiving Yourself

Close your eyes and imagine that you are at your favorite spot again. In both your hands you are holding a number of mud balls, some big, some small. They represent the bitterness and resentments you feel toward certain people who might have hurt you in the past; they may also represent things that you have done to yourself about which you feel full of shame. In this favorite spot, along comes Jesus again, and this time he is carrying a silver garbage can. He places it in front of you and tells you to put your hands over the garbage can, turn your palms downward, and let all of the mud fall out of your hands into the garbage can.

Watch Jesus put the lid back on the garbage can, seal it up with tape, and attach a bunch of brightly colored helium balloons—orange, red, gold, yellow, blue. As he lets go of them, the silver garbage can rises into the sky and heads toward the sun. As it enters into the light of the sun, it completely disappears from view because the light is brighter than the can.

Now picture Jesus as he wrap his arms around you. Hear him whisper in your ears, "Just let it go. Let it go and lean on me." Picture yourself leaning against Jesus breathing restfully. You notice that there is still a little dirt on your hands, but you don't worry about that because the Spirit of the Christ is available so that each day, walking with the Spirit of light and love and forgiveness, you are healed and set free. Relax in this experience and let the Spirit of the Christ fill you and make you aware of God's love for you. He will never leave you or forsake you.

## Alternate Group Exercise in Forgiveness

*Please note:* If you are fortunate enough to have a group of like-minded souls who are willing to undertake an exercise in forgiveness, you can use the following text. One person can read it in a slow, calm voice, and you may use music of your choice in the background. I use *Om Nama Shivaya* by On Wings of Song with Robert Gass. If you use a different tape, omit the first paragraph of the following.

Realize that you are Spirit, that you were created by God, who is love, and so you were created by love, in love, for love. Allow the vibrations of the ancient Sanskrit song that is playing to enter your heart as you realize that you and God are one. Imagine the voices on the tape as the voices of angels.

You were created by love, in love, for love. Picture yourself being embraced by the person of Jesus and recognize that Jesus knows your faults, your mistakes, the times you have failed. He certainly does not consider any of us failures, nor does the Father, who is tender, compassionate, merciful, and totally understanding. Feel yourself bathed in this Divine light. Feel the lightness as you enter into that light and live in that light. It seems as if the heavy burdens on your shoulders, the burdens that are weighing you down, are being lifted layer by layer.

Get in touch with your sacred Self, your true Spirit. You are an elegant Spirit who is coming home. Take a deep breath and be aware that you are breathing in the breath of God. As you breathe in, say "Father," and as you breathe out, think *love*. You are breathing in the Father's Spirit that fills the whole world, and you are exhaling that Spirit of love back into the world. Let God love you.

As you are doing this, picture the hand of the person next to you as the hand of Jesus. As you take the hand, keep in mind that it doesn't matter to Jesus who you are, because he is always there representing the Father. Sense his love for you, as you sense the smile on his face.

Now imagine the light coming from his heart, down his arm, and out his hand into your hand, up your arm, and into your heart. Dwell in that light for a moment, feeling the bliss of this moment, knowing that God is for you, not against you.

In your imagination, open your eyes and see that Jesus is not the one holding your hand now. He has been replaced by a person you perceive to be your enemy, the one person with whom you have the most difficulty. It could be a parent, sister, brother, or child, someone you encounter at work, a troublesome neighbor. See that person holding your hand now. But notice the same light in you that was in Jesus now moving down your arm, out your hand, into your enemy's hand, up his arm, and into his heart. Just let it happen. Even if the person is deceased, this still works. And you may want to say to that person in your heart, "I forgive you and I release you into the light."

Now see that the person whose hand you are holding is once again Jesus. He is smiling and you are smiling and you feel absolute peace. Rest a moment in that feeling.

You may want to express your gratitude to God, however you conceptualize God: "Thank you for the peace of this moment. Thank you for helping me begin this healing process. Thank you, God, for drawing me together with brothers and sisters who are on this same path and who want fullness and fulfillment in life. Thank you for showing us the way. We don't have to live in this dark tunnel any longer. There is a light at the end of the tunnel. The light is love and freedom, and the process is forgiveness. Thank you, Father, for your Spirit."

While you rest in that feeling of gratitude, read this poem, which I wrote years ago in an attempt to describe forgiveness:

> *I traveled the country roads*
> > *and big city streets,*
> > *the grassy plains*
> > *and desert wastelands,*
> > *the rocky mountains*
> > *and seven seas,*
> > *longing to be free.*
> *Sweet thoughts,*
> > *bitter memories.*
> > *I sweated*
> > *and slaved*
> > *to be free.*
> *Happy songs,*
> > *sad songs.*
> > *I heard them all,*
> > *seeking to be free.*
> *I fought,*
> > *cursed,*
> > *and cried*
> > *in my struggle*
> > *to be free.*

I sought heaven,
    found hell,
    looked for angels,
    embraced the devil.
I wandered far
    from home
    in my search
    to be free.
In place of freedom
    I found a prison
    without a guard
    or a guide.
The miles were long
    the roads winding
    and steep;
    an empty heart
    until I saw
    the familiar
    country road.
Tears stopped.
    Fresh air.
    A white house peeking from behind
    the dense pine trees.
People waving,
    joy so deep,
    memories revisited.
    Love—
    Embraces.
I was home.

Let yourself be home now in the embrace of God's love. Remember that your concern is only this present moment, not the past or the future. You may want to picture yourself as a little child on God's lap. Picture God as a benevolent grandfather or grandmother, if that's what you would like. You are a little child sitting on His lap, your head against God's chest, His arms around you. We know that God is not a man, but contains both masculine and feminine traits in His personality. Let Him be tender with you, and when He puts His arms down, put your own arms around yourself in your imagination while still seated on His lap. Love yourself as God loves you. Be tender and merciful with yourself as God is tender and merciful with you. This is the way God wants to treat us. Thank you, Lord.

Now if you would like to share the forgiveness within, you can again shake hands or embrace each other. Imagine that the person you are embracing is the person who has just appeared to you, the one that you have just released and let go.

# Afterword

t one point near the end of *The Way of a Pilgrim,* the itinerant narrator, having mastered the art of continuous prayer, is discussing the practice with a magistrate in whose home he is a guest. The magistrate is well educated and already very devout, but he has not read the mystical literature concerning the continuous Prayer of the Heart.

"Ah, but the attainment of interior prayer is a very big business and almost impossible for layfolk," he exclaims when he is informed of the technique. "We are lucky if we manage to say our ordinary prayers without slothfulness."

"Don't look at it that way," the pilgrim replies.

> If it were out of the question and quite too hard to do, God would not have bidden us all do it. His strength is made perfect in weakness. The holy Fathers, who speak from their own experience, offer us the means, and make the way to win the prayer of the heart easier. Of course, for hermits they give special and higher methods, but for those who live in the world, their writing shows ways that truly lead to interior prayer.

I agree with the pilgrim that it is not out of the question "for those who live in the world" to learn to pray continuously, to make of prayer a constant part of our interior life, and one that also guides and directs all our external actions. If I had to sum up the basic message of my book in one sentence, in fact, it would be that prayer and healing are as natural as eating and drinking. By "natural," I mean both that they are intuitive and inherent in us—that we are "wired" for prayer and healing—and that we need to make them as much a part of our everyday awareness as any other natural function.

Like the anonymous Russian pilgrim who authored the passage above, many of the greatest mystics were relatively uneducated in the advanced study of theology. What they were very good at was practicing the discipline of prayer until their experience of union with God progressed from a momentary event in their lives to a state of constant communion. That is the goal to which each of us is working, and toward which I hope this book has in some small way helped you to move.

Most people naturally want to know how they can determine whether they are actually moving in the direction of that goal. Physical healing is by its nature quite apparent, whereas the more important emotional and spiritual healing that I have been discussing are more subtle and harder to discern.

What are the signs that significant healing has begun and that you are making progress through the five stages that lead to Divine union?

Genuine communion with the Divine, whether momentary or more prolonged, can express itself only as love and compassion for others. As Padre Pio put it, if your prayer practice is not leading you to love, then whatever you are doing cannot be prayer. And so as you work through the exercises and prayers in this book and attempt to chart your course along the five stages of healing, be alert to the levels of love and compassion in your own life. I don't mean the kind of love that expects certain behavior in return, but the love that manifests as a desire to serve others unconditionally. If manifestations of love and service in your life are increasing, however subtly, then know that you are moving in the right direction.

Someone has speculated that all we actually take with us when we die is the spiritual wisdom we have accrued and the love we have shown to others while on Earth. Assuming that is true—and I see no reason to doubt it—then being prayerful in a way that causes you to manifest more love in your life may be the most valuable thing you can learn to do.

# Compassion in Action

"When we ultimately go home to God, we are going to be judged on what we were to each other, what we did for each other, and, especially, how much love we put in that. It's not how much we give, but how much love we put in the *doing*—that's compassion in action.

"One's religion has nothing to do with compassion. It's our love for God that is the main thing. . . . . Religion is meant to help us come closer to God, not meant to separate us."

— Mother Teresa

(from *For the Love of God: New Writings by Spiritual and Psychological Leaders*, edited by Benjamin Shield and Richard Carlson, Ph.D.)

# APPENDIX

# Efficacious Novena to the Sacred Heart of Jesus

(This novena prayer was recited everyday by Padre Pio for all those who asked his prayers.)

1. O my Jesus, you have said: "Truly I say to you ask and it will be given you, seek and you will find, knock and it will be opened to you." Behold I knock, I seek and ask for the grace of _____. Our Father (etc.) Hail Mary (etc.) Glory be to the Father, and to the Son, and to the Holy Spirit. Sacred Heart of Jesus, I place all my trust in you.

2. O my Jesus, you have said: "Truly I say to you, if you ask anything in my name, he will give it to you." Behold, in your name, I ask the Father for the grace of _____. Our Father (etc.)

3. O my Jesus, you have said: "Truly I say to you, heaven and earth will pass away but my words will not pass away." Encouraged by your infallible words I now ask for the grace of _____. Our Father (etc.)

4. O Sacred Heart of Jesus, for whom it is impossible not to have compassion on the afflicted, have pity on us and grant us the grace which we ask of you, through the Immaculate Heart of Mary, your tender Mother and ours.

# Native American Prayer

O Great Spirit, whose voice I hear in the winds, and whose breath gives life to all the world, hear me! I am small and weak; I need your strength and wisdom. Let me walk in beauty, and make my eyes behold the red and purple sunset.

Make my hands respect the things you have made and my ears sharp to hear your voice. Make me wise so that I may understand the things you have taught my people. Let me learn the lessons you have hidden in every leaf and rock. I seek strength, not to be greater than my friend, but to fight my greatest enemy—myself. Make me always ready to come to you with clean hands and straight eyes. So when life fades, as the fading sunset, may my spirit come to you without shame.

# Selected Bibliography

*A Course in Miracles.* Glen Ellen, Calif.: Foundation for Inner Peace, 1992.

*The Amplified Bible.* Grand Rapids, Mich.: Zondervan Publishing House, 1965.

Anand, Margot. *The Art of Sexual Magic* (audiotape set). Boulder, Colo.: Sounds True Audio, 1996.

Barks, Coleman with John Moyne. *The Essential Rumi.* San Francisco: HarperSanFrancisco, 1995.

Besant, Annie, and C. W. Leadbeater. *Thought-Forms.* Wheaton, Ill.: Theosophical Publishing House, 1969. (Originally published 1901.)

Beumer, Jurjen. *Henri Nouwen: A Restless Seeking for God.* Trans. by David E. Schlaver and Nancy Forest-Flier. New York: Crossroad, 1997.

Broughton, Rosemary. *Praying with Teresa of Àvila.* Winona, Minn.: St. Mary's Press, 1990.

Cataneo, Pascal. *Padre Pio Gleanings.* Translated by Maureen McCollum and Gabriel Dextraze. Sherbrooke, Quebec, Canada: Editions Paulines, 1991.

Charlton, Hilda. *Hell-Bent for Heaven: The Autobiography of Hilda Charlton.* Woodstock, N.Y.: Golden Quest, 1990.

——. *Saints Alive.* Woodstock, N.Y.: Golden Quest, 1989.

——. *Saints Alive.* (Audiotape set with saint cards) Boulder, Colo.: Sounds True Audio, 1997.

Chorpenning, Joseph F., O.S.F.S., *The Divine Romance: Teresa of Ávila's Narrative Theology.* Chicago: Loyola University Press, 1992.

Chopra, Deepak, M.D. *Ageless Body, Timeless Mind: The Quantum Alternative to Growing Old.* New York: Harmony Books, 1993.

Cowens, Deborah with Tom Monte. *A Gift for Healing: How You Can Use Therapeutic Touch*. New York: Crown, 1996.

H.H. The Dalai Lama. *The Good Heart: A Buddhist Perspective on the Teachings of Jesus*. Boston: Wisdom Publications, 1996.

D'Apolito, Alberto. *Padre Pio of Pietrelcina: Memories, Experiences, Testimonials*. Frank J. and Julia Ceravolo, trans. San Giovani Rotondo, Italy: Our Lady of Grace Friary, 1978.

Durka, Gloria. *Praying with Hildegard of Bingen*. Winona, Minn.: St. Mary's Press, 1991.

Fox, Matthew. *Meditations with Meister Eckhart*. Santa Fe: Bear & Co., 1983.

———. *Illuminations of Hildegard of Bingen*. Santa Fe: Bear & Co., 1985.

Glassman, Bernie. *Bearing Witness: A Zen Master's Lessons in Making Peace*. New York: Bell Tower, 1998.

Gomes, Peter J. *The Good Book: Reading the Bible with Mind and Heart*. New York: Morrow, 1996.

Griffiths, Bede. *Universal Wisdom: A Journey Through the Sacred Wisdom of the World*. San Francisco: HarperSanFrancisco, 1994.

———. *Vedanta and Christian Faith*. Clearlake, Cal.: Dawn Horse Press, 1973.

Harpur, Tom. *The Thinking Person's Guide to God: Overcoming the Obstacles to Belief*. Rocklin, Cal.: Prima Publishing,1996.

Kushner, Harold S. *How Good Do We Have to Be? A New Understanding of Guilt and Forgiveness*. Thorndike, Me.: G.K. Hall & Co., 1996.

Leadbeater, C. W. *The Science of the Sacraments*. Adyar, India: Theosophical Publishing House, 1975.

Le Mée, Katherine. *Chant: The Origins, Form, Practice, and Healing Power of Gregorian Chant*. New York: Bell Tower, 1994.

Magida, Arthur J., and Stuart M. Matlins, eds. *How to Be a Perfect Stranger: A Guide to Etiquette in Other People's Religious Ceremonies.* 2 vols. Woodstock, Vt.: Jewish Lights, 1996.

Markides, Kyriacos C. *Riding with the Lion: In Search of Mystical Christianity.* New York: Viking, 1994.

———. *The Magus of Strovolos.* London, England: Arkana/Penguin, 1985.

Matthews, Dale, M.D., with Connie Clark. *The Faith Factor: Proof of the Healing Power of Prayer.* New York: Viking, 1998.

Meyer, Marvin. *The Gospel of Thomas: The Hidden Sayings of Jesus.* San Francisco: HarperSanFrancisco, 1992.

Myss, Caroline, Ph.D. *Anatomy of the Spirit: The Seven Stages of Power and Healing.* New York: Harmony, 1996.

Occhiogrosso, Peter. *The Joy of Sects: A Spirited Guide to the World's Religious Traditions.* New York: Image Books, 1996.

O'Hara, Nancy. *Find a Quiet Corner: A Simple Guide to Self-Peace.* New York: Warner Books, 1995.

Pagels, Elaine. *The Origin of Satan.* New York: Random House, 1995.

Ramotti, Ottavio Cesare. *The Nostradamus Code: The Lost Manuscript that Unlocks the Secrets of the Master Prophet.* Rochester, Vt.: Destiny Books, 1998.

Sathya Sai Baba. *Namas Marana.* Tustin, California: Sathya Sai Book Center of America, N.D.

———. *Harmony.* Tustin, Cal.: Sathya Sai Book Center, 1997.

Slattery, Peter. *The Springs of Carmel.* New York: Alba House, 1991.

Spong, John Shelby. *Why Christianity Must Change or Die.* San Francisco: HarperSanFrancisco, 1998.

———. *Living in Sin.* San Francisco:HarperSanFrancisco, 1990.

Strehlow, Widghard, Ph.D., and Gottfried Hertzka, M.D. *Hildegard of Bingen's Medicine*. Santa Fe: Bear & Co., 1988.

Ware, Archimandrite Kallistos. *The Orthodox Way*. Crestwood, N.Y.: St. Vladimir's Seminary Press, 1986.

Ware, Timothy, ed. *The Art of Prayer: An Orthodox Anthology*. London, England: Faber and Faber, 1966.

*The Way of a Pilgrim and The Pilgrim Continues His Way*. R.M. French, trans. San Francisco: HarperSanFrancisco, 1991.

Wilson, Andrew, ed. *World Scripture: A Comparative Anthology of Sacred Texts*. New York: Paragon House, 1995.

# Suggested Inspirational Reading

Bernardin, Joseph Cardinal. *The Gift of Peace: Personal Reflections.* Chicago: Loyola Press, 1997.

Borysenko, Joan, Ph.D. *The Ways of the Mystic: Seven Paths to God.* Carlsbad, Cal.: Hay House, 1997.

Chopra, Deepak, M.D. *The Seven Spiritual Laws of Success: A Practical Guide to the Fulfillment of Your Dreams.* San Rafael, Cal.: New World Library, 1994.

Dalla, A.S. *The Hidden Forces of Life.* Twin Lake, Wisc.: Lotus Light Publications, 1990.

De Mello, Anthony. *Sadhana: A Way to God, Christian Exercises in Eastern Form.* New York: Image, 1978.

Drosnin, Michael. *The Bible Code.* New York: Touchstone, 1997.

Dyer, Wayne. *Manifest Your Destiny: The Nine Spiritual Principles for Getting Everything You Want.* New York: HarperCollins, 1997.

——. *Your Sacred Self: Making the Decision to Be Free.* New York: HarperCollins, 1995.

——. *Wisdom of the Ages: A Modern Master Brings Eternal Truth to Everyday Life.* New York: HarperCollins, 1998.

Durka, Gloria. *Praying with Hildegard of Bingen.* Winona, Minn.: St. Mary's Press, 1991.

Hay, Louise L. *Heart Thoughts: A Treasury of Inner Wisdom.* Carlsbad, Cal.: Hay House, 1990.

———. *Meditations to Heal Your Life.* Carlsbad, Cal.: Hay House, 1994.

Thich Nhat Hanh. *The Miracle of Mindfulness: A Manual on Meditation.* Boston: Beacon Press, 1975.

Mata, Sri Daya. *Enter the Quiet Heart: Creating a Loving Relationship with God.* Los Angeles: Self-Realization Fellowship, 1998.

Myss, Caroline, Ph.D. *Why People Don't Heal and How They Can.* New York: Harmony Books, 1997.

Nouwen, Henri J.M. *Life of the Beloved: Spiritual Living in a Secular World.* New York: Crossroad, 1992.

O'Brien, Justin. *A Meeting of Mystic Paths: Christianity and Yoga.* St. Paul, Minn.: Yes International, 1996.

O'Neil, David, ed. *Meister Eckhart, from Whom God Hid Nothing: Sermons, Writings and Sayings.* Boston: Shambhala, 1996.

Prakash, Prem. *The Yoga of Spiritual Devotion: A Modern Translation of the Narada Bhakti Sutras.* Rochester, Vt.: Inner Traditions International, 1998.

Simsic, Wayne. *Praying with Thomas Merton.* Winona, Minn.: St. Mary's Press, 1994.

———. *Praying with John of the Cross.* Winona, Minn.: St. Mary's Press, 1993.

———. *Praying with Meister Eckhart.* Winona, Minn.: St Mary's Press, 1998.

Yogananda, Paramahansa. *In the Sanctuary of Soul: A Guide to Effective Prayer.* Los Angeles: Self-Realization Fellowship, 1978.

# Index

Exercises are gathered under the "exercises" heading. The various stages of healing are listed under their individual names. An "*i*" after a page reference refers to an illustration. An "*n*" after a page reference refers to a footnote.

# About Ron Roth, Ph.D.

**Ron Roth, Ph.D.,** is an internationally known teacher, spiritual healer, and modern-day mystic. As a leading-edge voice bringing us into the New Millennium, he has appeared on many television and radio programs, including *The Oprah Winfrey Show.* Ron is the author of several books, including the bestseller, *The Healing Path of Prayer,* and the audio-cassette *Healing Prayers.* He served in the Roman Catholic priesthood for more than 25 years and is the founder of Celebrating Life Institute in Peru, Illinois, where he lives.

# About Peter Occhiogrosso

**Peter Occhiogrosso** has been a journalist for 28 years and has written or co-written many books about religion and spirituality, including his guide to the world's great religious traditions, *The Joy of Sects.* He also co-authored *The Healing Path of Prayer* with Ron Roth.

Peter's e-mail address is: **PeterO@hardpress.com**

For more information on Ron Roth's Spiritual Healing Retreats, Holistic Spirituality Five-Day Intensives, Workshops and Seminars, or to send in your Prayer Request and be placed on his mailing list, please use the address below:

Celebrating Life!
P.O. Box 428
Peru, IL 61354
Email: **ronroth@theramp.net** • Fax: 815-224-3395
Please visit Ron Roth's website at: **www.ronroth.com**

The following materials are available through **Celebrating Life:**

## <u>Book</u>
The Healing Path of Prayer

## Audiocassettes
The Lord's Prayer, Teachings on the Aramaic Our Father
Take Control of Your Life's Direction
Celebrate Life! Choices That Heal, *with Paul J. Funfsinn*
Forgiveness Therapy: A Christ-Centered Approach
Holy Spirit: The Boundless Energy of God
The Path to Answered Prayer
Healing Meditations and Affirmations
Prayer As Energy Medicine
Transformed by Love: The Healing Power of Self-Love
Prayer: A Therapeutic Tool for Spiritual Healing

## Videocassette
Spiritual Healing: Merging Mysticism and Meditation with Medicine

Ron is interested in hearing from readers who experience healing—whether physical, psychological, or spiritual—as a result of performing any of the prayer and meditation exercises or rituals he prescribes from his books, tapes, and/or from attending any of his healing prayer gatherings, seminars, or workshops. You may contact him at the address on the previous page.

# Other Hay House Titles of Related Interest

## BOOKS

CHAKRA CLEARING: Awakening Your Spiritual Power to Know and Heal,
by Doreen Virtue, Ph.D.

THE EXPERIENCE OF GOD: How 40 Well-Known Seekers Encounter the Sacred,
by Jonathan Robinson

EXPERIENCING THE SOUL: Before Birth, During Life, After Death, by Eliot Rosen

HANDLE WITH PRAYER: Harnessing the Power to Make Your Dreams Come Through,
by Alan Cohen

MEDITATIONS TO HEAL YOUR LIFE, by Louise L. Hay

THE POWER OF MEDITATION AND PRAYER, by Larry Dossey, M.D., and
Other Contributors, with Michael Toms

THE WAYS OF THE MYSTIC: Seven Paths to God, by Joan Borysenko, Ph.D.

THE WESTERN GUIDE TO FENG SHUI: Creating Balance, Harmony, and
Prosperity in Your Environment, by Terah Kathryn Collins

## AUDIOS

HEALING, LIVING, AND BEING, by Mitchell May, Ph.D.

HEALING MEDITATIONS, by Gene Egidio

THE HEART OF SPIRITUAL PRACTICE, by Jack Kornfield, with Michael Toms

MEDICINE, MEANING, AND PRAYER, by Larry Dossey, M.D., with Michael Toms

MEDITATIONS FOR MANIFESTING: Morning and Evening Meditations to
Literally Create Your Heart's Desire, by Dr. Wayne W. Dyer (also on CD)

THE SERENITY PRAYER: Affirmations and Meditations for Recovery,
by Emmett Miller, M.D.

All of the above are available through your local bookstore,
or may be ordered by calling Hay House at (800) 654-5126.

We hope you enjoyed this Hay House book.
If you would like to receive a free catalog featuring additional
Hay House books and products, or if you would like information about
the Hay Foundation, please contact:

Hay House, Inc.
P.O. Box 5100
Carlsbad, CA 92018-5100

**(760) 431-7695** or **(800) 654-5126**
**(760) 431-6948 (fax)** or **(800) 650-5115 (fax)**

Please visit the Hay House Website at: **www.hayhouse.com**